THE GREAT MAVELLO

Colin Spong Jones

Percy Hunt

The Great Mavello

Life and Times of a
Health & Strength League Athlete

Colin Spong Jones

One-Off Publishing

First published in 1999
by One-Off Publishing
7 Ynys Street
Port Talbot
SA13 1YL

British Library Cataloguing in Publication Data
A catalogue record for this book is available from the British Library

Printed by Redwood Books
Kennet Way
Trowbridge
Wiltshire

Jones, Colin Spong
The Great Mavello
1. Title

ISBN 0 9534061 0 5

Contents

List of Plates

THE GREAT MAVELLO

The four poses of Percy Hunt are set against the backdrop of the partly
demolished old Aberavon town centre. The Municipal Buildings stand in the
background. To the left of the figures can be seen the back-end of the Walnut
Tree Hotel. Above lock-up shops next to the hotel is the Public Hall.
(Photo montage by the author)

Preface

That secret interlude, that kind of limbo where youth awakens to the physical man within, was for me somewhat remarkable in the intensity and naivety of my struggle to develop the culture of my physique. As a novice working my way through training routines, I lacked the ability to do so effectively, and indeed safely, until I came upon the redoubtable physical culturist* and Health & Strength Leaguer Percy Hunt, who ran a gymnasium in my home town of Port Talbot.

Once aware of his presence I began to hear all manner of claims in praise of his prowess as an athlete under triumphant sounding and rather intimidating flag-waving titles: 'World's Undefeated All-round Athlete', 'Britain's Best Developed Man over 40', and 'The Great Mavello'** stage name of his music hall days. Steeped in traditions pioneered by European physical culturists before and at the turn of the century, coupled with the Health & Strength League movement, he was renowned in Wales, and in particular the industrial valleys of South Wales, for the novel and sensational style of his displays of athletic versatility and virtuosity. Farther afield he had come before appreciative audiences in England and was also a respected all-rounder of the old school within the fraternity of a number of gymnasiums in the United States of America. From between the two World Wars until the early 1970's his place of exercise had become an oasis for numerous schoolboys, young men, and occasionally young women, intent on quenching their physical thirst in Percy Hunt's Health & Strength gym. If somehow you had missed or denied yourself the opportunity to become a pupil of the great man then your education, indeed your life, regarded by most young bloods as sadly incomplete.

It was with a generous infusion of reserved hope that I too followed the well-trodden path to enlightenment; a journey which led me before a man still vigorous in exercise in his autumnal years. Percy Hunt was in his 62nd year

---

* An old term used at best to describe physical ability and development. The culture of the physique was seen in high society before the First World War as a necessary prerequisite for gentlemen.

** A curious corruption of 'marvellous', the mis-spelling of 'Marvello' (without the 'r') was deliberate, supposedly necessary to avoid possible infringements of a brand name of an analgesic product 'Marvello Ointment' (with the 'r') manufactured in Abertillery by the Marvello Company. Percy was to sample the ointment before the First World War and, having found it inferior to other preparations, including his own concoctions, would probably not have wished to be associated with such a product.

when I, to touch on the Dylanesque, in my 16th year to heaven first attended his gym. The memory is quite distinct; it was December in the Coronation year of 1953, on a Monday, with Christmas Day not far off, when I strode through the dark of a cold winter's night towards the distant light marking like a beacon the position of his gymnasium in the back garden at the rear of Percy's family home, 15 St. Mary's Street, Aberavon,* Port Talbot. Sounds of gym activity arose sharp and clear in the still frosty air, the clanging of weights, the taking-in and letting-out of laboured breath. Opening the back garden door the unshaded dazzle of electric light above the gym entrance cast deep encircling shadows in eerie definition revealing in reflection the burnished gold of a large brass plate fixed to the door upon which was engraved in bold lettering: Percy Hunt, Teacher of Physical Culture, Massage and Physicultopathic Treatment. Pausing at the threshold of the gym I was unsure what reception a novice would invite from the weight-clanging, breath-exploding, muscle-hardened pupils within, before quietly clicking open the door and then noisily and clumsily brushing aside a heavy crimson curtain hanging like a trap for unsuspecting newcomers like myself. The sounds of my entry arrested the movements of the exercising athletes and another unshaded electric light, hanging from a roof rafter, silhouetted their looming forms, casting shadows large and menacing among the vaporous exhalations of breath and body heat upon my first night. A moment's silence, stillness, and at the rising tone of Percy's voice in greeting the shadows of the athletes retreated and slunk to my feet as they continued clanging weights and exploding breath in their lifts. 'Hello, young man, what can I do for you?' he asked in the light tenor voice of welcome and enquiry which he usually used for newcomers to the gym. Before me stood a surprisingly small man, fair of complexion and refined of features, tattily attired in a well-worn track suit. Percy's alertness, however, belied appearances and we sat together on a bench while he briefly explained the clear benefits of physical culture as a way of life. I listened intently to what he said, as every new pupil probably did; 'Sacred thy body even as they Soul', he pronounced in prophetic tones at the close of his introduction. I did not know then of the Health & Strength League movement's existence let alone its high-sounding motto. After a pause he added complication by intoning what is taken to be the secularised origin of the League's principle, Latin writer Juvenal's *Mens sana in corpore sano*. He then translated in clear diction and a full voice, as if an orator speaking to the

* I have used the English spelling, as I have for other Welsh place names of the time, and not the Welsh as it is now - Aberafan.

multitudes, and said, 'A sound mind in a sound body', adding with humour and a warning, 'When you pick up weights never strain your curran.'

The first meeting with Percy Hunt was of no more nor less significance to the celebrated athlete than making the acquaintance of just another initiate into the techniques of physical culture. To me, however, it was an entry into a nucleus of much activity where slim-slack muscles were trained to bulge in triumph and boys believed they had become men overnight. There was an air of excitement about the place, acceptance as a pupil depending not merely the paying of a nominal fee, then of 5/-, but on whether one had the ability to apply oneself to exercising schedules within a body of athletes where a hierarchy of physical excellence naturally existed. Elitism was also evident among a number of pupils but not intolerably so to any initiate, for Percy would always avoid such a situation before it took a divisive hold.

My application of the hierarchical and elitist system was steadfast, with a mixture of optimism and wait-until-I-get-stronger attitude all disguised under an 'After you Claude' demeanour, attendance at the gym on Mondays, Wednesdays, and Friday evenings becoming second nature to me.

Here then, in the St. Mary's Street Health & Strength gym, so it seemed to me at the time, the culture of the physique was first founded and forged in Wales and there could be no better teacher to have led the way than Percy Hunt, 'The Great Mavello'. Here was the centre, the starting line in the race for athleticism of which I had become a part; a part of the flow of pupils appearing in the 1950's and 1960', this period of recollection became for me the stimulus for this biography of a man who sought to embody health and strength, pure and simple, with bravura flourishes.

Colin Spong Jones

Acknowledgements

In writing the biography I am grateful for the assistance given by the following persons: Mrs. Gwladys Hunt and members of the extended family of Mary (nee: Burton) and Blanche (nee: Thomas) Francis, Hubert Francis, Mrs. Arthur Leigh, Mr. and Mrs. Percy Leigh, Cyril Hunt, and Mr. and Mrs. Spear. Jack Acocks (Aberdare); J.D. Bowen (Swansea); Mike Brown; E. James Clifford; Gordon Davies; Mrs. Isaac Davies (Bryn); Donald Dennis (Bridgend); Mrs. Isaac Dupplaw (Maesteg); A. Leslie Evans; Keith Evans (Mold); Yorrie Evans (Haverfordwest); Idris G. Hale (Neath); J. Ivor Hanson; Oscar Heidenstam (England); Mrs. Murial Isaac (Porthcawl); Mr. and Mrs. Will James; Graham Jenkins (Porthcawl); Wendy Jenkins and Merril Jenkins (Hafodyrynys and London); Myrddin John MBE (Ammanford); Mr. and Mrs. John Jones (Aberdare); Mrs. M. Simon (Maesteg); D. Bryn Thomas BEM; Eddie Thomas MBE (Merthyr Tydfil); Hubert Thomas (Swansea); Ted Tuckfield; David P. Webster (Scotland); Philip Wells; Alwyn Williams, and Ray and Hugh Woodward.

For Stephen and Mark

Chapter 1

Early years and the emerging athlete

Percy Cardwell Hunt was born on Wednesday, 5 August 1891, at 4 Tymawr Street, in the Ancient Borough of Aberavon, the third child of Thomas and Elizabeth Jane, with brother Thomas (Taff), born 5 August 1888, and sister Eliza (Lillie), born 7 December 1889, arriving before him. Having survived breathing difficulties at birth, the frail infant nestled in his mother's warm caresses with much to prove to himself and to others in the years to come as a Health & Strength League athlete and entertainer. Given his career as a sensation-seeking, imaginative stage artist, it would not have seemed amiss to many of his friends if by some theatrical trick a bravura heralding of mythical gods had attended his birth, with muted fanfares of trumpets and sunbursts from parting cherubic cloud formations, conjured up by a group of itinerant illusionists.

There was no hint of illusion about the home welcoming the new birth, but an atmosphere of huddle, a place in which family bonding and discipline were thrust upon its occupants by the scant confines of the welling. The street itself, narrow and almost secluded, led off High Street into Talbot Square and was named in tribute to the presence nearby of its namesake Tŷ Mawr (Great House), a commodious residence built in 1762 by John David, a Portreave of the town. There was possibly an absurdity about the street's reference to greatness - although Percy did not think so - and it became known in the locality in terms more familiar to its residents as 'Butter Street' and 'Shutes Lane'. There was also something operatic about Tymawr Street with its cobbled alley of echoes for budding songsters mostly of nocturnal habit, Percy too finding good resonances in his boy soprano days.

The family remained in Tymawr Street until Percy was 13 years old; during that time a further brother and two sisters were born - Christopher James (3 October 1893), May Elizabeth (2 November 1894), and Violet Evelyn (1 November 1899) - with Blanche (30 June 1904), Albert (26 October 1906), and Cyril Charles (23 August 1908) completing the family of nine children, which had moved in 1904 to larger premises at 15 St. Mary's Street.

Neither parent was of Welsh descent, the father, Thomas, having been born on 17 March 1863 in Exeter, Devon, and the mother, Elizabeth Jane (nee Hendra), on 1 October 1866 in Redruth, Cornwall.

Linked by a Celtic heritage both families were to become a part of the exodus of migrants from the West of England and Southern Ireland seeking work with the expansion of heavy industry in nineteenth century South Wales. It is uncertain when the Hunt's and the Hendra's first settled in Aberavon and although both families were to live near each other in mixed street communities of Irish settlers and the indigenous Welsh in Richard Street and High Street, Thomas Hunt's parents first lived some distance away from town on Margam Moors in one of the Morfa Cottages near Morfa Colliery.

In Aberavon both families also lived in the vicinity of Zion Chapel, Clarence Street, a chapel particular to Celts from Devon and Cornwall. It was here, in Zion Chapel, that Percy's parents were to meet, although his grandparents on his father's side moved allegiance to the Primitive Methodist 'Bethel' in Wern Place, where Wern Congregational Chapel somewhat overpowered in stone and mortar its Primitive Methodist neighbour. When the congregation increased and moved to a more imposing place of worship built on an elevated site in High Street, Thomas Hunt was to say that 'Bethel' deacons were even more delighted than the minister, and the rest of his flock, to have moved away from the shadow of Wern Chapel into the light.

The eventual marriage of Thomas Hunt and Elizabeth Jane Hendra was not solemnised in either of their parents' chapels but possibly a compromise was reached to alleviate anxieties over the sensitive matter of choice, the ceremony taking place on 25 January 1888 in Neath Registry Office. Among those God-fearing chapel goers a Registry Office marriage probably caused a few tremors of annoyance and dismay in both parent households, such ceremonies often being regarded as a way out of an embarrassing situation if the betrothed was pregnant before marriage. It is also probable that both families anticipated the wagging tongues of neighbours counting the months diligently with bated breath. Although their first-born, Thomas, was a finely timed achievement, his conception was regarded as legitimate by the locals.

Employed before marriage as a miner in Morfa Colliery - a pit notorious for taking the lives of many of its work-force - Thomas Hunt had now moved to comparatively safe employment as a tin annealer in the local Mansel Tinplate Works, settling with his wife into the routine of establishing a home and a family.

Thomas Hunt, said to be one of the pioneers of the local Independent Labour Party, was a firm yet amiable father by all accounts, cosseted by a wife whom he adored, as did the children. Both parents were noted for their sense of humour, although Thomas Hunt was also perceived to have a bizarre inclination if prompted by particular circumstances. This is perhaps best seen when, with his right leg severely damaged in a saw-mill accident on St. Patrick's Day (his birthday!) and needing amputation, he had his departed member buried in the family grave ready, he said, to receive the rest of him much later.

With the lost limb replaced by a cork leg, which he often complained was riddled with 'rheumatics', Tom Hunt secured varied employment and, in the work sense, was something of an all-rounder like his son Percy was to become as an athlete. Thus he applied his hand as a street lamplighter, a fish and chip and ice-cream van proprietor, a conveyor of passengers to Aberavon Beach in the summer in his horse and brake, utilised in winter for delivering coal to customers and, as a council roadman, the last town crier in Aberavon.

Recollections of family life for Percy Hunt, in the immediate and the extended sense of eight uncles and four aunts, are almost non-existent and what we are left with are grandfather Hendra's exploits in South Africa, where he found and lost a diamond mine to an unscrupulous partner. The story Percy told is how in a drunken stupor his grandfather's partner had him to sign over his share of the mine on a piece of paper believing it to be an IOU, and promptly staked the claim only in his name. Unable to legally prove otherwise grandfather Hendra created such a furore that the authorities sent him to gaol and then deported him as a vagrant. If the adventurer had hoped to return home to the welcoming bosom of his grass widow and her little sweet shop in High Street, minus the promised fortune, he was to be very much mistaken, his wife refusing to have anything to do with him, leaving her willing daughter Elizabeth Jane and son-in-law Thomas to take him in and live with them in St. Mary's Street until his passing. Although the incident was romanticised by the grandfather as a fire-side tale of adventure for all his grandchildren, the story of deceit while under the influence was not lost on Percy in his 'Sacred thy body even as thy Soul' days as a telling warning against the pitfalls of demon drink.

Grandfather Hendra's repeated tale of high adventure gone wrong no doubt brightened Percy's home life from time to time, as seen through the eyes of a boy plagues with lung complaints since birth. Although the debilitating condition did not develop into tuberculosis as many feared, his illness nevertheless fragmented his elementary education while also keeping him from the often rough and tumble of childhood activities. These set-backs were more than compensated for by a ready absorption of everyday and main-stream motivations shaping life outside the home. The weekly markets and accompanying side-shows bustled with exuberance of commercial enterprise

1. Percy's parents and their first six children
L to R Back: Thomas, Christopher, Percy, Lillie.
Centre between parents: May. Seated on lap: Violet.

4

and were always places for gatherings and flowerings of characters. There were also many strange happenings for Percy to see, none more bizarre than the 'tooth-puller', a strong-wristed coloured man who extracted troublesome teeth by levering them out with a spoon handle. When the crude procedure began to cause inevitable pain to the patient, the tooth-puller's assistant attempted without success to drown the shouts and screams of anguish by energetically beating a large drum!

There were darker images of recollections when free fights could be viewed after 'stop-tap' on Saturday nights, usually occupying the large spatial area dominated later in the second year of the First World War by the Municipal Buildings. Here the abundance of nearby public houses spilled out aggressive customers into the assumed arena where old scores were settled and probably new ones established. These usually male dominated pugilistic confrontations were sometimes supplemented with fierce hatpin skirmishes among the wives of those husbands involved, the cut, parry and thrust often drawing blood. Always accompanied by his elder brother Thomas (Taff) and younger brother Chris, these 'free-for-alls', as Percy called them, were regarded as good entertainment by him and many other residents living in the area.

The coming of the Nonconformist revival of 1904-5 seemed to have been, in Percy's view, a restraining influence upon such pugilistic indulgence. Whatever one's religious persuasion might have been, the resurgent heightened sense of evangelic purpose enveloped the faithful with a fervour revitalised with each crusading itinerant preacher. Regular attendance at Zion Chapel had long been a purposeful way of life for Percy's mother; his father, even in the midst of the revival, still, it is said, being inclined to stray from the Bethel Chapel fold whenever his Independent Labour Party beliefs did not quite blend happily with the piety of some chapel elders and deacons. Percy recalled that, as Chapel Treasurer but not Deacon, his father was not above partaking of a frothy pint of ale and whenever he had consumed more than a pint measure his mother, or 'Mumma Ginnie' as she was affectionately called in the family, would say to her husband knowingly, 'You have stars in your eyes, Thomas'.

With Percy's parents being members of different chapels there was at first a shared experience among the children until preferences were made according to stability of Sunday School friendships and parental ties. Percy's brief recollections of chapel were centred around the spiritual impact made by the short-lived revival of 1904-5. Although he tended to follow his mother to 'Zion', the chapel's subdued classical facade in frowning distance from the then quiet-on-Sundays Red Lion Public House, the revival encouraged the family as a whole to support both places of worship and, as a consequence, he also attended 'Bethel' at that time.

In either chapel, as in other places of worship, itinerant preachers, expert in the high and low chants, sang the congregation into exultant choruses of acclamation and, no doubt, total subservience to the pursuit of a longed-for celestial bliss. For a thirteen year old boy restricted in health, religious fervour became a dramatic climax to the sermons; further visits Percy claimed to have sampled with even greater relish.

In direct contrast to the then impassioned mood of Christian inspiration experienced was the free-wheeling, pleasurable sense of fun for its own sake which came with the arrival of the Circus and, in April and September, the Amusement and Flannel Fairs in the borough. Here, in fairs and markets, Percy took in for the price of two pence the jerky, flickering innovations of silent films, offered in canvas-covered 'Bioscope' (real name Kinema) booths, presented by the familiar trio of Messrs. Dooner, Hagger and Wadbrooke. On a small stage before fronted facades richly ornate with gilded carvings surrounding a fair organ, he viewed pre-Kinema shows in music hall tradition with an assemblage of clowns, dwarfs, dancing girls, jugglers, and stage strongmen.

It is probable the might and muscle performances of the stage strongman were not only greeted with anticipation and admiration by crowds gathered outside the booths but also with intimidation at the revelation of a man possessed of herculean power. When confronted by one Continental strongman, who declared his once puny condition as a child cured by exercise with weights, Percy, at that precise moment, it is said, decided that he too would aspire to a similar state of health and strength. There is something of the bravura spirit here for the aspiration was easier than its achievement and it was put into effect at first by his father, who guided him surely towards achieving early physical conditioning. As did the father so too did the mother encourage their son, with at times a degree of humorous relief in the urgency with which Percy took to exercise.

Although boxing methods of training are regarded as the first forms of disciplined physical development, before this exercise was taken by means of mountain walking, for near where he lived in Tymawr Street stood Mynydd Dinas, the first of the trinity of mountains: Emroch and Margam were the remaining two overlooking the town. The closeness of 'Dinas' made it ideal for the purpose of strengthening both heart and lungs, with the added therapy of mountain air. Here, at its summit, he was taken on fine days by his father to inhale and exhale, as an exercise, slowly at first and then deeply, the salted breezes often blowing off the Bristol Channel. Here he would view, as one is compelled to do from this height, the panorama of the town and distant stretch and expanse of sea and curve of Swansea Bay to the right and following back the almost unbroken landmass of dunes in front and to the left of him of Aberavon, Taibach and Morfa beaches. Here on the heights of 'Dinas' he was free from the congestion of town life and the pollution of its industry. Percy believed that climbing the mountain helped provide the early strength and stamina to succeed as a Health & Strength League athlete. 'Life's aims', 'self-belief' and 'motivation' were encouragements from both parents and he was to be sustained by these principles.

An extension to mountain walks, after the family had moved to 15 St. Mary's Street, were daily trips in summer to Aberavon Beach with the horse and brake Thomas Hunt had purchased - presumably from the compensation received for the loss of his right leg in the St. Patrick's day accident - to carry passengers from town to the seaside and back. It was here by the briny, wave-lapping edge, amongst the green and gold of turbulent hillocks of 'marram' grass and sand, where dunes and marshes teemed with insect, bird and animal life, dewberry and blackberry, and a place of adventure when Percy was young, that he spent many happy times. This intriguing place, decades before the building of the Sandfields Housing Estate erased the natural habitat of flora and fauna in the 1940's and 1950's, was another contributory factor in the improvement of his health.

Although there is no denying the value of open-air therapy, the seasonal variations and general unpredictability of the elements precluded the serious training which Percy now needed. The first steps towards a way of systematising training began when the stable, where Thomas Hunt housed his horse and brake, became part of a make-shift gym. In the confined stable space, among the herby smells of horse and hay, boxing exercises, which were fundamental for stamina-building, strength, and limb co-ordination, were put into practice: ball-punching, skipping and shadow boxing. Percy also utilised discarded objects of varying poundage such as bricks, iron bars and scrap metal; even the two bells which his father rang as the borough town crier[1(a)] were put into good use as weights with their clappers bound and silenced.[1(b)] These ready-mades were applied to the first elementary forms of 'Systematic Progressive Resistance Training'. The combinations of skilful and simple means of exercise imprinted a sense of achievement and seems to have accelerated the development of abilities in a number of disciplines, the building blocks of a potential stage routine.

Boxing was, however, still a significant part of his athletic repertoire, just as to a greater or lesser extent did it preoccupy young bloods in town and district. Although dedicated to boxing, Percy's youthful involvement in all-round athleticism was regarded by the brotherhood of local boxers as no more than a superficial addition by a dilettante. He was nevertheless fist-fast and fleet-of-foot as a developing boxer and often invited to sparring sessions to increase the tempo of others. The best gathered in the Taibach area of town where Billy Beynon, Bantamweight Champion of Wales, and later in 1913 Champion of Great Britain, reigned supreme. Besides small financial rewards for his sparring services, he also gained valuable hints on technique from Noah (Mandry), a gifted trainer of boxers.

Of the two gyms in use by Taibach Boxers, Noah Mandry's in Goytre Valley remained the young athlete's firm preference, even though some distance farther to walk than the 'Gunroom' or armoury, formerly used by local Volunteers, situated on the lower side of West End. He was at home in the Goytre gym's rural, summer camp setting, the square-shaped, saddle-backed, wooden building a curious structure with its four sides split into three hinged half-flaps, like mechanical wings ready to take flight. When the gym was in use the flaps were lifted to varying levels, according to weather conditions, aerating and giving light to an otherwise darkened boxing ring space. Here, in this ingeniously-constructed building, the young Aberavon athlete would meet and spar with most of the boxers training in the 'Gunroom': Billy Beynon, Charlie Lucas (Middleweight Champion of Wales), Jack Lucas and Bob Phillips, with Jimmy Jenkins regarded as the most skilful of them all.

Among the rest of the town's boxing fraternity Percy was also much in demand from a rival group of boxing brothers, Jack, Will, Dai, and Rees Jones, living in Aberavon. In intimidating style they called themselves the 'Fighting Brooks' - 'Brooks' being a family name somewhere along the line. The four brothers were all to become Welsh champions in their respective weights which, it was said by fellow pugilists, owed much to the realisation of how slow they were in sparring sessions with Percy Hunt.

Of the many venues where the 'Fighting Brooks' trained a small room at the rear of the Port Talbot Hotel, Water Street, not far from Percy's gym, was the most convenient for him to spar. Situated near the 'Slaughter House', training sessions were sometimes set against a none-too-stimulating animal choral background of deep-throated bellowing of cattle awaiting their finale, the smell of death no doubt on their slobbering mouths. When the bellowing increased to operatic volume it demanded that everyone, Percy included, work with even greater urgency in hoped-for but unsuccessful attempts to drown the blood-curdling sounds from their minds. In more peaceful moments the real fighting began and in sparring bouts the Aberavon all-rounder's skill was finely honed to keep him well away from heavier opponents with knockouts in mind.

It is perhaps not surprising, integrated as he was within the local boxing fraternity, and having taken to boxing methods of exercising at an early age, that he should hold ambitions of becoming a professional. As common a practice as it was for some youths to take to the ring in the hope of gaining financial rewards for their efforts, his pugilistic intent was not greeted with enthusiasm by his parents as it was a game fraught with natural dangers for aspiring young boxers. Adopting boxing methods of training mixed within a versatility of disciplines had been an accepted means of overcoming illness and even demonstrations were not regarded as objectionable, but taking to boxing with any seriousness had his parents' total disapproval. To quell their concern, he reassuringly told them, 'Nobody will lay a glove on me. I am too fast to catch a cold!'

His boxing aspirations seemed, however, to have been as much a gathering of knowledge of other skills as it was about exorcising the ghost of being looked upon by boxing colleagues as a dabbler in disciplines without specialisation in any of them. Although a number of them took to lifting weights, swimming and rugby, their participation was subsidiary to boxing and they were therefore suspicious of Percy's increasing regard for the fashionable attraction, filtering through from London to the provinces, of the 'Physical Culturist' as the he-man of the day with refinements. His whole-hearted membership of the Health & Strength League movement of high ideals was again viewed as a soft option, although some of his boxing associates, if not all, might well have been members.

In 1910 a Physical Culture Display was organised by the brotherhood of Taibach boxers, the town's premier Health & Strength athlete Percy Hunt being invited to give an all-round exhibition of his skills. Held in the Drill Hall, Taibach, the Aberavon athlete's participation had already assumed bravura-like proportions before the evening's main event had taken place, he having laboured throughout the previous extended night-shift into the afternoon of that day, employed as a tin worker in the nearby Works of D. R. David. Then, in the mould of a Hercules, Percy Hunt set about his own tasks to prove himself. He began by wrestling Dai Beynon (Welsh boxing champion Billy's brother), a grappler of craft and vice-like grip, and completed sessions of Indian Club Swinging and Muscle Control, followed by a four round boxing match with a taunting pugilist Kid Jones of Tonna, before climaxing the challenges with another four rounds against champion Billy Beynon.

The display, although viewed as an exhibition, was seen by Percy and his followers, who were greatly out-numbered in the audience by Taibach supporters, to be a definite attempt to establish his credibility as an up-and-coming all-round athlete. Such a belief was sufficiently heightened when a group of backers, headed by Taibach boxer Jimmy Jenkins, were prepared to champion Percy Hunt against the formidable Billy Beynon with a side-stake of £500. Certainly the wager created considerable pre-match excitement among supporters on both sides and gave an extra edge to the encounter. Insiders, however, realised that as a sparring partner of skill Percy was conditioned to Billy Beynon's ring craft and capable of keeping out of harm's way while scoring points and staying on his feet. That the side-stake was never realised probably had nothing to do with the young Aberavon athlete's boxing expertise but the bout was a test of his courage, while keeping spectators in the right frame of mind for a possible bloody encounter and Percy Hunt on red-alert with expectation.

The versatile Aberavon athlete's performance in the display was recorded by local diarist J. Ivor Hanson, in his usual careful assessment of local happenings, '...as a remarkable physical culture display,' and of the boxing finale '...as a fine example of what boxing should be, and how Percy, as the lighter man, compensated for the deficiency by speed and cleverness.' Meeting challenges with skill, courage, and a sense of occasion, the young athlete had proved something to himself and to others that was to be a continuing process.

With his mind still set upon credible recognition in the ring, the only division open to him where Percy would stand a chance of success was in the Paperweight category of 7st. and under. Not as regulated as other more popular, heavier weights, challenges were thrown down in these early years, from gym to gym, as little terrier contests before the big guns took over in the main bouts. An eventual match was arranged for the Welsh title at a Rhondda Valley venue with leading contender Jim Lightning (so named due to his supposed electric speed) when Percy was about twenty years of age. His opponent being decidedly not fast enough on the night, the Aberavon all-rounder won the championship on points with an even greater charge of speed of hand and fleetness of foot. He was now 'Paperweight Boxing Champion of Wales'.

2. The Emerging All-Round Athlete
(Newark Lewis)

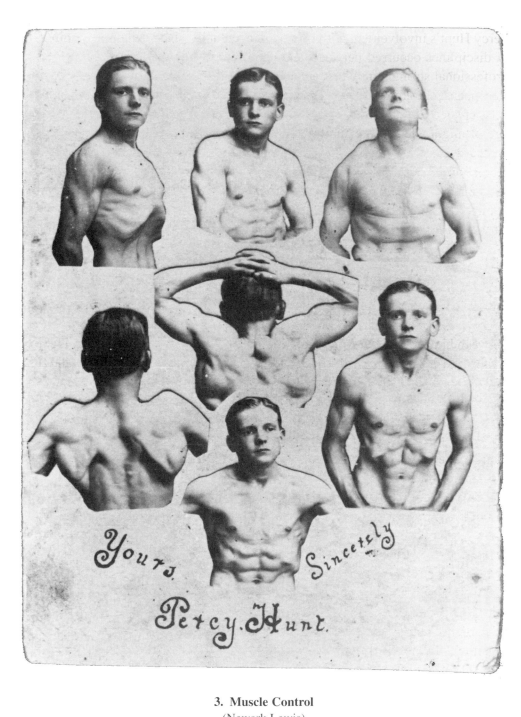

3. Muscle Control
(Newark Lewis)

12

Golden Age

Percy Hunt's involvement with boxing to eventually place the game within a list of disciplines occurred between 1900 and 1920 when the cumulative effect of professional strongmen, wrestlers and weight-lifters, many of whom were mid-Europeans, thronging London to participate in competitive stage and athletic acts, created the climate for the 'Golden Age' of Physical Culture. It was the age of might and muscle and the athlete heroic, with songs, poems and picture postcards celebrating the athletes' physique and achievements. The young Aberavon physical culturist was taken up by events published in journals and magazines. Athletes, he noted, were feted by the nobility, becoming fashionable enough with the Mayfair and Belgravia elite to mix socially with them, German strongman Eugen Sandow (b.1867, real name Fredrick Muller) and American all-rounder Bernarr Adolphus Macfadden (b.1868), being the leading pin-up idols of the day.

Both became inspiration sources; Sandow with his remarkable strength and physique, accentuated by classical good looks, and Macfadden with his multi-talent and eccentric behaviour. Percy believed there was a facial resemblance between himself and the American Macfadden, who was a visionary, an inspired writer, a film-maker, a sexologist, and, like Sandow a passionate crusader against social injustice and hypocrisy. Much of Percy's crusading attitude and versatile athletic realisation began with the American when he obtained an issue of a Macfadden magazine and a copy of his training chart illustrating quite advanced free movement exercises; the free limb movement method was to be supplemented with a pair of Sandow dumb-bells given by a friend bound for the Canadian Rockies.

Besides the influence of Sandow and Macfadden, Bavarian strongman Maxick and English athlete Monte Saldo proved a significant duo in presenting a system based on muscle control - a contraction and relaxation of voluntary muscles in isolation - combining their names to form 'Maxalding'.[2]

Percy was one of the first 'Maxalding' postal course pupils before the 1914-18 War. When devised in 1909, the system tended to be regarded by Percy's colleagues as a fanciful diversion from the hard graft of lifting weights. What Percy realised, apart from the discipline's many benefits, was the novelty potential. Taking the initiative, he claimed to be the first in Wales to introduce the system's original and sensational muscle control features before an audience. Calling himself the 'Welsh Maxick', he later received a Maxalding Gold Medal for his expertise, the discipline becoming one of the highlights of

4. Early Balancing Act with Bodyweight
Brothers Albert and Cyril cling respectively on to each end of a 100lb. iron bar.
(Newark Lewis)

5. A Family Pose
Percy with Albert and Cyril, and nephew Harold Tredree.
A signed photograph with Welsh Maxick written below.
(Newark Lewis)

14

his versatile style, establishing the physical culturist early on as a sensation-seeking stage athlete nurtured in the 'Golden Age'.

Health & Strength League

Percy joined the 'League'[3] in 1907, a year after it was founded. Formed by leading enthusiasts with intentions of creating a climate for physical improvement on a National scale, the movement's beginnings were as a consequence of threats and injunctions taken out against the *Health & Strength* magazine's publishing of erotic poseurs. Buttressed with moralistic intent, *Health & Strength* Publications[4] now declared, much to Percy's parents' relief, that the League movement's 'youth and maidens' will need '...no guiding lodestone to keep him or her on the straight, narrow track of virtue, honesty, sobriety, and truth.'

Much of this kind of moralistic purpose was off-putting to a number of his associates but not to Percy, believing so it seemed that he was uniquely different to them. It could be said at the time he had great ambition considerably laced with idealism, qualities not always compatible.

Another aspect of the League he took to which they did not, was the use of imagery defining in allegorical complexity the League motto: 'Sacred thy body even as they Soul' - a story heavy-laden with Christian symbolism in the style of Bunyan's *Pilgrim's Progress*. Although Percy had claimed no interest in literature proper, he sometimes read aloud passages of the story in his stable gym believing it gave him greater strength and purpose to the challenges and feats to come.

His readings in the quiet of the gym were, he admitted, to harken him back to his chapel days of revival and the minister in full flow in 'Bethel' and 'Zion'. It is probable that the material he read aloud ran a similar thread of meaning as the minister's. In these readings in the gym there was possibly something of the budding actor about him, as he developed a clear speaking voice essential for introductions in displays. The main passages of the story, allegorically told by Yorick Gradely in *Health and Strength Annual*, 1906, he underlined in another issue and are as follows:

"Arise!" the speaker said, "I am the Spirit of the Perfect Man, Arise and follow me."

...the Spirit took him by the hand...and he placed a strong sword in his right hand, and once again he said:-

"Follow me!"

..."This", said the Spirit, "is the mountain of Endeavour; steep, rugged, fraught with many perils. Will you climb?"

..."Take with you this ensign, and remember that the body, even as thy Soul, is sacred in the eyes of your Creator. There lies the way."

...From the springs that gushed forth from the hillside he quaffed refreshing draughts of Heaven distilled, and guiltless were the feasts of herbs with which the nymphs regaled him by the way.

From dark, impenetrable caves there came forth monsters who assailed him, but mightier than they was the sword, and stronger the arm that bore it;...The breath of heaven had filled and purified his lungs...his body glowed and tingled with the very joy of living...

Over the peaks the sun is rising, and his warm rays cast a halo round the hero as he climbs...he has gained a lovely fertile plain, which bears the name of Health, and through which the streams of Happiness flow on forever.

And he reached the City of the Strong. The massive gates fly open wide at his approach, for now he, too, is strong. He enters, and, amid that wondrous throng of men and maidens, perfect in form and beautiful beyond compare...he glanced into the crystal pool below. And then he knew that he had found the Spirit of the Perfect Man - for he had found himself.

Rich in metaphor, the allegory was written as an inspirational story; it was a journey of realisation and triumph over ignorance and reflected a British tradition in physical culture which, as Percy quoted from an article in *Health & Strength*, '...abounded with stories of weaklings who developed into strong men; cripples who overcame their infirmities, men who made marvellous recoveries from severe accidents and the rout of sickness by steady exercise.' He recognised himself to be very much a prime example of this tradition peculiar to Great Britain, which led the world in the scientific use of weights for curative and corrective measures.

Although the allegorical story was founded on religious symbolism, not many Christian leaders took whole-heartedly to the Health & Strength movement.[5] Physical liberation was there to be taken as a possible harmonising extension of the religious self. The idealistic enlightenment of the League's motto was two-fold within the sacredness of the body as well as the soul. For the uninitiated and the pious, the very idea of developing the physique on an organised scale seemed to encourage exhibitionism and the body as a temple syndrome could also incline towards narcissism. Such self-indulgence was not the way of the

Christian spirit. Such religious perplexities meant nothing to Percy who knew the worth of physical development. The Health & Strength League membership badge Percy wore daily and with pride upon his lapel held the accepted design that symbolised the movement's motto. The design, produced on badges, brooches and later pendants, certificates, diaries and journals, shows the athlete standing triumphant, sword in hand, upon the lifeless coils of a serpent he had slain, set against the radiant light of a new dawn.

The hero of Health & Strength League manufacture was much to his liking, and he was quick to take on the mantle of the gallant warrior battling against the barbaric hordes ignorant in matters of health and strength. In the role of the warrior, Percy was probably a near perfect example of what the League hierarchy wished every member to become, remaining faithful to the rules and objectives set out in the movement's Annuals and issues of the *Leaguer's Guide and Pocket Companion*:

"Health & Strength" Leaguers

In every corner of the Globe
this little book is dedicated.
May they live long, healthy, and happily
and die only as the result of old age.
When the race of life has been run
worthily and well, and as befits
the members of a body whose
maxims and Principles are
so intimately concerned
with health, progress,
and advancement.

The Objectives:

To bind together in a band of robust brotherhood all Physical Culturists and Athletes throughout the world; a band united for the purpose of disseminating the broad principles of, and in Nature's way promoting, the cause of Health & Strength.

The Rules:
  (1)   Every member shall pledge himself or herself to do all in his or her power to help forward the cause of Physical Culture

  (a)   By taking judicious exercise every day unless prevented from so doing by illness, or some other unavoidable cause.

  (b)   By encouraging others, whenever the opportunity occurs, to keep fit.

  (c)   By extending the right hand of fellowship to all brother Physical Culturists wherever they may be, and in whatever circumstances they may be found.

  (2)   Every member shall do his or her utmost to discourage juvenile smoking and all other evil habits. League members are not prohibited from a moderate use of the weed if extreme youth is passed.

Whenever Percy referred to the League rules, he would quote, not exactly verbatim, the last observance, No. 5 in the abbreviated set of rules.

  (5)   In short, to live a clean, wholesome, rational life generally and so cultivate a "Sound mind in a Sound Body."

      The Cardinal Principle of the League, as its motto implies, is "a recognition of the sacredness of the body, and the importance of physical education on the part of every individual within the radius of its circle."

The League also encouraged members to memorise passages of poetry which embodied the positive aspects of human endeavour and spirituality and to quote such poems at every opportune moment. Although not inclined towards such elevation of thought, apart from taking what he could from passages of the League definition he read aloud in the gym, Percy was said to have been the inspiration behind a verse composition in praise of the movement. It was also said that a poetic tribute was written as a collective effort by local members and sent by Percy Hunt, as leader of the group, before the 1914-18 War, to *Health & Strength*, and believed to have been accepted for inclusion in a League publication. Research has revealed a tribute was sent by a member in 1909, when the Aberavon all-rounder was eighteen, with the initials P.H., entitled "The 'Health & Strength League'", published in the *Leaguer's Guide and Pocket Companion*. It is of course uncertain if the initials imply Percy Hunt, but when we consider that pencilled remarks beneath the tribute state that the full name of the Welsh Leaguer should have been given, there is a distinct possibility that P.H. does refer to him and that the verse is the collective work of colleagues:

The 'Health & Strength League'

There is a League, a grand old League,
Of forty thousand strong.
It's cause is good, it's motto bright'
To cheer its sons along.

The badge we wear, and proud we are
To wear it on our breast.
It's worth is priceless to us all,
'Tis one that we love best.

The Motto, one we all know well
Betokens love and peace,
Of friendship to our fellow-men,
Goodwill that ne'er shall cease.

The aim of that great League is this,
To link us into one;
To bind us in a brotherhood
Which "Health & Strength" began.

In the years before the 1914-18 War, the influence of the Health & Strength League had gained momentum, enrolment reaching 50,000 by 1911, and in keeping with the popular use of photography to celebrate the physical culturist as pin-up stars of the time, Percy employed local photographer W. Newark Lewis, MPPA,[6] to record his athleticism for posterity. During this period he began to open up his campaign of awards with a number of medals and badges for various disciplines, culminating with a Health and Strength (London), 1914, Gold Medal for 'Physical Development', which he received in the capital before volunteering for the Great War.

6. Volunteers
Percy (left), Christopher (right),
and 'Buller' Heycock (seated).
(Newark Lewis)

Chapter 2

King and Country

For Health & Strength Leaguers of enlistment age the coming of the First World War might well have created an acute awareness of the challenges upon their physical condition, the patriotic call to arms for King and Country possibly rousing in them the League warrior image, ready and able; there could also have been motives of adventure and escapism too mingling with what was expected of local patriotic young bloods, which sent Percy Cardwell Hunt, his brother Christopher James and their brother-in-law John Ivor ('Buller') Heycock - feared pugilist married to sister May - as volunteering Leaguers in the Great War.

That they should volunteer was not, however, remarkable, for in Wales there was a greater upsurge to arms in comparison to the percentage of population elsewhere in Britain, encouraged by Lloyd George, with support from the chapels, to form a Welsh Divisional Army. Here then probably are the main reasons for their early departure to the war zone.

Of the three Regiments of the line - Royal Welch Fusiliers, the South Wales Borderers and the Welch Regiment - forming the 38th (Welsh) Division, Percy Cardwell Hunt enlisted at the age 24 years with the 10th (Service) Battalion, South Wales Borderers (1st Gwent), on 12 December 1915, the place of enlistment being Drill Hall, Stow Hill, Newport; his base for training was Colwyn Bay, North Wales, and his Regimental Number 39716.

Brother Christopher James Hunt, aged 22 years, joined the Cardiff City Battalion of the Welch Regiment and later transferred to the 10th Battalion South Wales Borderers for active service, his original Regimental Number changing from 50079 to 39717, a digit above his elder brother's. John Ivor Heycock served with the 2nd Battalion Welch Regiment, his Regimental Number being 24573.

Percy, Chris, and 'Buller' Heycock were attached to the 115th Brigade, composed of two Battalions (10th and 11th) of the South Wales Borderers, the Cardiff City Battalion of the Welch Regiment and the Royal Welch Fusiliers.

Army documents kept by Percy record that he was in France in 1916-17-18 and 19, which does not take into account the Battalion's involvement in the defence of the Ypres Salient, Belgium. His specialist military qualifications were as 'drummer' and 'stretcher-bearer', whilst Chris and J. Ivor Heycock served in the infantry. His medical class as expected was A1. Medals were campaign awards of British War and Victory Medals and upon demobilisation he was transferred to the Army Reserve and made up to Lance Corporal 36194, taking over the number of a soldier killed in action.

Before Percy, Chris, and brother-in-law J. Ivor Heycock left Southampton in the *Empress Queen* for Le Havre, France, Percy claimed that in concerts of a morale-boosting nature, in which he took part, it became apparent to him that he had a tenor voice worthy of developing alongside his athletic skills. There was in his make-up always something to discover that might benefit his chosen way of life as an H. & S. Leaguer, no matter where he was or in what circumstances he might find himself.

Percy Cardwell Hunt's recollections as a stretcher-bearer and band member in the First World War were fragmented, which probably resulted from an unwillingness to elaborate much beyond the voluntary, essential expression of physical culture displays given in Regimental and Battalion concerts. The inclusion of selected entries taken in the main from War Diaries of the South Wales Borderers thus places him within the wider context of the war.

All three Aberavon servicemen arrived in France prior to the 38th Division's commitment at the opening battle of the Somme, on 3rd July 1916. In subsequent attacks on Mametz Wood, defended in the main by crack Battalions of the Lehr Infantry and Bavarian Regiments, both the 10th and 11th Battalion's of the South Wales Borderers received their first real exposure to action, costing the 10th 180 lives and the 11th 200, the Brigade, after early confusion, forcing the enemy to withdraw.

The battles for Mametz Wood were to be horrific, awakening the unblooded to the realisation of the ease with which flesh and bone can be torn and fragmented out of all recognition. For physical culturists like Percy Hunt - and there were many on both sides - there was in all probability added futility in the knowledge that the toil and dedication to strength and physical perfection were meaningless before lethal contrivances for human elimination.

The most tragic image known to Percy and, no doubt, to his comrades, which symbolised not only the blind ferocity of the struggle for Mametz Wood but the absurdity of war itself, is of two soldiers - one from the Lehr Regiment and the other a South Wales Borderer - rigor-mortised in a deadly coupling by simultaneously bayoneting one another. Percy remembered that they were held in that position by the trunk of the tree against which they had fallen.

War Diary entries name officer casualties and other ranks in one attack by the South Wales Borderers followed by enemy retaliation:

Mametz	10/7/16 –	Attack on Mametz Wood by 38th Div. killed 2nd Lt. M.J. Everton & 2nd
Bivouac		Lt. R.P. Taylor & 21 other ranks.
Shts.Ameins	11 – 11/7/16	Wounded Major C.D. Harvey, Capt. Galsworthy (both on duty). Lts. Gill E. & Parry R.B. 2nd Lts. Davenport H.H. & Davies D.L. Missing totals 6.
		Battalion suffered an intense bombardment during night of 11 - 12th of July, 1916.
Frontline Trenches	16/9/16	Quiet day. Casualties 3 wounded, 1 suffering from S.S.

Some weeks after the three Aberavon volunteers arrived in France and the attack on Mametz Wood by the 38th Division, Percy was to hear from his brother Chris of the death of John Ivor Heycock, killed in action on 20 August, in the area of High Wood, a couple of miles from the infamous Mametz Wood. Although Chris was convinced their brother-in-law's death was caused by contracting pneumonia, a common killer alongside the bomb and bullet, after not fully recovering from a severe blow to the head sustained in a Regimental boxing tournament, army archives suggest (no known personal records remain) that he was one of a number of personnel who died during enemy shelling.[1]

It was some time before Percy Hunt was ready and able to enter the ring in Regimental boxing championships. When he did his record of successes was one hundred per cent in winning every bantamweight competition he entered in France and Belgium. He was never knocked down once and his wins were achieved on points decisions, due to his speed and skill.

Further War Diary entries are as follows:

Canal Bank	26/3/17	Batt. in support to 17th Batt. R.W.F. Physical training, Musketry, Bayonet Fighting, Passing messages, Box respirator drill. Work:- General upkeep of trenches.
Mon.	9/7/17	Batt. at Lairs "... All stretcher bearers (including 16 extra men drawn from the Band) received instruction from the M.O..."

After an uneventful winter in the trenches, Percy's reflections of the Third Battle of Ypres were centred along Pilken Ridge and Iron Cross Ridge when stretcher-bearers were kept quite busy. The attack by the Welsh Division started at 3.50 a.m. on July 31st and continued the following day with 'D' and then 'B' Company of the 10th Bn. assisting the 11th Bn. in repulse and attack and helping to smash up the famous German 3rd Guards Division, the 10th suffering 200 casualties while the 11th lost 350 of all ranks.

Pilken & Iron Cross Ridges N. of Ypres	... Facilities were afforded at RUDOLPHE FARM for making tea, and the constant supply was greatly appreciated by the men. During the night of July 31st/Aug. 1st a great deal of promiscuous shelling took place. AID POST at RUDOLPHE FARM received no little attention and Lt. G.L. Gall, the Medical Officer in charge, was wounded...

The most daring of attacks made by the 10th Bn, in which Percy's brother Chris was involved, was that carried out on the night of the 7/8th November 1917, by 10 officers and 270 men. The contingent penetrated 200 yds. into enemy defences on a front of 300 yds. blowing up three concrete dugouts, killing at least 50 Germans and taking 15 prisoners, at a cost of five killed and 45 wounded. In such attacks stretcher-bearers came into their own.

Estairs	25.12.17	Xmas Day: After Church Parade, Companies marched to places selected for dinner. A B D & H.Q. Corps dined all together

in the School Room & C. Comp. & Transport
were in the Sergeants Mess.

Christmas was celebrated with traditional fare in a free and easy festive spirit,
as Percy readily testified, with the main course of turkey or beef dinner followed
by cakes and jellies galore and a half-pound of plum pudding served to every
serviceman rounding off the feast. Christmas night was given to variety acts,
pantomines and humours sketches. It was thus inevitable and natural that in these
events Pt. Percy Cardwell Hunt would come into his own with performances of
athletic prowess, including the 'wobbly' delights of muscle control. The
significant difference compared to previous performances back home was the
spontaneous and playful practice by the Battalion Band of interpreting muscle
flicks, jumps and rolls in rhythmic forms to wind and percussion accompaniment.
Always seeking a heightened audience response to war-time performances, Percy
also let it be known that he had discovered what he described as a rousing tenor
voice and seized the opportunity to give solo renditions of 'Silent Night' and a
sentimental song called 'Mother'. Written by Irving Berlin, the chorus lyrics are
as follows, sung by the athlete as a melodic lament:

> M - is for the million things she gave——me——
> O - is on-ly that she's grow-ing old————————
> T - is for the tears she shed to save——me————-
> H - is for her heart of pu-rest gold————————-
> E - is for her eyes of love-light shin——ing————
> R - is right and right she'll ev-er be——   ——
> Put them all to-ge-ther they'll spell M-other,
> a word that means the world to me.

'Mother' became a firm favourite with Battalion and Regimental audiences,
and thereafter Percy introduced it in his shows of songs he sang to comrades in
the First World War.

> 1, 2 /1918   ...The Band paraded for Army drill under C.S.M.
>   Burgess. Drummers received instructions as
>   stretcher-bearers under the Medical Officer.

As the smallest member of both the 10th and 11th South Wales Borderers and other Welsh Regimental Bands, what could a hearty Health & Strength Leaguer have done but volunteer to beat the big drum with resounding effect and purpose?

Small in stature he most certainly was, but there was no denying his strength or indeed courage as a stretcher-bearer. The non-combatant duties of such men in carrying wounded to safety and medication, usually under constant fire in bomb-cratered terrain often turned into deep treacherous mud by incessant rain, were rightly held in high regard by the frontline soldier.

On active duty the most harrowing experience of the war was the carrying of his wounded brother Chris during the battle of Ancre, while the Battalion was in reserve, Aveluy Right Sector, in the Welsh Division's advance in the British offensive across the old Somme battlefield. The incident was also layered with irony when Chris, having borrowed money from Percy the previous day, wanted there and then to return the loan. With Chris seriously injured and urgently requiring medication, Percy did not realise his brother's attempts to repay him and it was weeks later in a letter from home that he knew of his demise from war wounds on the 13 August 1918. [2]

The war ended at 11.00 a.m. on Monday the 11th of the 11th month, November, of 1918, ninety days after the passing of Christopher James Hunt, one of 459 killed of all ranks of the 10th Battalion, South Wales Borderers.

Surviving the conflict physically intact was something Percy was thankful for, although the loss of both his brother and brother-in-law would run deep in painful memory for some years. Indeed, he was to find that even his duties as stretcher-bearer which, he said, stood him line for 'Mentioned in Despatches', came to nothing, as did his three recommendations for the Military Medal, the credit, he was convinced, having been taken from him by NCO's.[3]

It is probable he viewed military awards as another source of honours to be achieved as a physical culturist; certainly an MM and 'Oak Leaf' added for 'Mentioned in Despatches' would have gone well with the Health & Strength Gold Medal he had received in London, prior to the war, for 'Physical Development'.

The failure to achieve recognition as a stretcher-bearer was to be partly compensated for by the impending transfer to the Army Reserve as Lance Corporal and the privilege given him of sounding the 'Last Post' over the Somme Battlefield before Edward VIII, then the Prince of Wales. The latter he viewed as justifiably in keeping with having the greatest breath control among the trumpeters in the Division.

7. Band and Drums of the South Wales Borderers Regiment
Percy sits in front of the big drum, as he does in plate 8.

8. Band and Drums of the Welch Regiment

5/2/19   The Bat. billeted in Camp near Glisy. The Band
          & Drummers paraded for Inspection by the Adjutant
          at 09.15 hours. Dress-Drill Order.

On tour of the Welsh Division the Prince visited the 10th Battalion, South Wales Borderers, Percy taking the opportunity when spoken to by the Prince to mention to him his prowess as a Welsh physical culturist. The Prince of Wales, Percy claimed, responded with enthusiasm by telling him that he too had taken to physical culture, as did his grandfather, his Majesty King Edward VII, and his father his Majesty King George V, and that they had all been instructed by German strongman Eugen Sandow.

Glisy   7/2/19   H.R.H. The Prince of Wales visited Batt. at 11.00
                       hours and chatted with officers and men. He
                       inspected the Cook houses, Recreation Hut and the
                       men's huts. The officers and men cheered heartily
                       as the Prince got into his car to go.

Glisy   8/2/19   Training consisting of Physical Training
                       & football was carried out from 09.15 to 10.15 hours.

                       The remainder of the morning was devoted
                       to Educational Classes, consisting of
                       English, French, Geography and History.
                       The C.O. inspected the Transport at
                       09.45 hours in full marching order.

Glisy   10/2/19   Morning was spent in Physical Training & Education.
                       Afternoon all men turned out for football.
                       Inspite of snow - the games were greatly enjoyed.

While educational classes and sporting activities continued, Percy and his comrades found French classes useful when fraternising with local French women. Geography lessons of locality assisted too in the ability to find one's way back to barracks from a tête a tête with French families; the brief introductions to the indigenous population also helped to take his mind off the fact that he was going home alone.

A regimental Concert on the 21st seemed to have been a kind of finale; it was a gathering of all officers and men in one cultural pot-pourri of versatility and talent, although it was months before Percy and his comrades embarked for home.

Glisy 21.2.19 At 18.00 hours a concert was held in Sn.
Recreation Hut - Capt. W.T. Cobb took the chair.
Programme consisted of 2 playlets.
(I) "A Daughter of Thieves" & (II) "The Cure"
by Lt. T.L. Crawhall Bn. M.O. were well presented
and highly enjoyed.

Characters:-
(I) Major A.L. Bowen, D.S.O.
Capt. J. Morris, M.C. (T.M.B.)
Lt. T.L. Crawhall, M.O.
(II) Capt. J.W. Hughes, C.F. Lt. T.L. Crawhall
Lt. J.M. Lloyd, Lt. S. Hicks
Pianoforte Solos, Violin Solos, Songs,
exhibition club swinging.

It is probable that the 'exhibition club swinging' item mentioned was a part of Percy's contribution, as would have been his tenor solo under 'Songs'. There is also particular reference to his participation in army concerts in his Certificate of recommendation for employment:

This N.C.O. has a very good character. His conduct both in and out of action has been most praiseworthy - In action as a Stretcher-Bearer he was most gallant - Out of action he has been employed as Drummer and Bugler & has carried out his duties excellently - He is very conscientious, reliable & trustworthy - Has always assisted in Regimental concerts in amusing us with Club Swinging - Muscular Contortions & Music - I can thoroughly recommend his for a good job.

(signed)   C.D. Harvey, D.S.O.,
Lt. Col, Comdg, 10th Bn. SWB

9. Who is the Greatest?
(Photo montage by the author)

Chapter 3

Post-War and Onwards

'Our Brave Boys'

With hostilities over, Percy Hunt returned home in the Spring of 1919 to a post-war period not only to be enlivened by the rise of a Socialist Labour Party, but to the inhabitants of an Aberavon patriotic in preparation for 'peace' celebrations. In strolls around town dressed in uniform, his pre-war H. & S. Gold Medal for 'Physical Development' pinned alongside his campaign medals, Percy was, as all servicemen were, greeted as a hero as he familiarised himself with friends and acquaintances again. The weather was good and everyone seemed to him to have a ready smile on their face. Certainly it was evident that one of his friends and fellow comrades, Pte. D.A. Rees,* formerly of the Welch Regiment, projected a constant smile at the success of his campaign to attract back customers to his gentleman's outfitters by advertising his Spring sales as a chance to support not only his return home from 'active service' but from the point of 'patriotism'.

There was a 'Peace Sale' and a 'Great Victory Sale' by leading draper Abel Jones, and comparisons were made with Medieval Cloth Hall, Ypres, in Belgium, by W.T. Williams, who advertised post-war sales, as did his colleagues, in *The Aberavon and Port Talbot News*:

Ypres Mediaeval Cloth Hall is in ruins, but Aberavon Cloth Hall is replete with the choicest and most-up-to-date Stocks of Men's and Boys' Suits, Hats, Caps, Shirts, and Hosiery.
Be sure to go to W.J. Williams Boys!

* Regarded as the town's satirical voice, who was himself satirised with the nickname 'Dai-the-Nibs', Percy was not spared as a town personality ascending the plinth of public acclaim, being referred to as the 'Light of the World for seven stone weaklings'.

For Percy Hunt, his parents, brothers, sisters and other relatives, the day of patriotic celebration on Saturday, 19 July, was to be one of muted remembrance after the loss of Chris and cousin J. Ivor Heycock. The weekly tabloid, *The Aberavon and Port Talbot News*, recounting events of the day of celebration, reported that among the many flags and much bunting bedecking streets and roads '...it was a happy thought to erect a triumphal arch at the Aberavon end of the river bridge, just on the boundary between ourselves and the folk "the other side of the water".'

The casual mention of separation between street communities living each side of the River Avon (Afan), hid a hostility among factions which appeared in an invigorated form post-war and involved Percy Hunt as the town's leading exponent of the Health & Strength League movement. However, the day of the patriot, the day for celebrating 'Justice, Peace, Liberty' - words which decorated the inside of the triumphal arch, and their Welsh equivalents on the outer - 'Cyfiawnder, Heddwch, Rhyddid', ran its course with a cavalcade around the chosen areas of the borough. Displays of children in fancy dress contrasted with clashing resonances of many bands composed of discharged servicemen - 'Our Brave Boys' - Pte. Percy Cardwell Hunt, bugle to the fore, being part of the return of the conquering heroes. Parading through the streets he was to say that on that day he was not only marching for his Chris and Ivor Heycock but they with him.

The sense of family togetherness was carried by Percy throughout the rest of the celebrations to a rousing reception for the Mayor, S.H. Byass, JP, as he addressed the crowds gathered in Market Square from an open window in the Municipal Buildings. Percy heard little of what the Mayor said as he was caught up in pockets of the crowd that swayed and pushed their way nearer to hear something of what the first citizen of the borough was saying to them. It was the sense of occasion that had to be experienced even if what he had said meant little to the former South Wales Borderer when he and the family read the report of the speech in the local tabloid:

Ladies and gentlemen, I am afraid it is quite impossible for me to make myself heard, but I wish most heartily to thank you for the extraordinary reception you have been good enough to give me. I do not think I deserve any of it [Cries of "Yes, yes" and cheering]. We have met today to celebrate peace, and I ask you as you look round upon the children we have had the immense pleasure of seeing enjoying themselves today, to think what would have been their fate if the victory had been gained by the enemy. I ask you to accept my best wishes, and always to remember the brave men by whose efforts, bravery and self-sacrifice we are able to rejoice as we are proud to do today. I am now going to the schools to see the children having tea, and I again say thank you very much [loud cheering]. "Hen Wlad fy Nhadau" was sung, followed by "God Save the King" and "For he's a jolly good fellow".

The 'peace' festivities in Aberavon ended with a firework display set on the side of Myndd Dinas, above Springfields, that only served to remind Percy of the battlefields of the Somme in the cascading bright lights and explosions of celebrations. Nevertheless, like so many other discharged servicemen, he too, as if duty bound, climbed the mountainside and viewed not only the fireworks in Aberavon, but those in the parks at Taibach, Swansea, Briton Ferry and Neath. From where he stood on the mountainside, there was also to be seen the fiery glow of the largest bonfire in the Borough at the crescent-shaped, precipitous falling away of earth known as the 'Half Moon' on Mynydd Margam, despite the looming presence of Mynydd Emroch. It was a day Percy Cardwell Hunt was to remember with mixed emotions for some time.

Percy's Gym, Labour's Ramsey, and Hallelujah Nancy
With peace celebrations over, Percy began almost immediately to both extend and refurbish his stable gym with better made and acquired equipment. The establishing of a physical culture gymnasium proved not that easy a venture. There were standard requirements which the H. & S. League expected every gym affiliated to the movement to attain. It had to be well-ventilated and kept clean with facilities for hot and cold baths and fully equipped with suitable apparatus. The gym was also expected to be run in a way that fostered a mid-European regard for discipline and gentlemanly conduct, predominated by the Greek cult of the athlete - the ultimate pursuit of grace and beauty of physique.

All such requirements were eventually met, but in the early stages the venture was accomplished by a number of enthusiasts responsive to its setting up. For instance to secure enough weights one helper, Pat Flemming, acquired with Percy one evening a pair of disused 'dram' wheels near the Mansel (Byass) Tinplate Works, where suitable objects could be obtained with stealth. The wheels were carried and rolled over the 'Half-Penny' footbridge, arching the River Avon, some five hundred yards away. The dram wheels proved rather awkward weights to handle with their fixed axle, but in circumstances when professional equipment was expensive, and at a time when improvisation of materials was commonplace, they were an admirable substitute.

By January 1920, as part of a widening network of Health & Strength League-influenced physical culture clubs and gymnasiums in Wales,[1] Percy's St. Mary's Street gym was ready for custom, terms for pupils being 6d. weekly for three evening sessions - Mon., Wed., and Fri. 6-9 p.m. Cold baths were provided. Turkish baths and electric massage came later.

January also heralded the unanimous adoption of Scotsman, James Ramsey MacDonald, as prospective Labour Candidate for Aberavon Parliamentary Division for the General Election of 1922, and the long awaited visit in February of Salvationist 'Hallelujah Nancy'. Both crowd rousers attracted enthusiastic support, particularly Nancy with revelations of how her soul was saved by God's blessing, after she had been the worst woman in Spalding.

Saving souls possibly appealed to many townsfolk more urgently than the promise of Socialist utopia, Zion Chapel faithful Elizabeth Jane Hunt and members of her family, including her son Percy, joining the large crowds gathered at one of Hallelujah Nancy's open-air services in Charlotte Street. Here the Salvationist said, as recorded in The Aberavon and Port Talbot News, '"...there is not one of you as bad as I used to be, or as low." ...As a tramp on the road...she went from bad to worse...' One Christmas when Nancy was refused alcohol at a public house '...she heard a Salvation Army Band playing "Hark the Herald Angels Sing". The drummer said to the captain. "There goes the worst woman in Spalding, if we could only get hold of her it would be a great blessing", whereupon the captain went over to her, and placing his hand upon her shoulder, said, "God bless you, you have a soul to save".' Since then '...she has lived a sober and upright life.'

Whether Percy sensed any similarities between Hallelujah Nancy's misfortune and grandfather Hendra's experience with demon drink is unknown, for he seemed only to have remembered the energetic banging of boards and spirited waving of brushes by Nancy and her little band of Salvationists.

Against such a fervent background of Socialist hope and soul-saving, Percy began no less vigorous a campaign of his own to save from neglect and misuse the physical well-being of the youth of the town, declaring before audiences in his shows the benefits of physical culture and the H. & S. League. First he had to compete with and surpass already well established places of exercise. The gymnasiums of both the Mansel Works and Bantamweight boxer Billy Beynon were large and at the time better equipped. Many public houses also provided a backroom for customers with a punch-ball and weights, which probably encouraged greater demand for more alcoholic refreshment through the thirstful exertion of exercise. Then there was also the lone fanatic quite prepared to use his bedroom as a make-shift gym, with perhaps little consideration of the structural stresses on his home.

These places of physical endeavour flourished out of a competitive need for men to not only develop pure strength for weight-lifting but athletic physiques for aggressive contact games such as boxing, wrestling, rugby, and to a lesser extent soccer. When Percy Hunt came to the fore with the opening of his gym, it was said to be the one establishment in South Wales where physical development, or more precisely body-building, followed as a happy conclusion and not as a necessary preliminary to pure strength or a particular sport or game. Such an adoption by Percy in the early 1920's seemed to anticipate the movement in that decade away from strength feats to how well you looked physically, although progression of both disciplines ran parallel. With pure strength largely keeping hold of its grass-roots base in Wales until about the mid-1940's, it was a brave stance by the Aberavon athlete in the prevailing climate.

Much of the sporting contention in Percy's home-town arose not only from the geographical division of its population - the River Avon and the lesser flow of the River Ffrwdwyllt - but one's religious persuasion. The religious element compounded further allegiance to locality, which in turn fired greater abrasive rivalry in rugby matches between Protestant Taibach RFC and St. Joseph's Roman Catholic Church 'Saints' side, situated on the Aberavon area of the River Avon.

Percy was distinctly aware of the rivalry existing on his patch; his gym, as the street name implies, stood near the Church of England St. Mary's, which also had a rugby side and also in the vicinity of St. Joseph's Church, their clashing Victorian Gothic and Romanesque styles appearing to punctuate division in a symbolic sense. So intense was the sectarian conflict in sport between them that physical advantage was eagerly seized upon, Percy's gym becoming recognised as the main source of achieving athletic superiority with its progressive development of equipment better able to make use of training systems devised by leading British and European physical culturists.

Throughout this intense period of sectarian rivalry, which had the Taibach and 'Saints' RFC matches ostracised in town by Canon Kelly, of St. Joseph's, and played on neutral ground in Briton Ferry, Percy's gym was said to act effectively as a socialising mechanism against such prejudice. The so-called defusing effect was, however, of short, recurring, three evenings a week duration, rivalry

10. Percy and the Angels
An interpretation of the Health & Strength League
motto: 'Sacred thy body even as thy Soul'.
(Newark Lewis)

returning revitalised in sporting confrontations. With cordiality among pupils of opposing sects evident under Percy Hunt's supervision, physical strengths and weaknesses in training were noted by them and put to collective purpose on the field of battle. There was nothing more that Percy could have done apart from closing the gym to them, which would have harmed the continued success of his enterprise as they made up most of the membership. He did make a protest once, according to gym assistant Joe Manship, after one fierce confrontation between the opposing rugby sides, by ritually washing his hands of the continuing conflict in a bowl of water before a group of the culprits in the gym. The reputation of Percy's place of exercise was thus seen to grow in the early stages, and continued for some years, from the rivalry of sectarian factions training in his establishment.

To gain relief from the problems of often bitter rivalry among his pupils on the rugby field, he took on training duties with the Royal Ancient Order of Buffaloes Football Team. As a member of the Ancient order, he was also duty bound to help in the team's physical conditioning when the need arose. In his efforts to teach the side the rudiments of weight-training, Percy found difficulty in the short-term in convincing team members of the benefits and he returned to concentrate on his gym and the slow-burning fuse of pupil rivalry suppressed in work-outs.

As befitting a gym of distinctive character with Percy at the helm, there was to be a refreshing intermix of pupils over the years with students on vacation from college and university, manual and white collar workers, craftsmen, policemen and teachers. A number of pupils would make their mark in sporting activities, and there was a richness of endeavour in the continuity of seeking health and strength in a variety of disciplines.

Keep the Red Flag Flying High!
With the St. Mary's Street gym the focus of underlying sectarian rivalry among groups of pupils as much as a place for personal physical development, Percy had already resumed familiar employment as a tin worker in the Mansel Tinplate Works, whose proprietor was S.H. Byass, wealthy industrialist, landowner, and Mayor of Aberavon.

His manual employment at the 'Mansel' was varied and not regarded by fellow workers as being over-strenuous. He was always careful to lift correctly, in no way to jerk awkwardly, and to avoid injury from an incorrect stance. In all the lifting, pushes and pulls engaged in, Percy was always aware of the need for varying the demands imposed by leverages, in unison with correctness of breathing-in and breathing-out. To a number of 'Mansel' employees - and there were tough, rough men in the work-force - such a work ethic seemed, to put it mildly, rather ostentatious. Such disciplined methods of lifting at work were but an extension of his gym training, which steered him resolutely away from ruthless, mean-minded 'old hands' who would, if allowed, have mercilessly driven to over-exertion willing workers under their charge.

Only 4'-10" in height and 7st. 8lb. in weight, one of Percy's jobs demanded pulling, from one dark mill to another, 'carriages' of neatly stacked tinplate weighing about 5 to 10cwt. In moments of gymnastic skill and showmanship he would somersault over loads 4' to 6' in length and 3' to 5' in height; landing on his hands he would continue the movement in a back-flip through the open doorway of the nearby weigh-bridge office and alight nimbly upon his feet smiling before a startled weigh-bridge clerk, who was a company man through and through.

Such flamboyant acrobats were said by Percy to have been displays of exuberance at a time when the immediacy and popularity of the Labour Party began to gain momentum before the General Election of 1922. Opposing the Labour candidate and workers' choice, Ramsey MacDonald, were Major John Edwards, Liberal, and the Mayor of the town and Conservative hopeful S.H. Byass.

In expectation of a Labour triumph to come, Percy was at his father's side energetically campaigning for MacDonald as part of the onrush of political militants, prophets and fanatics blossoming forth in profusion in the Socialist Springtime before the election. Chapels, cinemas, halls and theatres, or any suitable spacious area in the open-air, were taken over by them, with even the modest elevation of Thomas Hunt's brake providing a platform for political zealots, as it was used before the 1914-18 War by Keir Hardy, chairman of the Independent Labour Party. The site for the brake then, as now for MacDonald supporters, was Bethany Square, the hub of local activities, where the elevation of Bethany Chapel, with its open face of a facade, surveyed the promised land of hope offered by the tongues of politicians.

When stirring words were written, adding to the inspired flow of emotion, by an admirer of MacDonald, Miss Minnie Pallister, a teacher at Brynmawr, to the equally rousing battle-song 'Men of Harlech', Percy included the refrain as a solo ending during pre-election displays:

Refrain:
Ramsey, Ramsey, shout it
Don't be shy about it.
Labour's day is bound to come,
We cannot do without it,
On then Labour, on to glory
'Twill be told in song and story,
How we fought at Aberavon
On election day.

The Labour victory which followed proved a harrowing defeat for Sidney Hutchinson Byass, the last Mayor of the Ancient Borough of Aberavon and the first Mayor of Port Talbot when the old borough was absorbed in 1921, losing as he did to an outsider like MacDonald. The victorious politician too would soon fall from political favour and this would be symbolised by Thomas Hunt telling his children to tear their red Labour rosette into shreds.

There were few commiserations for Byass amongst his employees; the long awaited day of Socialist triumph had arrived and they celebrated, Percy recalled, by dipping frayed ends of short lengths of thick hemp rope in grease, igniting them and marching in victorious procession up and down the 'Bottom Mill', singing 'Keep the Red Flag Flying High!'. Jubilation was rife among MacDonald supporters, Percy being staunchly Socialist as a crusading Health & Strength Leaguer.

Political gestures by Byass's employees were plentiful, but when the Abcravon physical culturist arrived in work before Byass himself (whether intentionally or not is unknown), not long after the election, his lapel emblazoned with a large rosette, it was enough for the proud, devout churchman, and donor to local causes, to dismiss Percy Hunt instantly from his employ. As a man who thrived on sensationalism his sacking popularised him as a hero before the radical element in the local Socialist Party.

Nom de Guerre
When Percy's enforced departure from the Mansel Works opened up a period of what the Aberavon athlete claimed to be ten years without full-time employment, events became duly romanticised before audiences. He was thus a victim of political conscience and the industrial depression, unemployment providing space, time and opportunity to devote energies fully to the culture of

11. Introduction Card

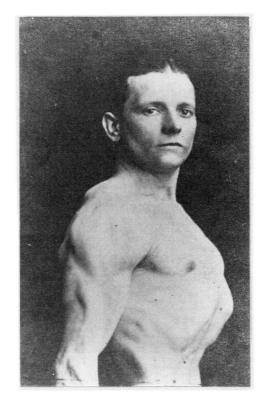

12. Percy in Fine Fettle
(Newark Lewis)

the physique and commitment to the H. & S. League. Nothing was said by him about his unemployed situation being partly due to his unwillingness to work shifts, which would have interfered with the furtherance of his stage act. He was after all a man with a mission and no obstacle should prevent him from attaining this state of being.

Now the time was ripe for Percy Hunt to take on the mantle of 'The Great Mavello', to consolidate his professional standing as a stage athlete and entertainer. With breathing space to secure theatre engagements, supported by the partial, financial security of his gym - having missed much of his mid-to-late twenties through war service - Percy became the driving force in bringing a Physical Culture Display to his home-town. Held at the Drill Hall, Ynys Street, the star of the event was former 'Britain's Strongest Man', Edward Aston,[2] who, unable to resume his career as a champion lifter after injuries sustained in the 1914-18 War, formed a famous adagio act with his female partner Xenia.

Besides theatre and promotional work Percy had already set about taking full advantage of post-war H. & S. award schemes. The awards of badges and certificates for various feats involving strength, agility and balance were usually made upon the recommendations of officially appointed League District Officers (LDO's), who were also expected to co-ordinate League activities in their district. One of their prime purposes was recruitment and they were themselves graded according to the number of new Leaguers enrolled by them. When Percy's H. & S. League gym had become established as a popular place of exercise in the 1920's, he was duly appointed an LDO and later awarded a God Medal[3] for recruiting over 100 pupils to the League. So it was that, on the 20 September 1926, Percy affiliated the gym to the League movement striving to add to his awards while encouraging pupils by his example to follow him in his athletic versatility.

World's Greatest Versatile Athlete

In his efforts to establish himself post-war, having taken an appropriate stage name, 'The Great Mavello', as a kind of defiance in the face of adversity, Percy was also bringing together a composition of feats or 'items', as he called them, in a twenty-one test challenge,[4] entitled 'World's Greatest Versatile Athlete'. Most of the feats chosen were reflected in his H. & S. 'Certificate of Merit' awards, the challenge against opponents under 11 stone all being performed in one evening. Written on sheet music the composition of feats, as Percy announced them, while not accounting for occasional changes in the list of 21, are as follows:

1. **Muscle Control**
2. **Fancy and Trick Skipping**
3. **Novelty Club Swinging to Music**
4. **Ball-Punching**
5. **Boxing**
6. **Wrestling** (Catch-as-catch-can)
7. **Running** (Sprint)
8. **Swimming** (Free-style sprint)
9. **Cycling** (Sprint)
10. **One-Hand Planche on a Chair**
11. **Standing on My Head on a Chair**
12. **A 12 Stone Man Jumping off a Chair onto My Stomach**
13. **Lifted up by My Hair**[5]
14. **Strand-pulling**
15. **Weight-Lifting** (3 feats: 2 set and one chosen)
16. **Tearing a Pack of Cards in Two**
17. **Driving a 6″ Nail through a 1″ Plank of Wood**
18. **Making a Chain out of 6″ Nails**
19. **'The Man They Could Not Hang'**[6] Suspended by my neck in a hangman's noose, I will pull out a 200 lb. chest expander while a metal plate hanging in front of my abdomen is hit several times with a 6 lb. hammer
20. **Showing Winston Churchill's Face in my Abdominal Muscles**[7]
21. **Finish with a Tenor Solo**[8]

Twenty-one as a number was at once a reference to celebration and coming of age as an all-round athlete of distinction, Percy eager to challenge athletes in a throw-down-the-gauntlet campaign by advertising in domestic and international editions of *Health & Strength*, one advert even appearing in a Malaysian issue.

By 1921 he had received his first challenge which was quickly withdrawn when the English athlete realised the scale of the feats, including for good measure ju-jitsu not often employed in his scheme of things. Percy claimed to be the leader of the British Society.[9]

Another challenger was a Scotsman who included the marathon in his 12 feats. Although capable of running a number of miles during training sessions with pupils, Percy would never have conceived taking on such a

13. Hair Gladiator Feat
Gym assistant Joe Manship lifting Percy by the hair.
(Newark Lewis)

14. Colossus
Eugen Sandow: Father of Physical Culture and Showman Supreme.
(Photo montage by the author)

distance due to muscle wastage. He thus not only refused the challenge on the grounds that the marathon was excluded from his feats, but that the Scotsman's programme also fell short of his number of items.

He did however, receive a more threatening challenge from a muscle man living in Japan, who claimed to be the 'World's Greatest Undefeated All-Round Athlete', which brought out in Percy an audacious sense of geographical bias. The story was given to me by an admirer of Percy, Keith Evans, a former Director of Education for Clwyd, and I quote him. 'Totally incensed by this oriental's temerity, Percy issued a challenge to him. Not only would he match him skill for skill, activity for activity - he even offered to meet him on neutral ground - in Cardiff!!' The bombing of Pearl Harbour in the Second World War was to put an end to any hope of such a meeting between the East and the West.

Many other rivals took up the challenge but they too found difficulty in the main with the variety of feats and number and Percy rightly claimed the 'World' title. With an inclination for home ground advantage challenges were doubly effective in his favour, having already compiled and perfected the 21 feats. He now looked forward to placing 'retired' within the title, ensuring its preservation for posterity.

Somewhere a Voice is Calling

The tenor solo finish to his stage act did not consciously present itself as part of his stage routine until Percy's return home at the end of the 1914-18 War when he sought the services of local singing teacher, Cornishman John H. Moody, receiving tuition once a week for three years.

Well versed in the mechanics and techniques of singing as part of a sound musical education, J.H. Moody was the brother of prima donna Madam Fanny Moody, the female partner and wife of Charles Manners of 'Moody-Manners' Opera Company. Further opportunities to improve Percy's tenor voice thus became readily available through his singing teacher's intermediary contact with his sister Fanny Moody, probably helped by family connections with Redruth, Cornwall, where both Madam Moody and Percy's mother were born and in the same year, 1866. Such a convenient source of influence was to enable the Welsh tenor to favourably approach Madam Moody's husband, the Irish Bass and impresario Charles Manners, for professional assistance.

With their opera company disbanded in 1916, after touring the provinces since 1896, the meeting and subsequent advice given on singing techniques is recollected by Percy Hunt as having taken place when the retired opera stars, holidaying in South Wales, visited J.H. Moody. While staying in Aberavon, rooms were taken at the Walnut Tree Hotel, High Street, and it was here that the all-round athlete and tenor met Fanny Moody and Charles Manners. Percy seems to have recounted little of what took place between the ageing Irish singer and himself, although he took note that Manners was quite tall, with piercing eyes, a large grey moustache, and all these distinct features were complimented by a deep resonant speaking voice.

Charles Manners in his prime had indeed been tall in stature at 6'-3", a lusty extrovert with a powerful singing voice and an impressive stage personality. A one-time teacher of singing at the Royal Irish Academy of Music in Dublin, the Royal Academy of Music in London, and later in Italy, he was notable in roles as the King in *Maritana* and as Mephistopheles in Gounod's *Faust*. It is said he was cast in the rugged mould of the Russian basso profundo Charliapin. Here then, before Charles Manners, stood the diminutive Welsh light tenor of supposed promise, all 4'-10" in height, and about 7 to 8 stone in weight. Despite the Irish bass's operatic pedigree and physical presence, Manners was said to be sympathetic to those in his employ, or potential operatic singers in need of his professional help. It is therefore supposed that he received the Welsh all-round athlete and tenor in the same manner.

Whatever assistance Charles Manners gave the Welsh tenor, the few brief sessions he received could only have been cosmetic. Nevertheless, the fact that he had received singing instructions from the celebrated Irish bass and met his wife Madam Moody, whose soprano voice was likened to Melba's in timbre - although Percy found her personality overbearing - was something positive to juggle with in moments of one-upmanship impressing a theatre manager for a booking.

Despite John H. Moody's groundwork and Charles Manners' professional finishing touches, Percy's tenor voice at best was not regarded by local people with musical discernment as anything special. They deduced that the finale solo in his display merely excused and hid vocal deficiencies in what had preceded. It was remarked by them that the Great Mavello's singing was the least memorable part of his stage performance. Such remarks, though possibly not entirely without justification, were in response to Percy's belief that if he ever gave up his versatile stage act he could turn to solo singing without difficulty as a professional singer. For those not so inclined for various reasons to make such judgements of his singing, it was enough for them that he was able to sing at all after his strenuous stage routine. Here then perhaps was another aspect of the bravura element emerging in Percy's performance.

One peculiarity of his vocal training was the unorthodox and dubious method of supposedly strengthening his light tenor voice by shouting the high notes. This shouting technique was wisely practised from the isolated nearby summit of Mynydd Dinas, which elevated him conveniently away from would-be irate neighbours. Shouting the high notes was a practice not unknown in Percy's days, prevalent with tenors who found the rigours of the opera circuit forced them to have recourse to this reprehensible method - hence tenor 'shouters'.

It is uncertain which of Percy's singing teachers advised such a risky and crude procedure, for he made no outright claims as to its origin. There is a possible clue as to the source in that Percy was advised by his father to adopt the thespian technique of 'throwing the voice', so to speak, in his talks on stage, a method used by Thomas Hunt as town crier. Whatever the source, he absorbed the method into his training, viewing the top notes as equivalent to the exercising of more muscular areas of his anatomy. He even attempted to authenticate this equivalence by implying that the practice was a natural progression for a true all-rounder to adopt. He might have had in mind the American all-rounder Macfadden who believed in singing while he developed himself to physical perfection.

It is debatable what quality of vocal volume was achieved by the shouting technique, although its use according to a few colleagues was unique in challenging two renowned operatic 'belters' - Leoncavallo's 'Your Tiny Hand is Frozen' from La Boheme and 'On with the Motley' from Pagliacci.

Besides the two arias, the remaining store of tonic-sol-fa and stave notation sheets for the pianist, and books kept in his small leather music case, were traditional songs and ballads mainly of English, Irish and American origin, with one Welsh ballad in English included. Although the following items are not the complete selection of what he sang they were the nucleus of his repertoire:

Somewhere a Voice is Calling	(Percy's favourite) Eileen Newton and Arthur F. Tate, 1911 (English)
I'll Walk Beside You	Edward Locton, 1936 (English)
It is only a Tiny Garden	Hayden Wood and Lillian Glanville, 1916 (English)
Watchman! What of the Night?	Words anon. Music J. Sarjeant, 1905 (English)
Lamentations of Nelly Jones	N. Jones 19th cent. (Welsh)
The Rose of Tralee	C. Mordaunt Spencer, 1912 (Irish)

Danny Boy	Fred L. Weatherly, 1913 (Irish)
Your Eyes Have Told Me So	Gus Kahn, Walter Blanfuss and
	Egbert van Alstyne, 1919 (USA)
Just Awearing for You	Carrie Jacobs-Bond, 1901 (USA)
Dear Old Pal of Mine	Gitz Rice and Harold Robe, 1918 (USA)
Mother	Irving Berlin, 1914-18 War (USA)
Italian Salad	F.R. Genee, 19th cent. (German)[10]

The arias, songs and ballads of which Percy invariably gave renditions in the gym, were thankfully for a number of pupils and colleagues, often of the first verse only. His favourite solo 'Somewhere a Voice is Calling', like 'Mother', although given full verse treatment, was of a short duration. Percy's singing of his favourite song in the gym often included, as he sang, a few of the musical interpretations as written in the score:

Slowly and with expression:-   **Dusk, and the sha-dows**
fall — ing _____ O'er land and sea; _____
Some-where a voice is call–ing, _____ Call — ing for Me! _____

The first verse was then repeated with promptings of 'Slightly quicker-urging on' and 'mysterioso'.

'Con sentimento' interpreted the last verse, which was repeated with change in emphasis of 'Slowly and with intense expression':-

Night, and the stars are gleam-ing, _____ Ten-der and true;
Dear-est! my heart is dream—ing, _____ Very Slowly, dying away:
Dream-ing, of you._____

No doubt the musical session would have been all very informative and effective in a master class situation, but for pupils in the gym romantic sentimentality needed to be soundly hit on the head before it caused problems concentrating on exercise.

The most dramatic of songs in Percy's repertoire was 'Watchman! What of the Night?' A popular Victorian duet for tenor and bass or bass-baritone, Joe Manship recalled that Percy gave the song an airing in the gym when a miner friend, who was an H. & S. Leaguer from the Cynon Valley, paid him a visit.

Standing at the gym's threshold the miner boomed a deep-throated greeting to Percy, who suddenly responded by taking up a theatrical pose and singing in earnest the opening lines for tenor:

Say, watchman, what of the night?   Do the dews of morn-ing fall?   Have the or-i-ent skies a border of light, like the fringe of a fu-ner-al Pall?

Before Percy could complete the rest of the opening for the bass part to come in, the entry of pupils boisterous in their eagerness to begin exercise ended the intended duet, his singing stance quickly taking up an abdominal isolation pose with great hisses of air as he formed a cavity beneath the rib cage and pumped out a rope-like column of muscle. Vocal renditions by Percy in the gym were not unusual, but it seemed to Joe that he had been caught in a serious vocal mood and was not prepared for the intrusion of pupils, and novice ones at that; the moment had passed for 'Watchman! What of the Night?', never to return in the gym.

Sacred, Operatic and Popular Music

While seeking the limelight exposure of a stage, participation in local cultural activities proved not only a satisfactory continuity but a necessary avenue for a celebrated athlete to take, demonstrating further his versatile qualities.

In the early 1920's Percy joined one of the many small male voice choirs in town, known as Harry Lewis's Male Voice Concert Party, after the choir's conductor, who was the brother of Newark, the visual recorder of the aspiring athlete's progression from the 1900's.

Chorally well-balanced, the male voice choir of about 16 voices gained a sound reputation in a repertoire of sacred, operatic and popular music. The highlight of the season was the annual week's tour of Devon at Easter and Cornwall in August. Although these events were regarded as holiday periods, the choir always committed themselves to a Grand Concert given on the final day, a Sunday, of each tour, at both Exeter and Truro Cathedrals.

Whenever an opportunity arose Percy, the athlete, would manage to include an abridged version of his stage act, although never on the Sunday event. His performance was slotted between choral pieces of sombre timbre like 'Abide with Me' and music in a lighter vein, such as the song, popular with choral members, known as 'Johnny Peg-Leg'. The chorus gave an effective and amusing transposition of the character's lameness by rhythmic stamping of each choir member's feet, with a heavier tread upon the supposed peg-leg!

15. Harry Lewis's Male Voice Concert Party with Mascot
Back Row: J. Grey, Haydn Daniels, Will Lewis. Second Row: Tommy H. Rees,
Harry Green, Jim Johnson, Frank Cronin, D. Phillips, R. Thorne. Third Row:
W.G. Rees, Bryn Wright, Dai Morgan (sec), Harry Lewis (conductor),
D. Dyer (piano), G. Henry, D. John. Front Row: M. Thomas, Percy Hunt.
(Newmark Lewis)

16. 'A Wond'ring Min – strel I…'
Percy as a Coolie in the Mikado.
(Newark Lewis)

Percy, the tenor, remained with Harry Lewis's choir for some years and extended, as did other members, his musical activities by joining both the Port Talbot and District Mixed Choral Society and the Port Talbot and Aberavon Operatic Society.

A Short Life but a Gay One

For the opera-lover the arrival of the annual amateur season was a much-awaited climax in the cultural and social calendar of town and district, the Aberavon athlete's association with the premier operatic society coming during a period when there was not only one, but two to enjoy and compare in the latter part of the 1920's and the early 1930's. The productions followed one another in the early months and so intense and sustained was the rivalry between them that in the pre-season any new musical which appeared on the London stage brought to the surface fierce competition to obtain permission to present the production first.

The story of operatic rivalry and the rift which fuelled its continuance was aired by Percy in response to a pupil's tenuous and unintentional cue in the gym that he had received a St. Valentine's card on which was written the much-used opening Shakespearean line from *Twelfth Night*, Scene 1, Act 1: 'If music be the food of love, play on; ...' That the metaphorical reference to music as a possible aphrodisiac should register in the Great Mavello's mind in all probability speaks of his amorous interludes with maiden members of the chorus. The gay - if I may use the adjective in its former sense - abandon of the hitherto comparative reserve of playing members before the full-tilting, music-lilting week's production, tended to encourage romantic interludes and Percy on these occasions was said to be ardently amorous. The rift itself, which he spoke about, was essentially a dramatic unfolding of jealousy and division among warring factions, the principals of which effected an unbridgeable split within the premier society Port Talbot and Aberavon, ultimately leading to a break-away group forming a rival society, Afan and District.

The roots of division even manifested themselves in Percy's H. & S. League gym, affecting recruitment, with parents of schoolboy pupils supportive of the rival society forbidding their children from attending his place of exercise. Such alienating measures stemmed not only from publicity of the town's physical culture personality's enrolment with the original society by Concert Party conductor Harry Lewis, who was himself a member, but from Percy's recruitment to the society of a number of his pupils. Among operetta-loving patrons, even those supportive of the premier society, such resentment of the celebrated stage athlete was soon put into perspective by the oncoming drama of two operatic productions awaiting expression in performances. The intensity of it all had taken over the daily routine of town life and Percy's endeavours to refresh the minds of those who did not believe in the benefits of physical culture, exciting public opinion far beyond the boundaries of the borough in 1927.

From the ensuing discord contrasting operettas emerged triumphantly in the following year, 1928, with the Port Talbot and Aberavon production of the Gilbert and Sullivan favourite *The Mikado* commencing on 30 January and the break-away Afan and District - with a fine sense of rivalry - staging *The Rebel Maid* on 3 March. Both productions were held in the New Theatre, Talbot Road.

Against a backdrop of considerable post-operatic ill-feeling over which production was the better, Percy sallied forth in the town proclaiming to friends and colleagues, and those prepared to listen, that his tenor voice had reached its peak in *The Mikado* and would be sustained in forthcoming stage appearances. It is difficult to imagine any genuine enthusiasm for such a singularly mundane claim of peak voice quality in a climate still enthralled as it was by collective voices of two charged-up operatic society productions still not yet cold to emotive acclaim.

The follow-on from Percy's vocal peak was the belief that if it were not for his commitments as a professional stage artist, an LDO, a gymnasium proprietor, and countless time-consuming displays given free for charity, he would have sought auditions for principal operetta roles. Even if capable of such a transformation from the chorus, which his colleagues and pupils inclined to doubt because of the light quality of his tenor voice, he could assume no other role than of himself. Indeed many pupils would probably have frumpled their muscles at the thought of a more complete musical treatment of items sung in the gym by their mentor in the months of operatic rehearsals and production. The consensus of pupil opinion at the time was that it had been enough to listen to Percy's singing of the lines of *The Mikado* favourite, as sung by the Mikado's son Nanki-Poo: **'A wond'ring min-strel I ____ A thing of shreds ____ and patches, Of bal-lads, songs and snatches, And dreamy lul-la-by!____'** without the added musical intensity and impetus of purpose which principal roles would have demanded upon him.

Such had been the musical conditioning during operatic rehearsals that Percy would extend notes playfully in a tour de force of breath capacity and control. For the duration of some months, and on every gym evening in the final four weeks through to the week of operatic production, resonances of athletes at exercise played their discordant counterpoint to Percy's tenor flourishes in dominant tempo. One thing in the pupils' favour was the poor acoustics of a small gym, which thankfully reduced the decibels of his high notes, sometimes sustained by the 'shouting' method. 'The commotion was really something,' Joe Manship recalled, 'with often a pupil retaliating by clashing the weights harder and exhaling breath louder than normal.' This kind of strategy was sometimes taken up by other pupils for fun, drowning Percy's singing, which of course did not entirely please him.

It was noticeable among colleagues and pupils that the placement of Percy's tenor solo of song, ballad or aria, as an item in the order of athletic feats indicated that to him it had attained great significance. There were moments, possibly, when Percy might well have believed that he was a singer caught up in the variety of his versatile act. He remained, whether believing this or not, locked into a series of feats that had become like old companions, reliable and compatible.

17. Percy in Repose in the Garden of 15 St. Mary's Street, Aberavon
(Newark Lewis)

Chapter 4

Before a Captive Audience

Percy Hunt's rise as a stage athlete and entertainer 'before a captive audience', as he referred to them, came at a time of decline in Music Hall acts as they met competition from silent films and later 'talkies'. The irony of the situation was not lost on him and he wasted no time in seeking engagements.

From 1912 to the end of the Second World War his performances were staged in a mix of venues from Public Halls, YMCA's, Workmen's Halls, Miners' Institutes, Welfare Clubs and Variety Theatres to castellated mansions. Although a number of Music Halls/Variety Theatre-cum- Cinemas still clung to traditional programmes of variety 'turns', live acts were now relegated to interval 'spots' in film entertainment. So it was during the fall in popularity of music hall acts, in which the stage strongman/athlete had featured, that Percy appeared as an interval artist.

As a learning process the physical culturist's initial stage appearances were in local halls and theatres, which brought him into close contact with professional artists, theatre managers and musicians of colourful repute. With gathered experience and when the opportunity arose, the all-round athlete extended his professional act beyond the comparative bias of local audiences to more critical receptions in other areas of Wales and England. In due course the novelty aspects of his act were said to gain the praises of stage colleagues and there was more than a hint of an aspiring star in ascendance at Health and Strength League rallies and displays in London, where he met many of the greats of the international scene. During this period of his stage craft Percy's engagements were numerous and I have curtailed description and accounts making reference only to his experience as a jobbing professional strongman in England, his tours of the South Wales valleys and his participation in war-time charity shows during 1940 to 1945.

In the early pre-First World War engagements Percy was sometimes assisted by his brother Chris, with whom a close bond had been forged, while often employing young neighbourhood boys (usually in pairs) so as to use their lively bodyweight as convenient poundage until brothers Albert and Cyril were old enough to take their place (Plate. 4). Nephews and nieces were also to assist Percy on stage or take part in gym exercise. They were Eliza's son and daughter, Harold and Elizabeth Tredree; Violet's sons, Percy and William Leigh;

Blanche's youngest daughter Mary - her elder sister Blanche was more of an absorbed onlooker of her uncle's gym and stage exploits - and stepson Hubert Frances. The introduction of human poundage was not so much a novel way of covering up Percy's lack of weight, but an improvisation in the classical tradition of stage strongmen, which continued throughout his performances when the opportunity arose.

Public Hall

Before the 'Great Mavello' stage name of the early 1920's marked Percy's emergence as a professional stage artist, his first engagement proper took place before the First World War in the Public Hall, Water Street, Aberavon. Popularly known as the 'Puby', the hall had been built in 1873 and, as usual for such buildings, was the corner-stone of local events including religious and political gatherings, and various musical, cinematic and sporting shows.

Although well acquainted with the art of boxing, Percy's appearance in the boisterous intervals between boxing bouts was perhaps not the ideal situation for a stage athlete to show off the finer points of balance, club swinging, muscle control, novelty lifting of weights and a solo finale to an audience who gorged their appetites for entertainment in pugilistic encounters of blood and guts. The experience nevertheless became a valuable learning process for the all-round athlete.

Continuing his displays in the hall into the 1920's he began to show what might be taken as an aesthetic interest in the structure of the 'Puby' - as he was to do with other venues - and noted that the exterior of the building above lock-up premises was hardly worthy of a glance while the interior displayed Nonconformist chapel overtones in the plain, but gaudy-coloured, cast-iron pillars supporting a gallery around three sides of the hall. The available seating was, he remembered, from the luxury comfort of red linoleum, lift-up seats, to hard-on-bottoms wooden benches at the rear and in the gallery. On the narrow, end side of the gallery short pillars supported a projection box and on the opposite end wall was the projection screen awaiting the moving picture, with an improvised stage or boxing ring assembled on the floor when the need arose. These recollections of aspects of the Public Hall's architecture and interior decor were unusual, for the athlete previously seemed solely concerned with his own physical development and performance, structural detail not registering again with quite such perception. There was, however, to be vividness in his descriptions of the hall's atmosphere and audience, which carried on to other venues where he gave his displays.

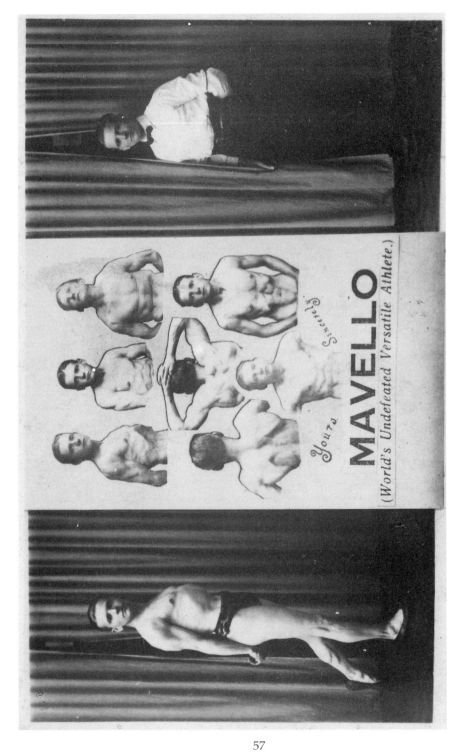

18. Mavello
A promotional image
(Newark Lewis)

19. (Newark Lewis)

The showing of silent films at the 'Puby' were, Percy recalled, lively affairs with customary patriotic singing before the commencement of the film show of 'Soldiers of the Queen' long after the reign of Queen Victoria ended. With an orchestrated accompaniment of stamping of feet the scene was then set up for varying kinds of behaviour as the evening progressed. He knew from experience that for some young boys it was common practice when viewing films to urinate freely upon the gallery floor rather than pay a visit to the 'gents' and miss a second of the film drama or comedy situation unfolding before their eyes. A more controlled and wilful act of misbehaviour, but regarded as great fun by them, was the accurate dropping of dried peas or even spittle - if peas were in short supply - upon the bald pates of unfortunate men seated below. Such wayward practices infuriated some victims and this was rather off-putting at times in Percy's performance when he required concentration.

These water-closet outlets and boyish pranks were as much a part of the provided entertainment as the reactions of a member of the audience living the dramatic action of the ever popular 'Cowboys and Indians' films. Here, Percy recalled, regular Western fan Tom (Moan) Davies would attempt to come to the rescue of a celluloid cowboy about to be bludgeoned from behind, by jumping up suddenly from his seat shouting, 'Look behind you!! Look behind you!!' Such outbursts did not disturb the musical interpretation of film action of the resident ensemble familiar to Percy in his act. Headed by pianist Jim Batt, renowned for his run-away accompaniment of silent films, he was assisted by two brothers, Bill (the fiddler) and Dai (double-bass) Davies.

On the night of Tuesday, 14 October 1924, when Percy booked for an engagement, the Public Hall became the latest cinema to succumb to the potentially high flammability of nitrate-based film stock. The stage athlete had been sitting in the back of the hall - the film having just commenced - awaiting the interval, when a women, upon seeing flames leaping out from the projection box, suddenly screamed with alarm. Although the fire quickly took hold in the gallery, Percy was more than surprised to find that there was no panic. In the early stages of the burning he found himself not quite panicking, but near enough, when he and the three members of the ensemble were the last to evacuate the building. In fact, they were held back by those in the audience standing on the stairs demanding their money be returned. Even when the four entertainers managed to leave the burning hall they found great difficulty not only distancing themselves from the impending inferno, with hundreds of onlookers congesting Water Street and High Street, but in hauling Percy's large leather bag of equipment totalling about 70 lb.

and the double-bass player's bulky musical instrument. With Percy leading the way the group eventually pushed through the throng to safety as the fire took its final hold on the building. It seemed to him that most of the inhabitants in the surrounding district witnessed the end of the Water Street Public Hall. There was also an added concern among the crowds for the safety of James Ramsey MacDonald who had booked rooms in the nearby Walnut Tree Hotel.

As if to compensate for the loss of a popular venue a hero was sought and found in the figure of projector operator Mr. Cotton, who was slightly burned about the arms in his efforts to put out the fire while saving the projector and slides. With an early hall lost to him for engagements, Percy was to miss the special 'Puby' atmosphere of film shows and reminisced about the resolve to succeed in his athletic skills before an audience during those interval displays between boxing contests.

Palace

'Vint's' Palace of Varieties, Water Street, opened briefly as a live theatre in 1911 by owner Leon Vint, but it was not until the early 1920's and 1930's, after a lengthy period of disuse, that the theatre opened again as a cinema hosting Percy's interval 'turns'.

It was the most intimate venue in the structural sense of the variety-cum-theatre cinemas Percy played in, the narrow sloping limited ground floor seating and steeply raked gallery occupying an exceptionally tight site, pushing spectator viewing almost to within touching distance from a small stage erected above the theatre's main entrance. So confined was it in fact that when one of the Great Mavello's Indian clubs slipped from his grasp, in an attempted high throw, the wayward flight it followed terminated in the hand of a wag seated in the front row of the gallery, who retorted, "Howzzat! Percy? Howzzat!!?"

Despite the Palace's cramped interior, which required gallery patrons trekking outside the theatre after purchasing a ticket to gain entry at the rear, the front of the theatre, Percy recalled, was visually impressive In the early years he found the 'Classical' elements of Greek and Roman influence even more spectacular with thinly-draped, muse-like, female stone statues, ensconced in each of two elevated niches, holding an oil-lit torch. In the night with a whipping wind flickering the flames and casting ghostly shadows, there was also the hazard of burning oil dripping on patrons with flaming consequences. Percy claimed that the fiery effect was to inspire him years later to construct an electric torch and mirror display in his act that was equally spectacular without any near member of the audience going up like a Roman candle.

One of the most colourful of theatre musicians Percy ever worked with was the Palace's wizard on the keys, Edward Llewellyn Spragge. Remembered as a fine though somewhat eccentric musician, the pianist gained a reputation as an exceptionally fiery interpreter of silent film chases, becoming known because of this as the 'mad' pianist. Percy could not help but notice that his enthused dramatic thumping often inflicted chaos upon the piano keys, with a collection of maimed ivories left like bones upon the piano top. At best Edward Llewellyn Spragge fused music with image and was regarded by the Aberavon athlete as a re-defining influence in his muscle dancing routine,[1] from its first expression with members of the 10th Bn. Band of the South Wales Borderers.

Grand Theatre

Formerly Prince of Wales Theatre and later the Assembly Rooms, the Grand Theatre in Clarence Street/ High Street stood large as a play, variety and cinema venue at the rear of a single row of terraced cottages in the cul-de-sac of Clarence Street, a number of the dwellings being shadowed by the northerly facing side wall of Percy's mother's 'Heavenly Jerusalem', Zion Chapel.

No 'Palace' facade blessed the 'Grand', only a plain side of red brick and glass-topped entrance before alterations placed it in High Street. The interior decor and the gallery Percy found no better, although the stage was reputed to be at one time the largest in Wales.

Involved in the running of the Grand Theatre at the time of Percy's engagements were two brothers, Gwyn and Trevor Saunders, the latter a wax-moustached all-round sportsman sympathetic to his H. & S. League cause and nursing ambitions as a stage athlete. Trevor Saunders with his wife also ran the Red Lion Public House, convenient to its situation at the threshold of Clarence Street, where itinerant stage artists and members of the audience quenched their alcoholic thirst in a pall of cigar, cigarette and pipe smoke. As a teetotal, non-smoking Leaguer, Percy always felt duty bound to join them briefly as part of his brand of public relations stance against the evils of alcohol and smoking, while he drank lemonade with a cheerful smile and exuberantly condemned both addictions to those about him. It is unknown what kind of reaction Percy received from the addicted.

During occasional engagements in the 'Grand', Percy came into contact with the talented musician in residence, P.W. Peat - stage names Jules Frascati. Very much aware of the often intense rivalry between theatre managers for the services of the best musical interpreter of silent films Peat, Percy noted, had

20. Posing with Rose Bowl and Bovril Silver Medal
The rose bowl was presented by pupils in recognition of Percy's all-round
prowess as a Health & Strength League athlete, and the medal awarded by
Bovril for 'Body Control'.
(Newark Lewis)

been employed in the 'Vint's' Palace before being lured to the Grand Theatre with financial inducements.

Similar rivalry existed for the engaging of interval 'turn' performers like Percy Hunt, but as a local product well known to audiences in town he would not have had the same impact as an English outsider or, more exotic still, a European artist. There was a reversal of this in that 'The Great Mavello' was to receive more praise for his act in parts of England and, if he had contacts and a contract with an agent, might have taken the opportunity of trying his luck on the Continent. He had to accept things the way they were and this he did by developing and adding to his stage presence and content in the name of Health & Strength and the League.

Picturedrome/Capital

Of the town venues in the 1920's and 1930's the 'Picturedrome', High Street, later 'Capital' in the 1930's, became a more permanent stage for the physical culturist's displays, offered, as was customary, in traditional variety ' turns' in the interval of silent films.

Built during the First World War, the theatre became ideal for Percy to view professional acts by itinerant artists so as to repolish, extend and refine his athletic performance after the war years, such opportunities being given by theatre manager Johnny Rees, who seemed to have had a bias for employing versatile stage athletes. The preference possibly arose from the fact that his brother Billy had himself been an athlete, winning a coveted 'Powder Hall' professional sprint championship. There were also distinct family ties with the theatre for not only was Percy's father the doorman and elder sister Eliza one of the usherettes, another sister married the then resident pianist George Bowen.

The Picturedrome/Capital stood slightly back off High Street, the entrance elevated by broad flights of stone steps with niches in a plain facade. Percy believed they should have held statues of the famous strongmen Eugen Sandow and Bernarr Adolphus Macfadden. The interior he found suitable, with just the bare essentials of a modest proportioned stage, upon which a number of promotional photographs of Percy were taken by Newark Lewis[2] (Plate. 21), an orchestra pit for silent films and live performances and a curved gallery extending audience capacity.

Separated from the prominence of the Walnut Tree Hotel by its namesake Walnut Tree Lane, the theatre was connected on the opposite side to 'Rees the tea shop', owned by the manager's brother Billy Rees, where Percy enjoyed a

21. Age-Span
Percy between the ages of 44 years (left) and 29 years (right).
(Newark Lewis)

regular cup of tea in keeping with his teetotal attitude. The unconnected side of the tea shop was separated by Pear Tree Lane which then belyingly held no possible imagery of such luscious fruits, but rather did it slink its narrow, dog-legged, grubby pretence to a blacksmith's forge, adjacent to the rear of the theatre and Auction Rooms, where boxing bouts took place. Percy took advantage of their sitings as convenient venues for casual employment as a blacksmith's striker and sparring partner, which improved his strength, speed and stamina for his stage exploits.

When unemployed as a blacksmith striker, sparring partner or stage athlete, he accepted invitations to join the ranks of touring companies at the theatre, which sometimes meant being drafted as a member of the chorus of an opera/operetta or review. From *Uncle Tom's Cabin* to *Madam Butterfly*, he gave of his best in professional company, as one professional to another.

Through some of the acts encountered, Percy became acquainted with a family group of performers known as 'The Musical Seymours', who toured the provinces in England and Wales. Assisted by their three children (there might have been further additions), both parents were capable of playing a variety of musical instruments and were, according to Percy, expert in all of them: string, wind, or percussion. Their act was composed of a medley of popular and sometimes classical music intermixed in novel and amusing arrangements.

In the theatre he was often challenged by rival athletes in the audience, or any strong man who fancied his chance, and they tested him to his limit as a versatile athlete. Although not always successful in challenges he would nevertheless claim, in most instances, that he had lifted with ease the weight in question the previous evening in the gym. Whatever the truths surrounding these inconsistencies, Percy was to find through direct contact with professional strongmen that equipment was often tampered with by a number of strength athletes in their acts, which gave them distinct and unfair advantage. For instance, he was introduced to variations of barbell circumference devised to suite the grip size of the athlete and, by using sand, lead shot or mercury, he could also make the hollow globes of the barbell heavier for the challenger or lighter for the so-called strongman by means of a bung-hole secretly filled or emptied by an assistant. When Percy realised how prevalent cheating was he made it quite clear to audiences that he followed combinations of skill, strength, and practice without recourse to trickery in his display.

In this part of town given to commercial enterprise, where closely sited theatre-cum-cinemas/halls rivalled one another for audience patronage; where mazed streets and lanes seemed failingly to attempt some definite order from the jostle of buildings which piled and pushed almost carelessly for recognition and dominance over decades; where the ancient town cross once stood in the space in front of the red Lion Public House, near Zion Chapel and Grand Theatre in Clarence Street; where Church Street slid past the South wall of the Red Lion and terminated its line, following across High Street, almost direct to Percy Hunt's birth place in Tymawr Street; where the Picturedrome/Capital - the crucible of his professional stage ambitions - was dwarfed by the commodious corner pile of the Walnut Tree Hotel in High Street and the elevated 'Puby' Hall at its rear in Water Street, the Ancient Borough of Aberavon was reassuringly imprinted and energised with intimate reminiscences of Percy's early childhood and maturity as a Health & Strength League athlete.

Palace Theatre

In Wales the Palace Theatre in High Street, Swansea, remains, in terms of a music hall and cinema of distinctive architectural design and historical pedigree, one of the more prestigious of Percy Hunt's venues. Opened in 1888 as the Swansea Pavilion, the name changed several times during the building's lifetime as a variety theatre and cinema.

Erected on a dramatic triangular site in renaissance style, the 'Palace' was to the Aberavon athlete a theatre of strange, deceptive illusion to play in. Without room for stage boxes the two steeply-raked balconies curved to the proscenium arch and confined stage with orchestra pit, situated in the wedge-end of the building, creating an auditorium of deceptive, spatial, fan-like depth. Percy admitted that he seemed to be squeezed even smaller than he really was on stage until be became used to the theatre.

Although Percy Hunt had taken on the title of 'Great Mavello', the *nom de guerre* did not appear in the *South Wales Evening Post* 'Postscripts from the Past' account of the programme of events in 1924, an omission which he put down to printing error:

> Top of the bill were The Four Lagoons, a clever quartet who delighted everyone with their high musical standard. An exhibition of difficult dances was given by Ciss and Phyl, and Gilbert and Mather brought the memories flooding back with their old fashioned melodies.
> To cap it all there was Percy Hunt, the weight-lifter and Great Musicus, who could drum up any tune on his kitchen utensils.

Remembered by Percy for the similarity of his own stage name to the 'Great Musicus', he considered the latter act to be novel entertainment with renditions of popular tunes drummed up by using spoons of various sizes. After the show both the 'Great Mavello' and the 'Great Musicus' exchanged rudiments of their performances. While Percy demonstrated techniques of hand-balance his fellow artist revealed how to conjure up tunes from deft clashings of two spoons on different parts of the anatomy - elbows, thighs, head and chest cavity areas. Percy found the different areas for spoon clashings gave off varying sounds and related the effect to throwing the voice in the thespian manner from the throat and chest resonances.

Holborn Empire

The Holborn Empire, High Holborn, Holborn, London, became a favoured venue before the Second World War for the Annual Health & Strength Displays,[3] Percy taking his part as an invited guest artist from Wales in four shows. The most memorable of the Holborn Empire displays was in competition on 21 March 1936,[4] to find the 'Best Developed Man in Great Britain over 40 years of Age' (both amateur and professional and between the ages of 40 and 45 years). The event was to be seen by the Welsh athlete as a perfect opportunity for him to crown his middle years with an official title of some worth and qualification. *Health & Strength* presented the competition as '...a chance for some of the glorious old time athletes to prove that physical culture life is the best and healthiest life'.

Chosen as one of four candidates in the final - the remaining three selected being W.H. Jay of London, C. Izod of Kettering, and Thomas Jarvie of Glasgow - Percy travelled early by rail on a day return to London with gym assistant Joe Manship, having heard rumours of difficulties in picking a winner from photographs in categories of amateur and professional.

Intent on making up the minds of the judges with a personal appearance, the journey to the display had thus been held in some secrecy, but once on the train Percy did not seem to Joe Manship unduly troubled by events. On the contrary he had brought with him the *Health & Strength* magazine issue that had published his favourite classical pose taken for the competition of that year on the stage of the Capital Theatre back home. Printed next to the editorial introduction to the competition he would from time to time on the journey turn to the photograph, captioned with 'The Great Mavello', and read aloud to Joe, or anyone else who happened to be with them in the compartment, the apt poetic companion-piece to the image, in which the editor recalled the lines of American poet J.R. Lowell:

Lgr. C. Izod, Kettering. (48)

G/Lgr. Percy Hunt. (44)

Thomas Jarvie, Glasgow. (44)

Lgr. W.H. Jay, London. (60)

22. Finalists for Britain's Best Developed Man over 40 Competition
(Photo H.&S.)

In life's small things be resolute and great
To keep thy muscle trained; know'st thou when Fate
Thy measure takes, or when she'll say to thee,
'I find thee worthy; do this deed for me?'

There was no doubt in Joe Manship's mind that while Percy Hunt accepted the poem as particular to him, the prize of £5.5s.0d., plus a silver cup valued at £10.10s.0d. for the winner, were also encouraging.

Health & Strength Displays and rallies held in the Holborn Empire were seen as a meeting of kindred spirits in health and strength, Percy having already made known back home the euphoria experienced from previous displays, and here he was again not as guest artist but as a competitor.

The sense of camaraderie is perhaps best described by acquaintance and special *Health & Strength* correspondent Gilbert E. Odd, in his rather high-flown introductory account of the eighth annual display, which irritated both Welshmen with the passing blinkered implication that Britain contains no other nation than England:

A Great Show - A Wonderful Audience - A Splendid Tonic

Spring is the time of youth and what more fitting day for the gathering of the youth of England could be selected than March 21st, when winter is ended and life bursts forth anew so gloriously?

Once more the mecca of the healthy and strong, the Holborn Empire, is the venue on this glorious Spring afternoon, for the eighth annual banding together of the 'Health & Strength" League. The sunlit streets of the metropolis are filled with the nation's fittest men and women, wending their way to where they can meet and enjoy a veritable olympiad of Physical Culture.

Friends meet friends, strangers are welcomed and made friends; into the theatre they troop, laughing and care-free, with badges and brooches of like pattern, to show the rest of the world that they are brothers and sisters of one great fraternity of radiant health and physical beauty. Every seat is filled, standing room is taxed to capacity; the programmes they already know by heart eagerly scanned and when the call comes to join together in the lusty singing of ballads of national tradition, they use those capacious lungs of theirs to full advantage and "raise the roof".

It was in the singing of the accepted League song, written in 1934 by Leaguer N. Castle, of North London, to the surging tune 'Marching to Georgia',[5] that the Welsh all-rounder first sensed that special feeling of belonging to a family of athletes. Inspirational as it was when compared to other contributions, Percy encouraged pupils to sing 'The League Song' at all local physical culture displays from the mid-1930's into the 1940's, with an occasional solo airing after his act.

The lyrics of the song display a triumphant rejoicing embodied within the pursuit of health, strength and happiness, heightened in line three, verse two with an apparent miraculous curative faith which Percy, in his own way, tried to instil in others. So it was on Saturday, 21 March that 'The League Song' was given its usual lusty mass voicing, with Percy Hunt (tenor) and Joe Manship (baritone) giving a rendition in Welsh hwyl style:

The League Song

Leaguers lift your voices and proclaim your joyful song!
Sing the battle to the swift, the triumph to the strong;
Sing the joy of living as you pass the road along;
Right round the world set it ringing!
Chorus:
Hurrah! Hurrah! Ring out the Leaguers Song!
Hurrah! Hurrah! Proclaim it loud and long!
Body, Mind and Spirit, balanced true and going strong!
That is the song worth the singing.

Sing a life of fitness for yourself and all mankind;
Sing a perfect Temple for the Spirit and the Mind;
Sing until the deaf shall hear and sight come to the blind;
Sing till the world's with you singing!
Chorus:

Sing the Body Beautiful as God who made it planned;
Sing the Body Supple, quick to move at His Command;
Sing the Body Strong to help a comrade help and hand;
Fill all the Earth with your singing!
Chorus:

With the completion of the opening address given by T. Bowen Partington, Vice-President of the League, and 'The League Song' voiced under the leadership of T.P. Ratcliff, Percy was to hear from reliable sources that a mix-up had taken place over photographs, and the amateur/professional status of contestants, in the over-40 competition. While the show began with the Walthamstow Ladies H. & S. Club Physical Training champions, 'Percy suddenly took off', Joe remembered, 'like a coiled spring!' to look up the judges of the competition, returning for the Perfect Physique Tourney and ladies' Physical Excellence contest won by W.F. Archer and Violet Butterfield. Having found the officials involved, Percy declared his position as a famed G/LDO and professional stage artist from Wales, lest they forget. To make a further point he stripped to the waist in front of the judges and gave them a posing routine in the flesh, in protest against competitions judged purely on photographs. With the officials duly impressed there was little for them to do, he told Joe Manship, but declare the competition invalid and have a further check of photographs and details. This they agreed to do, although it was some time before a decision was made naming Percy Hunt, 'The Great Mavello', the winner in the professional section of the 'Best Developed Man in Great Britain over 40 years of Age'.

The first prize of £5.5s.0d. and the large, two-handled, ornate, urn-like silver cup were presented to him the following year at the London Palladium, and not the Holborn Empire, where the Annual H. & S. Display had once again been held. To celebrate his belated triumph a photograph of the all-round athlete holding the trophy in the back garden of his lodgings at 81 Tydraw Street was included in the *H. & S.* journal of 25 October 1937.

Music Hall Tours & From Russia with Love

Seeking at every opportunity to establish himself as an all-round athletic stage entertainer, Percy found engagements with a number of provincial touring companies of dancers, hand-balancers and musicians. The best of them was to provide a six month tour in the late 1920's and early 1930's with a troupe of Russian Cossack dancers and acrobats called 'The Kessells'. Percy's contact with the company and subsequent tour, as a versatile strongman in their act, had taken place on one of his migratory journeys from Wales to seek employment in a number of English variety theatres in Manchester, Birmingham and London. Engagements up to that time were often short-lived and very much one-off and weekly terms. Although no detail of the background and circumstances of 'The Kessells' are known, it would seem they were one of a number of up-and-coming supporting stage acts striving to make a success.

23. Britain's Best Developed Man over 40
Posing with Health & Strength cup award in the back garden of his lodgings in
Tydraw Street.
(Press photo)

On completion of his six month engagement he did not renew his contract. Severance with the company was attributed to an unfettered rivalry for his affections among the female dancers. Percy, although completely devoted to the welfare of his physical prowess and development, was quite willing and able to exert, when appropriate, his boundless energies to the advantage of the shapely female dancers of the troupe. There is a point, I suppose, at which amorous preoccupations of this kind can incur and inflame jealousy and when it became apparent to him much inflaming had taken place the only sensible option left was to retreat with grace and as much good will as possible. It would seem that he was still held in their affections a year later when the dancers visited him at his parents' home in 15 St. Mary's Street, while they were booked at a theatre in Swansea.

It was inevitable that while on tour of a number of English music halls, Percy would eventually meet renowned personalities of the physical culture world. The list was like a 'Who's Who', which included German strongman Eugen Sandow; world champion heavyweight wrestler George Karl Julius Hackenschmidt, 'The Russian Lion'; weight-lifter Thomas Inch[6] and rival W.A. Pullum; [7] strongman Edward Aston; Polish all-round athlete Otto Arco; muscle controller and strongman Monte Saldo and his son Court Saldo.[8] Percy would bring the athletic personalities he had met into the conversation with a forthrightness that seemed to deny any hint of name dropping.

The Welsh physical culturist also became acquainted with professional heavyweight boxing (and wrestling) brothers Max and Buddy Baer (Max in particular as a boxer), their meeting being recorded in a photograph signed by them. This was possible because photographers sometimes made themselves available behind stage to take pictures of the stars of the shows, Percy taking advantage of this to organise a novel arrangement. Although the photograph is no longer in existence, presumed lost or sold along with a number of H. & S. medals in times of financial hardship, the composition by all accounts had 'The Great Mavello' standing in straddling position on the left and the right palms of the hands of the massive Baer brothers.

The Welsh athlete's journeys in times of economic depression were no exception, for there were many professional strongmen, all-round athletes and manual workers of strength prepared to travel the music hall circuit in the hope of success. Such work in many instances did not extend to the securing of a professional engagement with a theatre or better still a contract with a touring company but were open challenges, which included members of the audience.

Percy was familiar with this kind of popular competition back home but the outcome was seen by him as more fun-based.

Following the music hall circuit in England, Percy found open challenges to audiences more intense; although the all-round nature of the feats of strength, such as tearing a pack of cards into pieces, bending steel rods, driving six inch nails through a plank of deal, and balance and agility, were merely a part of his repertoire, the inclusion of lifting sacks of flour was troublesome. Shrewd professionals like Percy would first practice a way of dealing with such an awkward weight, for there was a mocking sting in the tail for challengers who were unprepared in the lift. To see men in attendance with hungry families to feed unable to lift the sacks of flour, which they could either have sold or used to make bread to eat, break down in tears before sections of an audience given to jeering at failure, was not to Percy's sense of professional conduct or that of anyone who looked upon strength challenges as akin to something heroic in the attempt. He found it brutally demeaning to see a lifter who had not covered his nose and mouth begin to choke from inhaling clouds of flour dust (the sting in the tail), squeezed out in the act of lifting, to cover him clownishly like a snowman. There was no place here for the comaraderie of spirit so valued by Percy; the reality of trying to earn a living from strength challenges precluded such quality of feeling. In these circumstances he came upon the cheating Samson having a field day. It was the name of the game.

As a professional stage athlete and entertainer protective of his claimed position as a pioneer of Welsh physical culture, who also challenged audience members in his act, Percy was wary of such competitions. Whatever the financial inducements, the possibility of failing and losing face before audiences he might confront later was said to have been uppermost in his actions. He was however successful in those challenges he undertook after having with knowing wisdom trained for such undertakings back home.

Despite the growing success of his versatile act before audiences, encouraged by the senior member of 'The Musical Seymours', whom he had met again on tour in the provinces, trawling the music hall circuit for engagements was demanding and soul-searching, involving much moving to and fro from home. Responsibility for Percy's inability to sustain enthusiasm and establish himself on the professional stage, with its brief intimacies, cannot be solely placed upon the decline of the stage strongman in the face of competition from silent films. His failure to establish himself and move beyond the support artist stage might possibly be due to his disregard of the services of a theatrical agent. The reasons for his penny-wise attitude were said to have resulted from a frugal upbringing and a stubborn independence which influenced him to go it alone and ruled out any understanding of the procedures of making a living from the variety stage. The disappointments of the period arose, he believed, from the Englishness and ordinariness of his surname, and he concluded that, 'If I was a Huntski, instead of a Hunt, I would be famous!'

Miners' Institutes, Workmen's Halls and Welfare Clubs

Of all Percy's engagements the most rewarding and eventful, in terms of audience reception and programme of events, were those given from the stages of Miners' Institutes, workmen's halls and welfare clubs, in support of morale-boosting, charity fund-raising concerts for the benefit of the unemployed and their families in the 1920's and 1930's.

Accompanied as usual by strongman and gym assistant Joe Manship, with sometimes one or two of his talented younger pupils in attendance, Percy was emphatic, as was Joe, that they were the only Welsh Health & Strength Leaguers who whole-heartedly took upon themselves the tortuous task of travelling very nigh the length and breadth of the industrial areas of the counties of Glamorgan and Monmouthshire.

Charity fund-raising excursions at first took in the near valley villages and towns of Afan, Lynfi and Garw, with venues at Bryn, Cymmer, Glyncorrwg, Abergwnfi, Nantyfyllon, Maesteg and Blaengarw, before travelling to farther valley regions of Rhondda, Cynon and Rhymney, with venues at Treorchy, Porth, Aberdare, Mountain Ash, Treharris, Bedwas, Bargoed and Tredegar.

The Aberavon duo had come upon the valley scene where chapels and churches were declining as focal points of the community, their position being taken over by miners' and workmen's halls, institutes and welfare clubs. They were to find that in a number of instances these structures appeared like chapel facsimiles, with a showy spread of classical frontal eloquence often equalled by a music hall style interior, in attempts to bring traditional variety acts to the valleys while they were on the decline elsewhere, before they too became interval 'turns' in cinema shows. Although at home before a captive audience in the most undistinguished places for his act, he continued to find it pleasing to confront a valley stage with a flourish of decoration to its proscenium arch.

A number of the finest venues where Percy and Joe gave displays were the Parc and Dare Workmen's Hall and Institute, Treorchy; Messrs. Nixon's Workingmen's Hall, Institute, Library and Public Hall, Mountain Ash;

Workmen's Hall, Institute, Bedwas, and Miners' Institute, Tredegar.

Conveyance to these places and other locations was by train, with a bus or horse and trap used as an intermediate mode of transport if the venue was situated some distance away from the railway station. Journeys to nearby charity events were completed in a day, except where the inability to return home the same day, either due to wintry conditions or extended engagements, pressed them to stay overnight with a miner and his family. Whoever they stayed with Percy was always ready, indeed, as Joe Manship noted, duty bound to repay their hospitality with a muscle control routine followed by renditions of ballads and arias.

Audiences encountered on these engagements were not the often blasé ones of city and big town music hall, valley people showing a vitality that was often expressed in fierce warmth and robust good humour. Visiting artists like Percy and Joe, who gave freely of their time for the unemployment fund in Wales, were thus given rousing receptions for their support. They were to find that variety entertainment too had a vibrance and virility never seen before in England or even in the lower regions of South Wales. Essentially composed of a miscellany of local talent, much of it musical with choirs, soloists, bands, comic interpretations of classical music, and the clownish antics of individual instrumentalists, there was also a mix of boxing bouts, wrestling, weight-lifting and acrobatics.

Although traditional and topical ballads chosen were often in English the performances, Percy noted, were given rousing ovations, for example: 'The terrible murder near Cowbridge'; 'The working man's lament for the bad times'; 'Why did she leave him, because he was poor'; 'Just before the battle, mother'; 'The adventures of Miss Betsy Williams'; and Will Hopkins' 'Y ferch of gefn Ydfa' (The Maid of Cefn Ydfa).

One of the more popular of Percy's solos for valley audiences, besides 'Somewhere a Voice is Calling' and 'Mother', was ' Lamentation of Nelly Jones'. Sung to the air 'Isle of Beauty', the ballad is a seven verse account of the male deception of a young woman from Aberdare, formerly of Tregaron, Cardiganshire, who bids farewell to eighteen of her former sweethearts. Written in Liverpool by Nelly Jones before emigrating to America in the hope of better fortunes all-round, Percy found it heavy going to complete the seven verse lament, with interruptions of laughter and jeers from the audience when the names of her former men friends and their places of residence came up:

Lamentation of Nelly Jones

Farewell Wales, the land of pleasure;
  Farewell Tregaron evermore;
Farewell precious hills and valleys,
  That is full of earthly store.
Farewell lads and farewell lasses;
  Farewell people great and small,
To America now I am going,
  And I'll bid adieu to all.

Farewell all false-hearted young men-
  Eighteen of these I leave behind;
Once I loved them, now I hate them,
  They used to talk so very kind;
For to deceive me they did promise,
  That I should lead a happy life;
One by one they often told me,
  That I should be their lovely wife.

Farewell Dai and Ben and Billy,
  Farewell Dick and Tom and Jack;
To America now I'm going,
  And I'll give you all the sack;
Farewell English Hugh, from Dowlais,
  Who often said I could depend,
Before the parson he would take me,
  And keep me till his life would end.

Farewell Jim that was so pleasant,
  And Jenkin Jones that was so true!
Like man and wife we lived together,
  For two long years in Froedychiw;
Farewell Morgan Rees, from Mill Street,
  Farewell Timothy I declare;
Farewell old and young in Gadlys,
  I shall remember Aberdare.

Farewell Cwmdare and Aberaman,
    Cwmbach, Cymaman, now likewise,
Capcoch, and Mountain Ash, and Hirwaun;
    While I live I'll not despise.
Farewell delicate Dan, the tailor,
    Who caused me often for to sigh;
You went with others and deceived me,
    And with a frown you passed me by.

Farewell Teddy from Treherbert
    And Bob Treorchy now adieu;
Farewell Joe and Chris, from Ystrad,
    I am going far from you;
Farewell Martin from the valley;
    Farewell Patrick, farewell John,
Who said I must be in the fashion,
    And wear that dandy big chignon.

From Pontypridd and from Caerphilly,
    I am going far away,
Tredegar, Ebbw Vale, and Rhymney,
    Where I spent many a happy day.
I'll bid farewell to all my sweethearts,
    Whom I often did adore,
I must conclude, my voice is failing,
    I grieve too much, I'll sing no more.

The liaisons of a country lass too easy with her sexual favours in seeking a husband, can be considered a spicy inclusion by Percy in a repertoire of otherwise sentimental and romantic songs and ballads. It was a ballad which Joe Manship remembered as a 'brought the house down' ending to Percy's act.

Although Percy Hunt's stage performance was at best a virtuoso accomplishment of a finely tuned athlete releasing his powers in a miscellany of feats, with enough wind left for a closing solo, inevitably, over the years, it brought about occasional mishaps. Joe Manship's account of two such incidents are worth recalling.

Booked as the star attraction in Blaengarw Workingmen's Hall, situated at the farthest end of the Garw Valley, both Percy and Joe were greeted by an enthusiastic capacity audience of miners and their families. They were to find the confinement of a modest, proportioned hall filled more then usual in a pall of pipe and cigarette smoke not an encouraging prospect for the execution of feats demanding forceful intakes of air. Nevertheless Percy and Joe were there to entertain and they did just that in a novel and unrehearsed fashion.

Having survived respiratory problems in the first half of the programme, the opening of windows and doors relieving the situation to some extent, one of the feats chosen after the interval had Percy firmly secured astride the broad shoulders of Joe Manship. From this elevated position he was to bend backwards, pick up a 70 lb. barbell and then return again with the weight to an upright position. With the barbell in his grasp, Percy was in the difficult position of returning when Joe somehow caught his foot in some stage contraption, the result of which had him desperate to keep his feet before losing balance and toppling with a resounding crash upon the wooden floorboards. Percy sprang up in a reflex action that Joe believed was as much out of anger as fear of losing face and attempted to cloak the error by exclaiming in a shrill tenor voice, 'The Fall of Rome that was!!'

With Percy's stage routine more vulnerable to physical calamity than others of a more orthodox kind, there were moments when fate really sprang a surprise and events did go wrong. For audiences whose visual appetite was possibly whetted by exposure to silent film comedy, the routine offered great expectancy of some impending hilarious slip-up.

Journeying to an engagement in the Rhymney Valley, Percy was challenged to pull out a pair of powerful chest expanders fixed to the back wall of the stage. These old expanders had been well used over the years and were regarded by locals as giving a measure of a man's physical prowess. Well, it was a challenge Joe knew that Percy delighted in, as he considered himself something of an expander expert, and he took up the gauntlet before an encouraging and eager audience that Joe believed were ready for anything. With his arms outstretched, he was half-way through pulling the expander handles together in front of him when suddenly the apparatus broke away from the wall taking with it a sizeable portion of plaster, mortar and stone. The mass of ruinous remains must have been travelling quite fast when it hit 'The Great Mavello' squarely upon the back of the head, knocking him unconscious. There were a few gasps of dismay from sections of the audience before a surge of quite uncontrollable applause, laughter, four-fingered whistles, and shouts for 'More! More!' greeted the knockout, as if, it seemed to Joe, the audience thought the incident a part of the act. Amid continuous pandemonium, the prostrate 'Mavello' was removed, aided by Joe and a sympathetic miner, unceremoniously from the stage on top of the most convenient form of conveyance available - a battered old door. Still dazed after lavish applications of cold water and frequent wafts of smelling salts, Percy looked up at Joe and asked, 'How did I do?', to which Joe replied, 'Great! Perce. Great!'

Mishaps in novelty feats were inevitable and all part of the variety of occasion, although with free-wheeling entertainment much in demand it seemed to Percy that unintentional happenings in his act now enhanced the prospects of further engagements in some districts. The message of health and strength through scientific use of weights, which he gave audiences before performances, had to be more and more cloaked in a humorous style. The requirement for humour Percy and Joe put down to the depressed state of the minds of the unemployed present with their families in the audience.

One such charity fund-raising event for the unemployed in the 1930's took place in Bedwas Workingmen's Hall and Institute, Trethomas. For the event Percy had brought along one of his talented schoolboy pupils, Ray Woodward, with Joe given the task of refereeing a fun-time wrestling match between local lifter and wrestler, LDO Wilfred H. Pope of Trethomas, Wales, and the formidable wrestler and strongwoman Ivy E. Russell, of Croyden, England. Billed as the 'World's Strongest Woman', after becoming the 9st. champion lady weight-lifter of the world, Miss Russell, at 5'5" in height and weighing 125 lb., was well acquainted with the versatile athlete in physical culture shows and theatre engagements. Ivy Russell was herself an all-rounder and according to Joe Manship had taken a liking to the sensation-seeking little strongman from Wales.

Many years younger and heavier than Percy Hunt, Ivy Russell was stronger than many strong men, including the Aberavon athlete,[9] and proved her strength and speed in the show by successfully challenging men of her weight, or a stone or two heavier, to throw her. The wrestling exhibition itself in the show ended as expected in a sporting draw with Wilfred Pope and Ivy Russell entangling referee Joe Manship in a few well-rehearsed holds of slapstick intention. Percy Hunt gave his own routine, without clownish antics, in what he considered a novel mix of humour and serious intent in the role of 'The Great Mavello'.

While on the same billing with stage personalities of note, it was wise to lay claim to as many distinctions in the physical culture world as possible, however trivial, and thereby hopefully influence audiences for a return engagement. In the Bedwas display Percy announced that both he and Joe were the first in Britain to receive Health & Strength certificates after the 1914-18 War. Such public claims were always open to denial and, at another fund-raising event near Chepstow, a member of the audience had the cheek, in Percy's opinion, to denounce the certificate claim as bogus, saying, in an offended tone, as Joe Manship recalled, that his uncle, a Herefordshire man, had been the first to receive them. In response Percy stood to attention and gave a patriotic loud rendition of the opening lines of the Welsh National Anthem 'Mae hen wlad fy nhadau...', followed by a somersault and 'Howzzat!', seeking acclamation upon landing. The sudden action brought ovations from the amused audience and the effect of the counter-claim was diluted, if not forgotten. 'Percy was "stage-wise", Joe reflected, 'to any kind of audience reaction and, in his own style, gave as good or better than he received.'

Keep the Home Fires Burning

The war years of 1940-45 became a period in which Percy Hunt was again much in demand as a morale-boosting stage artist, entertaining both British and American Forces convalescing or stationed in Glamorgan, and in accordance with the patriotic mood of those days he gave freely of his time. In addition to these war-time displays he also made himself available for physical culture demonstrations and lectures to numerous Boys' Clubs, YMCA's, and both Scout and Girl Guide movements.

With engagements taking place in all kinds of venues, the most memorable were often those precarious performances where his act held in small, shabby buildings of timber frame clothed in either rotting wood and roof felt or rusting corrugated sheeting, which were altogether changed into strange, draughty, sometimes window-blind distortions urgently awaiting human interaction or demolition. In keeping with Percy's programme of introducing schoolboy pupils or youths of athletic promise in the gym to the public, the debut of Donald Dennis is a good example of circumstances falling foul of the best intentions before lively audiences in a structurally unsound building.

Donald Dennis at his initiation was, he admitted, a little apprehensive, the more so when Percy had declined to tell him who they were going to entertain and where the local venue was situated. The only information given him was that the display was for a good cause.

Arriving at Bridge Street, near the Aberavon RFC Athletic Ground, the building was no more than a large, elongated shabby shed. When Percy appeared on a kind of stage attired in a tatty leotard and black tights, and Donald Dennis in bathing trunks, the pupil was 'horrified' to find that the audience was a company of giggling Girl Guides - the shed being the headquarters of the movement in Port Talbot.

The demonstration proceeded apace until the potentially hazardous feat 'The Man they could not Hang'. Viewing the roof construction, Percy decided the rafters did not look secure enough and dispensed with the 'hangman's noose' in the act. There had been previous mishaps with the noose, which had resulted in near strangulation, and he did want to risk his neck over faulty rafters. The change in the act required Percy to pull-out the usual 200 lb. chest expander in a back not front press, with a metal plate hanging by a rope around his neck being hit with a 6 lb. hammer - this was the 'human gong' element in the feat. Aware of the young, penetrating, gleaming eyes of the Girl Guides sitting in the front rows, the pupil quickly wielded the hammer and struck the bakestone. He remembered Percy swaying backwards a little with a whispered request to hit harder. Donald dutifully obliged and hit harder than before, followed this time by impatient demands to strike with even greater force. Behind him he could hear teasing, muffled giggles. Donald, nervous, vulnerable, young and strong, suddenly dashed the 6 lb. hammer upon the cast-iron plate with considerable power. What followed was inevitable, the cast-iron plate fracturing into several pieces and shooting into the startled audience like shrapnel from a detonating bomb! Percy's physical and mental resistance too was broken, the expander snapping his arms backwards and upwards, almost dislocating his shoulders, which caused him to lose balance and topple back onto the makeshift stage. Amid virginal screams and hysterical laughter the show prematurely ended, and it was a considerable time before Percy Hunt ever asked Donald to assist him again in a display.

The use of a cast-iron bakestone in the act, instead of an implement of more robust properties, was due to its availability and splendid size and form. It's innate brittleness was another matter which Percy had suggested could be overcome if a limited amount of force and lots of pretence were applied; this was only said, of course, because of the pupil's lack of control. Unfortunately both Percy and his pupil had been swept away by the moment and pretence gave way to the reality of youthful temperament and metal stress. Needless to say, the cast-iron percussion implement was replaced by a more resilient one made of aluminium but, as the athlete was to say upon reflection, it lacked the character of a well-used blackened 'maen' with its history of baking Welsh cakes.

Many of Percy Hunt's wartime charity events were given appropriate press coverage, for he was without doubt his own best press agent. Coverage of displays were included in the *Port Talbot Guardian* and the *Glamorgan Gazette*. Below is a selection of engagements taken from the *Guardian* under the main column heading 'Around the Town':

May 1st '42

Port Talbot Athlete's Display

...physical culture demonstration was given by Mr. Percy Hunt, officially acknowledged as Britain's best developed professional athlete between forty and fifty, and leader of the British Ju Jitsu Society, before the Port Talbot Boy's Club last week. The demonstration included hand balancing, a novel tug-of-war, the 'human gong', skipping, novel club swinging, muscle control and breathing, and was greatly appreciated by the audience. Mr. Hunt also sang a solo.

April 9th '43

Port Talbot's Versatile Athlete

Percy Hunt...famous international athlete, paid a visit to the Presbyterian Chapel, Margam Road., Port Talbot on Tuesday. He was assisted by Clive Harvey, who is a gifted thirteen year old candidate for athletic fame.

March 24th '44

Aspired to be Athlete at 58

...gave a display and lecture at Swansea YMCA, so delighted the audience that a return visit was booked. Among those present was a veteran aged 82, who said he had seen Mr. Hunt give a display in 1920. "I really believe you are getting younger," said the old gentleman. "I was so impressed on that occasion in 1920 that I nearly made up my mind to take up physical culture again, though I was 58."

August 11th '44

Port Talbot Athlete's Demonstration

..."The Great Mavello", retired world's undefeated versatile athlete, who has been busily engaged lately in giving demonstrations to the Forces and Cadets, demonstrated to an audience at Penclawdd on Monday, feats of strength and skill, at which he is expert, despite the fact that up to 12 years of age he was constantly ailing. He was assisted by two members of the Health & Strength League, Messrs. Cecil Treharne and Joseph Stanton.

September 29th '44

Demonstrating Fitness

...recently gave a number of demonstrations and lectures to the Forces, and appeared at Aberavon Hospital for wounded servicemen, and at Margam. His future engagements include visits to Swansea Boys' Clubs, Porthcawl, Mumbles and Neath.

November 24th '44

Port Talbot Athlete as Model

Mr. Wyndham Lewis lectured to Port Talbot YMCA on physical fitness and development on Monday, using Mr. Percy Hunt, the Tydraw Street athlete, to illustrate his talk. Mr. Hunt demonstrated at St. Athans and Llantwit Major on Thursday of last week.

May 25th '45

Mr. Percy Hunt...has been greatly encouraged by messages from physical culture experts and champion athletes brought to him by returning soldiers, sailors and merchant seamen. "They came from all parts of the world." says Mr. Hunt, adding that he had the pleasure of entertaining a Liverpool weight-lifter, who has bright prospects of becoming a British champion at 10 stone, and who brought Mr. Hunt a message from the famous Siegmund Klein of New York. On Sunday last week Mr. Hunt gave a talk and demonstration to the Royal Army Ordnance Corps. at their victory social at Cwmavon.

June 29th '45

Crippled Athlete gave Display

Mr. Percy Hunt... was assisted, at the display he gave to wounded soldiers, as part of an entertainment staged by the Cymric Glee Party at Dunraven Castle last week, by Joseph Stanton and Clifford Webley, the latter a cripple, who nevertheless gave a wonderful exhibition of hand-balancing and muscle control.

Margam Castle

One local event, not given press coverage for one reason or another, was

Percy's engagement at the castellated mansion of Margam Castle, then occupied, since the latter part of 1943, by the 109th Regiment of the 28th (Pennsylvania) Division of the USA Army.

Previously one of the two Welsh country residences of the wealthy Mansel and Talbot dynasty, the mansion and its fine furnishings and artefacts had already been sold in October 1941 by Captain Andrew Mansel Talbot Fletcher, nephew of the previous owner Emily Charlotte Talbot, and bought, though not as a residence, by David M. Evans-Bevan of Cadoxton, Neath, before the Americans were billeted in the castle.

There is little doubt that the arrival of the 'Yankee Doodle Dandy' boys with their casual, gum-chewing confidence and distinct American accents, smart uniforms, American Dollars, and consequent popularity with some womenfolk of the town and the district, exposed all kinds of prejudices from sections of the populace. Despite underlying tensions, the happy-go-lucky Americans continued to make their presence known in town, Percy Hunt, the self-appointed ambassador of physical culture in Port Talbot, being quick to make contact and welcome them. Such acquaintance also provided the opportunity to give the Americans a swift verbal resumé of his versatile athletic prowess and his links with the American equivalent of H. & S., the reverse-named Strength & Health League.

Closer contact was achieved when an invitation from Percy to a group of Americans to visit his gym prompted a return invitation to appear before the Company Commander and his Staff assembled in the Tudor Gothic mansion at Margam. A staff car was placed at the athlete's disposal and both he and pupil Clive Harvey were conveyed to and from Margam Castle in style.

The chosen setting for the display could never have been more grandiose than when the athlete and pupil stood at the foot of the Staircase Hall with its Octagonal Lantern Tower above. Standing beneath the towering structure they were at the heart of the Castle's showpiece and able to benefit from the theatrical effects of sublime nuances of daylight and acoustic resonances, as used in the musical events once held by the Talbots. Whatever the ethereal ambience of light that day, no matter, Percy was there to entertain and if the majestic setting contained a possible hint for the Americans of a Hollywood musical stage set in the central flights of steps, supported by Tudor/Gothic columns, so much the better for his performance.

From the middle landing of the long flight of stone steps beneath the Lantern Tower, Percy gave his customary introduction to the benefits of 'clean living', including a description of the dramatic episode in the 1914-18 War of carrying his mortally wounded brother from the field of battle, which was even more appropriate before a military audience. With this said, Percy began his routine well: Indian club-swinging; double front and back cross-hands skipping; jumping frontwards and backwards over a 12″ length of hose-pipe; hand-balancing with pupil Clive Harvey; a good middle of strand-pulling; his pupil jumping off a number of stone steps onto his abdomen; 'human gong' feat; barbell manipulation; muscle control - which included the patriotic abdominal muscle control of Winston Churchill's bulldog features - ending with tenor solos 'Somewhere a Voice is Calling' and 'On with the Motley'.

The spatial elevation of the Octagonal Lantern Tower, Clive Harvey remembered, gave Percy's voice considerable operatic volume and resonance and he took the applause, and the sure certainty among those assembled that he would become a star in America, in his stride.

With Margam Castle now deprived of its once sumptuous artefacts and furnishings, the contrast of the Great Mavello's performance with the emptiness of the castellated mansion before a uniformed audience might have been considered surreal.

War-time displays were to conclude famously with a journalistic and colourful description of Percy Hunt's athletic versatility. Delivered with artistic licence, it first appeared in an item written by Ivor Davies in the Sports Round-up column of the British Forces Weekly *CRUSADER*, on Sunday, 12 August 1945:

54 - Year-Old Mavello is a Boys' Wonder

Take a portion of Joe Louis, a few stone of Samson, the limbs of the man on the flying trapeze and the voice of the inimitable Bing. Mix freely and you have the British product known as "The Great Mavello".

Chapter 5

Brave New World

Samson and Delilah?

The brave new world of the post-war years had already arrived in Percy's opinion in 1937 when he married a local spinster, Gwladys Mary Llewellyn, some fourteen years his junior, on 9 March, at Neath Registry Office. Indeed, there were to be many challenges in marriage to overcome or bare patiently as his sister May, who married three times before departing to Colchester,[1] discovered, but none more irritating than his wife's casual lack of interest in the ritual rigour of exercise and performance before captive audiences - the whole purpose of his life! Nevertheless, 1937 had a bravura spirit about it, with acclaim from American physical culture institutions in the form of certificates and a gold medal. He had been in correspondence with the institution leaders since 1932. Also, he received his Health & Strength trophy for 'Best Developed Man in Great Britain over 40 years of Age'. That year of athletic celebration and marriage was a good beginning to a new phase of his life in the continuum of keeping fit and healthy.

'Gwlad', as Percy called his wife, was similar in height to her husband, but thicker-set, and first met the versatile athlete through the most convenient of introductions by her elder brother Gwlym who trained, as did her younger brother Elved, in the St. Mary's Street Gym. As a professional stage artist he had little or no time to prepare for the final commitment, so courtship had been far from intense until amorous adventures with female members of 'The Kessells' finally helped concentrate his mind, with assistance from Gwlad, upon the bonds of matrimony.

Having cast aside the precarious living of the professional stage, Percy secured employment as an experienced blacksmith's striker at the village pit of Bryn, situated a couple of miles off the Avan (Afan) valley. The money received from full-time employment, supplemented by his gym earnings, which had increased significantly with further enrolment of pupils since his award from H. & S., provided a welcome income to keep his young wife, who was no fair maiden at 32, in blithe spirits in rooms taken with her uncle and aunt, Harry and Jane Vaughan, at 81 Tydraw Street.

24. Percy under the Hand of the Law in High Street
PC F.R. Owen on point-duty. c.1930's

Full-time employment in Bryn Colliery had not been an easy mantle for a former professional stage artist to assume, and when both of his parents died within ten days of one another - his mother on 28 January and his father 6 February - the year after his marriage he was even more restless to return to the music hall circuit with all its proven shortcomings outweighing the successes. As a reminder of those times he had still kept his hair of a length suitable for 'Hair Gladiator' feats popular with audiences; he held it in a hair-net at work for hygiene and safety. With his long hair trussed up in a woman's hair-net he was said to have been viewed by fellow workers as a curious cross between a thespian and a biblical character. At least he was not ordinary but stood out from the rest, even though not always for the reasons he would have wished. These were the soft edges of a versatile athlete with bravura longings.

Although the accolade of Percy's H. & S. award opened up opportunities for a surplus of engagements, gym commitments, combined with employment in Bryn Pit, imposed further difficulties in arranging availability even though Joe Manship and a younger gym assistant Will James, were able between them to run the establishment in his absence. Another difficulty was to arise, which in itself was a welcome bonus, with a further resurgence in pupil attendance due to a Government National Fitness Campaign to improve the population's health and fitness levels in preparation for a possible war that was feared at the time.

In a clime of increasing demands for the Great Mavello's return as an entertainer, there came a time when the lure of the professional stage began to exert its old compelling power to release the showman in him. His wife, sensing this, did a quick 'Delilah' on her 'Samson', shearing his locks to a then conventional 'short back and sides' hair style, seeming to convince him at the time that he looked much younger. As if anticipating the 'Samson and Delilah' taunt from colleagues, he promptly declared that the cutting of his lengthy hair would in no way lessen his strength. He later retaliated against Gwlad's persuasion to conform and grew his hair long again to accommodate the 'Hair Gladiator' act, though it was not as luxuriant as before.

The second eldest of six children, two daughters and four sons, of John and Elizabeth Llewellyn of 29 Lletty Harri, Penycae, Gwlad herself had left home on more than one occasion to take up domestic service in London, somewhat peeved at waiting for Percy to return home and settle down while he sought to establish himself on stage with theatre engagements in London and other cities in England. Forthright in manner, with an often robust sense of humour combined with a dry wit, possibly gleaned from her London experience, Gwlad found that her parents at first discouraged courtship with a man so many years her senior and little prospects as a stage strongman to enhance his eligibility.

Percy's father-in-law, John David Llewellyn, a signalman by employment, certainly could not have had any pretensions to social standing job-wise other than tenuous connections to the Llewellyn dynasty of Baglan Hall; they were a local family of some substance. Besides such links he also had academic inclinations, his main achievements being the gaining of Bardic honours at the Welsh National Eisteddfod and a correspondence BSc degree course in Astronomy. The reflected glory of family ties with Baglan Hall plus the father's academic attributes were said to have given a heightened sense of pride to the Llewellyn family, which Percy had to combat with his own brand of one-upmanship in spirited acclaim to the world of the benefits of physical culture!

If John D. Llewellyn was a quiet and contemplative pipe-smoking signalman/academic, then his bravura, sensation-seeking, stage athletic son-in-law was his absolute opposite in temperament and capabilities. It might well have been these somewhat clashing contrasts with her father which attracted Gwladys Mary Llewellyn to Percy Cardwell Hunt, who could be quite commanding and chivalrous, in the spirit of the Health & Strength League, with the age difference posing no problems in so youthful a man.

Although by her own admission Gwlad was happily oblivious to the ideals of the League movement and to Percy's stage performance, such lack of interest was not uncommon amongst wives of husbands who championed the cult of the physique. It was something you took to or not. Nevertheless her happy indifference to her husband's athletic ambitions did not erase willingness to at least listen to accounts of an audience's grand ovation to his act, neither did it prevent Gwlad from sharing in successes or the receiving of gym earnings, which he gave her to the last penny. Settling into a routine of compromise, there were to be no post-mortems between them as to why the marriage remained childless. It is possible that the young schoolboy pupils Percy took in the early part of an evening's training partially filled the void he apparently felt without a following bloodline.

In post-marriage appearances on stage, with the best of young pupils assisting him in his display, he was to make telling play of the difficulty in manipulating barbells and achieving balancing feats without his left index finger, amputated below the second joint in an accident at Bryn Colliery. Although the fact of the missing digit earned him extra ovations in difficult feats on stage, at work its loss could have posed safety problems in the accuracy of striking with the sledge hammer, which caused concern to his wife who advised he take other

25. Cloning
(Photo montage by the author. Backdrop after El Greco)

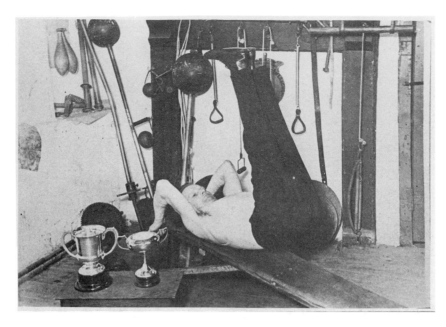

26. The Great Mavello at Exercise in the Gym
In front of Percy is displayed his H.&S. Over 40 Silver Cup and Rose Bowl
award from Pupils.
(Press Photo)

27. A Combined Bovril and Health & Strength Advert
(Newark Lewis)

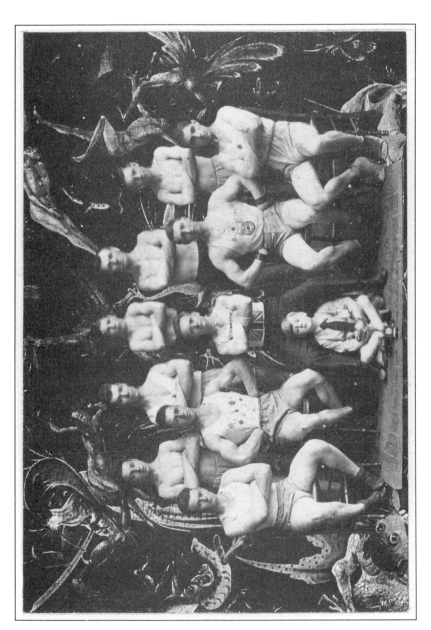

28. Percy's Health & Strength League Warriors

('From dark, impenetrable caves there came forth monsters…')

Percy with gym assistants and pupils.Graham Jones, Tommy Mayne, ?, Bob Yaylor, ?, Picton Lloyd, Will James (assistant), Joe Manship (assistant), Bryn Thomas, Bruce Mayne

(Photo montage by the author. Backdrop after Hieronymus Bosch)

employment lest further 'bits' of his anatomy be accidentally 'chopped off'. Always appreciating Gwlad's dry wit, he acted on her advise by obtaining a supposedly safer job as a general labourer in Vivian's Works, Taibach, before carving, or more precisely brushing out, a niche for himself as the most thorough and celebrated of Port Talbot Borough Council road sweepers.

For Gwladys Mary Hunt, Percy's expertise as a road sweeper was to have greater merit than all her husband's athletic achievements. The work after all was honest and safe with a regular wage each week to keep the wolf from the door and head held high. 'You are my Samson with shovel and brush,' she once acclaimed to him, to which Percy quickly replied, 'And you leave my hair alone!'

Knight of the Road

Percy Hunt's full-time employment with the highways and byways department of the local borough council began on 12 May 1941, and after five years extension beyond the normal retirement age of 65 years he unsuccessfully applied for another extension, retiring on 7 August 1961, at the age of 70.

Within the period of his final employment changes were taking place in physical culture, Percy gaining recognition and relishing the challenges of the new age reflected in the vigour with which he carried out his council road sweeping work to public acclaim. Nevertheless a common remark from relatives and friends was what they regarded as the unworthy nature of this employment for a man - whatever his educational shortcomings - who beside his athletic achievements had established not only one of the best known private gyms but one of the earliest Health & Strength establishments in Wales.

This said, the belief in the unworthiness of his work was emphasised in an article written by diarist J. Ivor Hanson, in his *Port Talbot Guardian* town personalities series 'Sketches from Life'. Of his employment Ivor Hanson concluded that 'A stranger, having learned something of Percy Hunt's unique record, might well ask, "And how do you employ him?" to which we, his townspeople, would have to reply, "As a road sweeper."'

However eloquent the reasoning of the local diarist, Percy's employment as a roadman suited him, whatever he had said to the contrary in the newspaper interview. With no displacement of physical energy his work in open-air conditions became a valued part of training in mid-to-late life and he benefited from the physical and mental harmony which prevailed. Proudly conscientious, he clearly symbolised the nineteenth century Romantic concept of dignity in physical labour. The quality of his roadmanship was highlighted when he worked in 'Penycae' - an area of the town overlooking a panorama of contrasting prospects of a densely industrialised Port Talbot hemmed in by natural forces of mountains and sea.

Riding a push-bike to and from home to Penycae via the Taibach Council Depot, the base for the versatile athlete's work from Monday to Saturday (later a five day week) became a test not only to his fitness but a stage for further recognition of the benefits of a healthy mind in a healthy body. Referring to the district of Penycae as his 'patch', he immediately, and on his own, set about keeping the elevated stretches and curves of a system of roads lacing the middle and lower slopes of Mynydd Emroch as immaculately clean as highways and byways can be kept. Apart from 'Bay View' and the 'Uplands', the rest of the roadways had Welsh names, and he became familiar with the English translations given him by old residents (for he was not Welsh speaking) in an effort to know more intimately, as a roadman with a professional approach, his area of labour.

His main roadwork took him along Pen-y-cae (top of the field) Road which snaked past a mix of residences. Here, in leafy seclusion, Percy's family practitioner, Dr. Donald Isaac, lived in an imposing house where Percy had been a convenient subject for a display of his muscularity before the good doctor and his colleagues. Farther along on the bend in the road stood Saron Chapel, where he was allowed to store his bicycle, his handcart and his shovel and brush in the chapel vestry boiler-house.

Where Pen-y-cae Road ended Lletty Harri (Harry's lodging) began and continued to merge with Dan-y-ffynon (under the wall), and then Caerhendy (field of old house). Junctioned with Pen-y-cae Road were Gwar-y-caeau (hay fields), the Uplands, Tydraw Hill (yonder hill) - with its tortuous 'S' bend - and Bay view, which viewed the town and Bristol Channel from its 'Graigavon' valley prominence.

Almost opposite the road from Saron Chapel, clusters of irregular flights of stone steps, 109 in total, known conveniently as 'Saron Steps', descended precipitously passing a pathway to Saron Cottages on their way to the old Lodge Lane below. The flights of stone steps became a great trial to his stamina and athleticism. Viewed by Percy in the category of a grade one assault course, his method of attack was to run up and then work on the steps on the way down. In winter no ice or snow ever dared coldly cling long while the versatile athlete was about, for no-one ever slipped on the steps, with every tread scraped and brushed vigorously clean - it was the only way, he would say, to keep warm. He was thus at his vigorous best in the cold months.

In the extreme elevations of the area, where houses had steep flights of steps either ascending or descending to their threshold, it was no trouble for the athletic road sweeper to clean them as well. His energy and commitment to his work beyond the call of duty was duly rewarded at Yuletide with a collective gift of appreciation from grateful residents.

In keeping with his fine work as a council roadman, he was also an active member of the National Union of General and Municipal Workers, taking on duties as collector of members' contributions while becoming a self-styled recruitment campaigner for the union. Considered successful in influencing pupils to join the H. & S. League, so to a lesser extent was he a keen campaigner for membership of the NUGMW. In due course a tribute was paid to him in the union's journal of 1953 by Bro. George Moseley, Port Talbot Branch Secretary and Chairman, South Wales District. The account inevitably gave prominence to Percy's professional athletic skills as 'The Great Mavello', concluding that '...Bro. Hunt is a great fellow and comrade, and I recommend him to the whole of our membership as a pattern to follow.' It is inconceivable that any of his comrades would have been prepared to follow his devotional work pattern, as it would have taken at least three work-mates to clean the energy-sapping district of Penycae with such style as he did.

With the altogether refreshing attitude of a man who took pride in his work and carried it out with a sunny disposition, inhabitants of his 'patch' would willingly fall in with his often infectious enthusiasm concerning his almost daily account of any occurrence, however trivial, which overtook him while at his labour. So it was no surprise when the rescue of a local damsel in distress became one of the acclaimed highlights of his road sweeping career. The lady in question, the daughter of a well-known high class greengrocer baron and a charming, gregarious woman of considerable Wagnerian, heroic proportions, had locked herself out of her car on a particular stretch of the road Percy was cleaning. With a commendable and instinctive display of gymnastics, he managed to insert his small, supple body through a convenient gap in the window and thereby rescued the situation. So much was made of the rescue in the locality that the incident began to take on the proportions of a medieval act of chivalry, partly through the praises of the lady in question and of Percy himself, so it raised amongst townsfolk well acquainted with both of them a sense of unrestrained delight and amusement. For lovers of operetta the very thought of a well-proportioned, talkative local operatic society soprano locked

29. Knight of the Road on Pen-y-cae
(Press photo)

out of her automobile and the appearance of a diminutive but energetic road sweeper, and former operatic tenor, briskly coming to her rescue had all the hall-marks of a comic operetta duet. It was this incident, his consistent gentlemanly conduct and the unstinting rigour of his labours which earned him the accolade of 'Knight of the Road', given in a courtesy campaign by the *News of the World* Tabloid in the 1950's, and commemorated with a badge. It was without doubt an honour which heartened him greatly, as he fixed the badge in turn on the lapel and on the front of his 'Knightly' black charger of a push bike.

In keeping with 'Knight of the Road' award Percy began to receive even more praise for the quality of his roadmanship, an occasion arising in which he claimed that a Llynfi bus driver en route to Maesteg alighted and congratulated him on keeping the cleanest stretch of road that he (the driver) had ever driven over! Another claim by Percy on the bus theme had a touring coach full of admiring German visitors who, upon seeing him working, and having possibly heard of his much publicised world's undefeated versatile athlete title, stopped and assembled before him to sing 'Der frohlicher Wanderer' (The Happy Wanderer).

Well understood by residents of his 'patch' as a kind of personage who viewed life's ordinary little everyday happenings as a background upon which he could express his athletic prowess and philosophy, he was thus his own script-writer, producer and director, and, above all, was ever ready to enter and sometimes manipulate the drama of events which unfolded.

Dramatic events did occur when the council were contemplating permanently transferring Percy to sweep the roads of the so-called 'crachach' (toffs) in the 'Pentyla' area of town - although it was said that he had moved for a short time to Margam. So incensed were the inhabitants of Penycae district, and members of Saron Calvinistic Methodist Chapel, that local bureaucracy should have the temerity to devise the unthinkable (for that was the said feeling at the time) and remove the acclaimed physical culturist and 'Knight of the Road' from their midst, a petition was drafted and signed by them and sent promptly to the council. It came as no surprise that the depth of feeling, whipped up by Percy himself as he did not want to leave his domain, implicit in the petition, changed the minds of the local authority and he was allowed to remain in the Penycae district until his retirement.

Deep Harmony versus The Great Mavello
Buttressed within the comforting bonds of marriage and permanent employment

as an A1 category road sweeper, Percy had entered the volatile post-war physical culture scene already a Health & Strength Leaguer of distinction.

Anticipating the changes to come in physical culture, acting League Registrar Miss Elma Whiteman, an admirer of the Welsh G/LDO, wrote in her final farewell letter of 1946, 'Remember the strength of the League does not depend upon officials, or formal organisations, but upon the unity of aim, purpose and ideal among Leaguers themselves. So, in wishing you all good progress, I cannot do better than repeat what Robert Crosbie, 'The friendly philosopher' once wrote: "May you have all power, health and courage, externally, internally and eternally".'

In the growing clamour for physical liberation and identity, which led to a rapid decline of all-round athleticism in favour of an increase in specialisation, stimulated by training and drug-taking methods from America, the new generation of Percy's pupils were like choruses of gym-land songsters awaiting a revitalised dawn of opportunity. Although none too melodious by all accounts, they put their energies into the formation of a weight-lifting group and thereby discovered deep harmony in the 'Military' lifts and later in the 'Olympic' set.

The pupils' demands to specialise in weight-lifting, although there was cross-fertilisation with body-building methods, posed considerable problems for Percy with an ageing gym under structural stress and his own preference for all-round training systems. Uncompromising attempts by the lifters to take over and dictate gym policy did not endear them to Percy. Determined to succeed in their aims, tables of poundage in lifts, in accordance with the individual lifter's bodyweight, were pinned around the walls of the gym. Although such preparation was a necessary discipline for serious weight-lifters to undertake, the procedure demanded the allocation of vital space to the weights and, for pupils who required less structured and more all-round training, a breaking of continuity. It was this kind of fractured situation which drove the group to train secretly in colleague Donald Dennis's father's joinery shop at 137 Water Street, Aberavon, situated at the rear of the Port Talbot Hotel, while still using the facilities of Percy's St. Mary's Street gym. It was the proximity of the Port Talbot Hotel that decided the name of the weight-lifting team, 'Talbot Barbell Association', nicknamed by rivals as the 'TB' Association.

As the accepted leader of the TBA, which was composed in the main of Sid Davies (Porthcawl), Will Thomas (Bryn), Roy 'Bingo' Williams, Doug Evans, Tom Hughes and Hugh Woodward, Donald Dennis was viewed with caution by

Percy as a born-again trouble-maker. He was to him, whether unfairly or not, all that was wrong about post-war physical culture with his smooth, salesman-like approach to selling radical change. So it was against a backdrop of intrigue that Percy compromised and gave support to the home-grown, weight-lifting team, allowing matches to be held against rival clubs in his gym; no doubt he did not want to lose their gym payments.

One of the few home-based matches against a formidable Llanelly YMCA team of lifters, against which Percy and pupils of the early-to-middle 1930's had competed successfully, proved a classic in terms of flagrant use of one-upmanship on Percy's part, and took place about 1947. The evening was cold matched by a definite chilly atmosphere of intense rivalry. One of the rival lifters, a stage strongman and Welsh Lightweight champion, Ted Jones,[2] was in the process of executing a two-hand snatch which, it was said, would have given him a personal best when, at the critical moment in no-man's-land between comparative inertia and dynamic movement, Percy's voice suddenly cut the silence from the back of the gym; 'What's on the bar, then?' Weight-lifting matches in those days tended to demand complete silence, any interruption being quite disconcerting. The Llanelly lifter slowly stood up and stated with commendable composure the particular poundage involved. Again he attempted the lift, squatting on haunches, arms wide apart, ready to hoist the weight at speed, when again Percy decided to intervene; 'Oh yes, I remember Ted Aston, in the early 1900's, did that six times to warm up!' The Llanelly lifter and everyone else in the gym were fully aware that Edward Aston won the title of 'Britain's Strongest Man' in 1911. Defying belief, these quite outrageous interruptions of varying degrees of devious intent were said to have carried on until the fifth attempt!! One must of course remember that Percy Hunt was a respected figure at that time in physical culture circles which probably gave him a privileged position of carte blanche in such instances, at least on home ground. On the fifth attempt, the versatile athlete remained silent when Ted Jones was in the process of lifting, interrupting with some utterance at a crucial moment when the weight was at the point of no return and travelling fast. Totally unnerved, the lifter's concentration suddenly gave way, the weight bursting out of his grasp to fall behind his head and crash with splintering force onto the once bouncy wooden floorboards. It came as no surprise at the time that Ted Jones never succeeded in a personal best, although the Llanelly YMCA team, according to TBA lifter Donald Dennis, beat the local competition despite Percy's marathon attempts at one-upman-ship.

The Ted Jones incident with the gym's floorboards was repeated when visiting British Bantamweight/Featherweight weight-lifting champion, Englishman Julian Creus, attempted a lift which crashed through the boards. The evidence of these incidents were covered in both instances with colourful metal plates advertising Bovril - 'It's the beef in BOVRIL that does you a power of good.'

After such mishaps on the stressed-out timber floor in a period fraught with considerable danger when weight-lifting sessions overlapped with the earlier class of schoolboys, and there was difficulty in arranging regular training schedules, Percy eventually found out about the secret venue to which the TBA lifters had drifted away from his place of exercise.

The exodus of most of the talented pupils was a bitter blow for Percy to take at a time when the forming of a Welsh National Physical Culture Association began to diminish post-war lethargy. With only gym assistant Will James and a few remaining potential athletes of promise, such as the talented body-builder Jim Hegarty and a young schoolboy of promise Alan Rees, whom Percy believed had the makings of a sporting champion, there ensued a battle for dominance in the town between Percy's band of pupils and Donald Dennis's group of weight-lifters.

There was only one possible outcome to the situation and that was a challenge opportunity provided by the full-fledged TBA, who sought to strive to a position of prominence in initiating and organising, in association with Health & Strength League, a physical culture display. Comprised of weight-lifting and varied athletic items, the event was held in St. Theodore's Mission Hall, on Saturday, 4 December 1948, and was highlighted by the final judging of 'Mr. Port Talbot', the first competition of its kind to be held in the town. Indeed, the affable, Rev. Glyn Bowen, BA, Curate of St. Theodore's Church, described the event as 'Unique in the history of the Mission Hall'.

On this unique occasion the scene was set for a lively but composed confrontation between members of the St. Mary's Street gym and the break-away Talbot Barbell Association. Seven competitors reached the final, the judging being carried out by Messrs. Emlyn Jenkins, Health & Strength League Councillor for Wales, Ike Davies of Bryn, and local barbell athlete Pat O'Neil. With seven competitors either current or former pupils and the latter two judges also former members of his gym, it came as no surprise when the versatile athlete declined judicial status in the competition.

The result of the competition was particularly pleasing for Percy Hunt with associate Will James, aged 39 years, normal chest measurements 38 inches and height 5'-8", taking the title 'Mr. Port Talbot' 1948; in second place was former pupil Donald Dennis, normal chest 40 inches and 5'-5" in height. Will James attributed his physical perfection to Percy's preferred method of all-round training, while Donald Dennis thrived on weight-lifting and sprinting. Both contestants received silver medals from Emlyn Jenkins, on behalf of Health & Strength, with the redoubtable 'Great Mavello' said to snatch more than a share of the applause with his display of athletic showmanship.

With the break-away lifting team having left Percy's gym some months before the display of physical culture of 1948, the result of the 'Mr. Port Talbot' contest was inevitably a great disappointment to competitor Donald Dennis and his band of TBA members; two years later, due to the failure to obtain permanent premises, the group disbanded.

The departure from Percy's friendly little gym to form an independent group was not abrupt and final; a number of lifters - minus Donald Dennis - were allowed to return and train there at the time when I became a pupil, but the break had been made and circumstances were never to be the same again.

We Stand for Positive Health

Within the new dawn of muscledom, while the veteran athlete remained in a flux of compromise and conflict with TBA members, League Councillor for Wales, schoolteacher Emlyn Jenkins, had already formed, with co-operation from Health & Strength League Organiser, Laurie Webb, a Welsh National Physical Culture Association, taking as its motto - 'We Stand for Positive Health'.

As elsewhere in Britain, the Welsh movement centralised the body-building and physical excellence competitions while integrating other responsive Welsh amateur sports organisations such as gymnastics, judo, and weight-lifting, along with the H. & S. League and its offshoot NABBA - the National Amateur Body-Builders' Association.

Directly involved almost at the beginning with the wider League movement from its absolute power base in London, Percy was at first unsure of the coming together of disciplines in a Welsh organisation that was intended to be free-flowing, idealistic, non-commercial, and self-contained without any external interference. His hesitation came from regular correspondence with American athletes who had warned him of the pressures to monopolise physical excellence events world-wide. Such intentions were expressed by Canadian brothers Joe and Ben Wider, co-founders of the International Federation of Body-Builders, whose hard-edged commercialism disregarded the idealism of the non-profit-making attitude at the root of the Welsh association.

It was evident to colleagues and pupils that Percy had no time for this kind of political intrusion, which would eventually permeate and nullify the aims of H. & S. and NABBA - as the British Amateur Weight-Lifters' Association (BAWLA) attempted to do with their claims of sole organising of physical excellence displays - his gym for the time being was registered only with the Health & Strength movement. When he did decide to extend his position in the scheme of things it was 1954 before he joined NABBA and not until 1957 did he find it appropriate to affiliate his gym to the Welsh National Physical Culture Association.

Although disenchanted by alien shifts of training principles and methods from America, combined with commercial forces diluting Welsh idealism, Percy ascended into the limelight as a re-charged celebrity of bygone days ready to tap the potential of the new regime, without need as yet to affiliate his gym to either NABBA or the Welsh association. He came not alone, but at the fore of a body of pupils themselves with high expectations in their quest to find a way in post-war physical culture. Their enthusiasm shone bright, gathering others to its flame before scattering into separate gleams and blazes of pupils' aims and achievements.

With associate disciplines involved in their own shows and all four supportive of each others, Percy was quick to make himself known to the main officials of the WNPCA as a versatile athlete whose life story had been told by influential physical culturist W.A. Pullum in his 'Random Recollections' in the H. & S. issue of 30 October 1952. For quick reference he had put the names of the selected members of that year on one of the walls of the gym. His use of such items of information was seen by pupils as an unconvincing response to their own pinning up of details of American methods of body-building-cum-weight-lifting which they displayed as if they were powerful slogans against suppression.

The officers of the Welsh National Physical Culture Association were:

President: Capt. Geoffrey Crawshay, JP, DL; Chairman: Mr. John Evans, Cardiff; General Secretary: Emlyn Jenkins, Pontypool; Treasurer: Alban H. Jones, Cardiff; Display Organiser: (West Wales) Idris Hale, Heath; Medical Adviser: Dr. F. Bridgewater, Newbridge. The executive officers were H.C. Llewellyn, John Hampton, W.G. Maidmant, Gordon Davies, Bert Sansom and John G. Jones, North Wales.

In the invigorated flow and mood of the Welsh physical culture movement Percy became popular as a guest artist with spectators of physical excellence

'Mr. and Miss', 'Adonis and Venus' Displays.[3] As a one-time accomplished, non-competitive Health & Strength lifter, the new-found glamour in Wales of poseurs in shows, and greater number of accompanying supportive associate disciplines and acts, suited the peculiar nature of Percy's versatile athletic performances more than the dour arena of weight-lifting contests.[4] Appearing in only a couple of gymnastic displays, aspects of which he had absorbed in the early days, it is unsure if he ever gave performances in judo events even though familiar with the discipline's root form of ju-jitsu. Yoga was to be another Eastern form of discipline in his displays, demonstrated by 'Indian Breathing' and the 'Cat-Stretch'.

With the convenience of a recognised stage act late in his athletic career Percy was now able to parade before spectators, many of them unfamiliar with music hall acts, his complex but seemingly simple combinations of clever dexterity, timing, balance, mobility, strength, quick reflex and rhythmic action culminating in his vocal finale. The manipulative gyration of tossing and catching a 60 lb. barbell and the request for a member of the audience to stand upon the abdominal area of his body while he was supported between two chairs by head and heels, were just a couple of stunts from the old days he included, the latter feat being a variation on the abdominal theme in which the area is either struck with a hammer or jumped upon by a colleague.

At once welcomed as a link with a pioneering past, Percy was also seen by athletes of a certain temperament and ambition as a little meddlesome all-rounder unwilling or unable to understand or appreciate the progression achieved in muscle size and increase in strength among body-builders and weight-lifters. It was discovered in conversation that he had little, if any, knowledge of anatomy to satisfy even casual enquiries. He understood the basics of a precise movement but the mechanics, the kinematic relationships involved, were quite mysterious to him. The intellectualising need among ambitious, younger physical culturists for often copious detailed anatomical knowledge, with mind ready and able to grasp and formulate any new training systems and principles that might arise, was not Percy's way; the path he trod was practical and intuitive in approach. Nevertheless he shared the stage and applause with the best of athletes, renewing acquaintances from pre-war years while establishing new ones post-war. In such shows he was to meet progressive body-builders Hubert Thomas of Swansea, and Dennis Stallard of Tonyrefail, who caused Welsh physical excellence to surge to new heights, winning Welsh and British titles respectively in 1950 and 1951. When exchange visits of leading Welsh and English athletes across Offa's Dyke became fashionable, Percy too made guest appearances at English displays. His engagements were in many ways a return journey to the land where he had become popular as a bravura style artist in theatres, and a defiant Welsh G/LDO crusader at Health & Strength League displays.

One-Upmanship

Although out-moded as an all-rounder in the mainstream of herculean principles of sectional development of a mighty chest, arms, legs, back and abdominals, Percy took to one-upmanship by claiming that he had pre-empted the trend of corresponding with American athlete Bob Hoffman, proprietor and editor of *Strength & Health* publications, and of following his 'York' Barbell Training System.[5] A letter from Percy Hunt to Bob Hoffman was published in the magazine of 1939:

It is now 1939 and I have just finished reading the December number of your valuable magazine. I am pleased to state that although I am so far away I have not missed a single issue of your magazine since the first one in December, 1932. I am always delighted to read S. & H. magazine.

I am a life member of the A.C.W.L.A. and Hon. Vice President of the American Strength & Health League, you may remember. I would like to congratulate the American weightlifting team on their improvement.

I am enclosing one of my latest photo's, taken at 29 yrs of age and also at 48 (Percy means age-span image). After twenty years I am still the same size and weight, and can perform most of my feats of years ago. I am enclosing a photo. of one of my favourite stunts, being lifted five feet high by my hair. I can still do the following programme in spite of having attained the age of 48. One hand anyhow and bent press 112lb. Wrestler's bridge of 148 pounds and a 168 pound man sitting on my stomach. While sitting on a pupil's shoulders, I bend back and pick up a seventy pound barbell. Hanging by my neck I press out a 200 pound expander, while a man strikes a steel plate which is hung on my neck. I do double and single cut offs on the rings, also dislocation, etc. I can still hold my own with the boxing gloves with the boys which goes to prove that weightlifting athletes do not get old after forty. I can perform a great many other feats of acrobatics too numerous to mention.

I hope this letter will be of interest to you and help to prove that your methods

of training are best. It's the system I have followed for over twenty years and I can still claim to be one of the fittest men in the world of my age.
Lgr. Percy Hunt, 15 St. Mary's St., Port Talbot, South Wales.

He also made much of the fact that he had corresponded with other influential American athletes, including physical culture organiser Ray van Cleef;[6] the acclaimed weight-lifter-cum-body-builder John Carl Grimek, who became the first H. & S. (NABBA) 'Mr. Universe' in 1948; and Steve Reeves, 'Mr. Universe' 1950.

Taking a different approach to further himself as a personality in the thriving Welsh scene of might and muscle, Percy found a convenient niche in prophecy predicting that a young Aberdare physique poseur, Myrddin Palmer, a former 'Junior Mr. Wales' and 'Mr. Britain' 1950 champion, would gain further Welsh success in the 18 to 40 category. Sure enough, on Saturday, 18 April 1952, at Cymmer Colliery Workmen's Hall, Porth, outsider Myrddin Palmer beat both Hubert Thomas and Dennis Stallard to become 'Mr. Wales', remembered by Percy in Emlyn Jenkins' biblical metaphor of the sensational result as '...a David who killed two Goliaths with one stone'.

As an athlete supportive of women taking their place with men in Welsh physical culture,[7] he came up with another correct prophetic judgement when he tipped Mary George, of Aberdare, to win 'Miss Britain' 1957 - the second Welsh woman to lift the title achieved previously by Abertillery's Marianne Gill-Evans in 1944. Percy regarded the 1944 winner and League Councillor for Wales, who ran one of the top ladies' keep fit classes at Llanhilleth H. & S. Club, as the pioneer of the Welsh women's movement. Warming to the task, he declared that the presence of women in shows, with their graceful routines of 'Miss' and 'Junior Miss' or 'Venus' Contests, and club group displays of wand drill, tap dancing, callisthenic ringwork and club swinging, gave that special feeling of a family get-together. Keeping things simmering, he announced to Emlyn Jenkins that the enthusiasm of women athletes in particular, along with their male colleagues, and warmth of audience reception, equalled anything experienced at Health & Strength League events in the Holborn Empire, London.

Emlyn Jenkins echoed similar sentiments when he wrote, 'What a grand reunion this has become. The friendly handshakes, the smiles, the cheers, the jolly camaraderie make everything worthwhile and the miracle occurs again'. The 'miracle' referred to arose from the unrehearsed condition of the display when '...the jig-saw pieces drop into place in a surge of enthusiasm from both sides of the footlights, and the job is done'. In fact, it was the unrehearsed condition of Welsh shows which appealed to Percy who possibly found the benevolent chaos of events a suitable platform for bringing out the definite order of his act and preparatory talk on how he kept his all-round fitness and health with increasing age.

Although there were without doubt fine muscular specimens exhibiting the physique and strength existing in Welsh body-building and weight-lifting, Percy put out the belief that combinations of all-round fitness and health - more so than their associate disciplines - did not always apply to them. Such athletes he regarded as surely neglecting the definite dangers of immense stresses imposed upon joints and internal organs of the body through illegal stimulants and cheating manipulations in lifts and as a result he denounced their way of training.

Inevitably these accusations brought response from the more reactionary and possibly vulnerable of athletes, rendering Percy and his act unpopular with them in a dismissive way. It was said that physique poseur Dennis Stallard, whom the Port Talbot veteran physical culturist had heard was setting his sights on separating Welsh body-building from the unifying links of the WNPCA, hardly concealed his dislike and annoyance among colleagues over Percy's remarks. Dennis Stallard's rival to Welsh and British physical excellence titles, Hubert Thomas held different views of Percy Hunt and did not take exception to a situation in which the veteran athlete's censure rang true in certain circles. The Swansea athlete knew, as did Percy, that his (Hubert Thomas's) health and strength were A1.

Another Swansea athlete Harry Pelta, a former British 42 lifts category heavyweight record holder, some twenty years younger than Percy but years older than both Stallard and Thomas, found the criticisms rather obnoxious. Straddling years before and after the Second World War, he was a man of natural, prodigious strength, who had no time for the versatile routines of the so-called 'Great Mavello', or his joy of mind and body happily attuned in health and Strength. At the age of 14 he had been able to tear a pack of playing cards into quarters compared to Percy's tearing of similar cards in half in his prime.

The Swansea strongman's younger colleague, Welsh Featherweight Champion Teify Jones, was one weight-lifter who had a measure of affinity with the Port Talbot veteran in muscle control performances, the feat probably being more acceptable to the new era of physical culturists for its novelty aspect.

Stickability

When athletes were stimulated to develop muscle size of massive proportions or strength to lift record poundage after suspicion of drug use, Percy's move from his 'one-upmanship' stance to denouncing such methods had been like the proverbial voice in the wilderness. The herculean athlete glamorised by Grimek and Reeves, among others, was in irreversible ascendance while, looming ahead, with all the hazardous, chemical concoctions produced, was a further increase of the highly muscle-defined physique with venous proliferation and super-aggressive drive of the weight-lifter.

The controversy began to appear then in the late 1940's and early 1950's, but the reliance on good old 'stickability' of the clean-cut, grafting, work-out in the gym ideal, was still said to hold sway in Wales, although Percy was unsure of this from chatter circulating in the gyms, including his own. Although the WNPCA was officially against the use of illegal stimulants in aiding physical development and performance, Percy had heard from sources close to the grass roots of Welsh physical culture that a small number of officiating members secretly condoned the practice. By nature something of a free-spirit, he was not shackled by brotherhood ties and would say, when condemning anabolic steroids, and other potential harmful substances, 'Clean living; clean life in physical culture makes you beautiful and keeps you young'.

Gwlad, his wife, also had to listen patiently on the sensitive matter of drugs, apparently developing an encouraging pattern of response followed by the down-beat, 'Yes, Percy, but nobody will listen.' To this negative response he would reply, 'When people will see how happy, fit and healthy a person I am, they will listen, Gwlad.'

To add to this belief Percy noted, reading in a biographical account 'Health versus Crime', published in the 1957 issue of *Health & Strength*, that physical culture in a weight-training manner was even capable of restoring self-respect in a hardened criminal serving time. He responded to this social engineering in a telling manner, quoting the heading of an article which appeared on the cover of the first issue of *Health & Strength* - 'Ill Health is a Crime, Don't be a Criminal.'

Guest Artists and Supporting Acts

Although Percy viewed his versatile act as a unique highlight in displays among the considerable efforts of younger athletes, the long-awaited special guest appearances of English stars such as Oscar Heidenstam and then Reg Park were as often as not the measure against which the Welsh compared their skills, strength and physiques. Indeed, as an acrobat and hand-balancer himself, Percy found much to admire in the 'Les Trois Milles' acrobatic team of herculean hand-balancing bearer Reub Martin and partners Len Talbot and Rusty Sellars. Nevertheless it was the home-grown supporting acts he claimed to be the raising agent for high drama.

A fun event for audiences was roller cycle racing, each machine, nothing like Percy's old push bike, being anchored to the stage with sets of rollers upon which to race and large speedometers facing the audience to display distance achieved by riders over each other in a set time. He was to say that compared to the comparative unanimity of a delighted vocal audience for cyclists as they wobbled to the limit of their momentum, physique poseurs and more so weight-lifters carved out sections of ardent biased support.

Among the novelty Welsh display personalities, Percy recognised SLDO Alban H. Jones of Cardiff - WNPCA treasurer, organiser, gymnast and the force behind the Central Boys' Club - to be one of the few younger physical culture officials who had the unifying ideals of the movement at heart and the grit to sustain this idealism against increasing dissent.

Considered a fine gymnast and supreme both in muscle control and yoga, the Cardiff physiotherapist was said to surpass Percy's expertise in producing startling tensions of muscular tremors, flicks and abdominal isolations. Although Jones's muscularity was greater, the veteran athlete was not convinced that he had as yet achieved precise timing to music.

Physical Culture Displays and Contests

Percy's favoured displays of physical excellence were, like weight-lifting championships, usually held at venues in South Wales where the greatest enthusiasm was to be found, performances in the North taking place in Mold, Port Dinorwic or the Health & Strength League summer gatherings in Prestatyn Holiday Camp. With difficulties in travelling to North Wales, such events remained isolated for the versatile athlete.

It had long been evident to Percy that displays in the South were at their best when staged in the Rhondda and Rhymney valley areas, much of which entailed retracing journeys undertaken by him in pre-war times. From Parc and Dare Workmen's Hall, Treorchy; Cymmer Colliery Workmen's Hall, Porth; Coliseum Theatre, Aberdare - to name but a portion of Percy's valley venues - to Cardiff's Cory Hall, 'The Great Mavello' marched forward in no uncertain optimism as advocate and proven example of a healthy life-style.

Although not as frequent as he would have wished, most of the veteran athlete's displays occurred in the decade of the 1950's. Below certain events are described using a combination of *Health & Strength* magazine and newspaper write-ups, recollections by Percy himself, former stage colleagues and pupils, and occasional added information. However, the first major WNPCA physical excellence display Percy took part in as guest artist was not at a valley location, but at nearby Briton Ferry, Neath. Programme introduction as follows:

> 1951 – Festival of Britain' Mr. and Miss. Wales held at the Public Hall, Briton Ferry, Sat. April 28th at 6.30 p.m. Introduced by His Worship The Mayor of Neath, Ald. R.W. Perrott, JP Programme 6d.

As it was a 'Festival of Britain' occasion Percy had chosen the right time to make his entry into the Welsh National Physical Culture Association in a year of celebration in the land, with over 60 competitors from all parts of Wales entering the area physical excellence contests. Compered by Emlyn Jenkins, Percy Hunt, his stage name boldly printed in capitals on the programme, appeared in the second half, item 4, before a packed audience of one thousand enthusiasts, who gave him, by all accounts, including Percy's, a rousing reception.

The athlete's recollections of the celebration year's display, apart from the success of gym assistant Will James in winning the 'Senior Mr. Wales' competition and two pupils, Jim Hegarty and Doug Evans, both being finalists in the main physique event, were focused on the result of the 'Mr. Wales' contest when Englishman Henry Downs won the competition but not the title.[8] With London-born RAF St. Athan-based Downs not domiciled in Wales it was inevitable he would be ineligible for the title, which was thus awarded, as Percy clearly remembered, to an embarrassed Dennis Stallard of Tonyrefail, who had really come second, with Graham Hale, of Neath, third. The occurrence was to be one of a number of such controversial results, which in their own way revealed the quality of English body-building personnel in RAF St. Athan's School of Physical Training,[9] in the Vale of Glamorgan. It seemed to Percy the WNPCA left the risk of a winner not living permanently in Wales to chance.

Alfresco
The variation of acts and rivalry of competitions in WNPCA displays were sometimes transferred in summer from the usual theatre or hall setting to outdoor venues. In the 'Festival of Britain' year a number of open-air events took place;

30. A WNPCA Out-Door Display
Percy in balancing performance with a pupil.
(Photographer unknown)

Percy undertook the first with schoolboy pupil Philip Wells as his assistant. Remembered by exiled pupil Donald Dennis, who accompanied them both, was the 'Display of Physical Culture and Skill', which included 'Miss Rhymney' 1951 in one of the heats for 'Miss Wales'. Commencing at 4 p.m., the event was held on the MacDonnell Football Ground, Bargoed, on Saturday, 30th June, proceeds going towards the establishment of a Pensioners' Club House.

In a programme of 17 events Percy was placed 6th - '"The Great Mavello", Retired World's undefeated All-Round Athlete. At 60 years of age, in feats old and new.'

What was most memorable to Donald Dennis about the day was not that the display was attended by Post-Master General, the Rt. Hon. Ness Edwards, PC, MP (Labour), or that it heralded the return to his native Bargoed of Welsh and British Midheavy/Heavyweight weight-lifting champion, 'Tiger' Mel Barnett,[10] but the pre-show incident (it was more of a happening) which occurred on the bus journey with Percy between Cardiff and Bargoed. The bus was full of noisy, chattering old ladies returning from shopping in Cardiff, so it was hard on the ear-drums, but the sudden decision by the exuberant 'Great Mavello', after an enjoyable summer's day, to reveal a wonderful cure for constipation caused disbelief among passengers. Given no doubt from a genuine sense of therapeutic concern it also lessened the unceasing chatter of the gang of elderly women. The revelation revealed, Percy rose to his feet in the bus gangway and pulled up his jersey, shirt and vest, lowered his trousers just below the navel region and performed the central isolation, with multiple abdominal rolls and ripples in demonstration of the exercise for bowel-relief. Donald Dennis vividly recalls that 'All these dear old ladies were shaking like mad and I couldn't tell whether it was from fear or laughter, and I crouched in a corner pretending I wasn't with the great man.' The laxative exercise was regarded as a potent remedy but for the ladies its execution came as quite a surprise.

Another open-air engagement was the 'Miss Tredegar' 1951 Competition and Physical Culture Display, staged in Bedwellty Park, Tredegar, Saturday, 14 July. Compered by Emlyn Jenkins, Percy was placed 5th in a varied programme of 18 items, including: Wand Drill - Llanhilleth H. & S. Club; The Three Across - Comedy Tumbling; Free Standing - Welsh Festival Team featuring Ken Buffin, British FS Champion 1951, Coach - W. Buffin (former Welsh Gymnastic Champion); Yoga Asanas - Peter R. Horton; Judo - Ryugakwai Judo Club, Cardiff (Principal - Frank Baldwin); and a weight-lifting match between Mel Barnett (British Heavyweight Champion) and Yorrie Evans (British 11 stone Champion).

When Percy's turn came to present his act the veteran all-rounder said that he was greeted in sunlight by a crowd of several hundred. The modest turn-out for such events he believed to have been due entirely to inclement weather the previous couple of days, which had muddied the ground and kept away many of the locals and surrounding valley street communities. On the whole Percy remembered that open-air displays were blessed with sun and excellent crowd attendance.

Among the physical excellence champions present for the public to meet, Percy was said to have been the quickest of them all to get into his stride. With a beaming smile he stood alongside Hubert Thomas, Swansea (Britain's Perfect Man 1951, Mr. Britain 1950); Dennis Stallard, Tonyrefail (Mr. Wales 1951); Joan Richards, Briton Ferry (Miss Wales 1951); Myrddin Palmer, Aberdare (Junior Mr. Britain 1950); Jean Bridgewater, Abertillery (Junior Miss Wales 1951); Trevor Jones, Dowlais (Welsh Physique Team); Bill St. Roas, Cardiff; Elsie Baines, Chepstow; Bert Davies, Abergavenny (Senior Mr. Wales 1949); Valerie Jones, Crumlin; and Elwyn Rees, Port Talbot.

That Yorrie Evans won the lifting contest against Heavyweight Mel Barnett came as no surprise to Percy, for the West Walian was regarded, pound for pound, as an outstanding example in Welsh and British weight-lifting. He was also a modest man and because of his lighter bodyweight category he, unlike his opponent, was not prone to obesity; what power Yorrie Evans had was packed in a dynamic muscular body.

Apart from the weight-lifting match and parade of physical excellence champions, with an ex-pupil of Percy's, Elwyn Rees, finding his way into the physique team, the 'Miss Tredegar' title was won in that Welsh valley area by an English 16 year old, one Joan English. There was much good humour, Percy was to recall, over the surname, the young woman being a popular winner and member of the Glanhowy Youth Centre. We, the St. Mary's Street gym pupils, were surprised that the physical culturist of the old school had bothered to remember such trivial details of a past event until we found that he sometimes looked up *H. & S.* magazines or press-cuttings about particular displays to maintain an ongoing interest in proceedings.

Another two alfresco displays covered in 'Welsh Window', are as follows:

1951 – Latest open-air display at Pontnewydd on Tuesday, July 24th was the best of the series, and congratulations are being received from many quarters. The evening display attracted an audience of a few thousand and the team work of the performers was excellent. Top marks therefore to the Welsh Festival Teams under **W. Maidmant** and **Pop Buffin**, the Ryugakwai Judo Club, Llanhilleth H & S Club, **Peter Horton**, the Three Across, **Percy Hunt**, Cwmbran Youth Club, Llanhilleth H & S Club and PE Parade led by **Hubert Thomas** and **Dennis Stallard** (Mr. Wales).

1951 - Several clubs gave up their holidays to entertain the crowds at Ebbw Vale on August Bank Holiday. Notable among these were the Ebbw Vale Gymnastic H & S Club; Star W L Club, Tredegar and Llanhilleth H & S Club. Percy Hunt appeared on two days with his well known act.

With the 'Darian Weight-Lifting and Physical Culture Gym, Aberdare, generally regarded - despite the claims of the Manselton Gym in Swansea - as the post-war successor to the dominant Llanelly YMCA, H. & S. Club (which was operated by world weight-lifting record holders Sid Frost[11] and Cliff Hall), it was inevitable Percy would follow the mountainous route to Aberdare as guest artist in one of the club's shows. It was founded and run by Lightweight lifter Jack Acocks[12] and Heavyweight brothers John and Walter Jones.[13] They were to view 'The Great Mavello' with the reservations of young lifters in full tilt of reforming and sustaining the discipline in Wales. Although deprived in the veteran stage of many of his credible strongman feats, Percy's performance still held enough items displaying skill enlivened in novelty of application for audiences geared to weight-lifting to be well pleased. Jack Acocks, who had revived post-war Welsh weight-lifting to become the movement's first secretary and dynamic leader, found Percy's act rather eccentric, but admitted 'He was an original - without people like him the game would not have progressed.'

One of Percy's guest appearances took place in a combined weight-lifting and physical excellence event staged in the Coliseum Theatre, Aberdare, recollected by Welsh and British record holder, Lightweight lifter Yorrie Evans of Haverfordwest. His account does not deal with details of Percy's act but rather takes in the health-wise effect the all-rounder had on some members of the audience, which, in this instance, led to a teasing leg-pull of female manufacture. The situation that arose was directly motivated by the stage artist's traditional pre-performance pep-talk concerning in part the nutritious benefits of 'Marmite' and what he called 'correct diet' contributing greatly to his longevity, although he was then only in his early 60's. Percy's 'correct diet' did not however prevent him from helping to consume large piles of sandwiches and cakes spread before guests and competitors in nearby Siloh Chapel Vestry.

The comic situation in question occurred at breakfast after Yorrie Evans and an older colleague, strongman and weight-lifting referee Tom George of Letterston, known as the 'Welsh Sandow',[14] stayed overnight after the show at the home of friends of Heavyweight lifter John Jones of the 'Darian' club and wife Sally, in Glanant Street. With John joining his companions and Sally helping the ladies of the house in preparation for breakfast, the women were genuinely full of praise for Percy's youthfulness and vigour. With special reference to his 'Marmite' claim, and aware of the lifters' pride in their own physical prowess and hearty appetites, a mountainous plateful of the said sandwiches was placed before them, and nothing else! The implication was that if the nourishing spread was good enough for Percy Hunt then it was obviously good enough for them. Well, just when these crestfallen, desperately hungry strongmen had resigned themselves to the eating of this most healthy but rather unsatisfactory breakfast, the ladies saved their morning appetites, and no doubt their day, by bringing forth plates of steaming hot bacon and eggs with all the trimmings.

For those strongmen present with thinning hair, nothing was said about Percy's 'Hair Gladiator' feat, in which he claimed that if tufts of his hair were dislodged by the stressful grip of a colleague or invited member of the audience lifting him bodily by the hair or attempting to pull him off a certain spot on stage, rapid growth stronger than before would result[15]. Later Yorrie Evans felt inclined to say, 'For an old age person to have any hair to pull or lift was a bonus!'

If 'Marmite' to Percy was health-giving, Myrddin John (Penygroes) was, in Percy's opinion, the slow fermenting yeast in Welsh weight-lifting. A convert from gymnastics, he won the Welsh Bantamweight championship (Olympic set) a couple of times, but his strength resided in organising and transforming, as secretary, the Welsh Amateur Weight-Lifters' Association.

Other class weight-lifters of Percy's acquaintance in the 1950's were: Featherweight John Heywood (Swansea) - Welsh Lightweight Champion in 1954, and Featherweight in 1958; Lightweight Ron Jenkins (Aberdare) - won bronze medal in Vancouver Commonwealth Games 1954, and British Featherweight Champion in the same year; Middleweight Gordon Newman (Bargoed) - Welsh Champion 1956, 1957 and 1958; and Midheavy Alwyn Evans (Cardiff) - lifter-cum-body-builder, won Welsh weight-lifting championship several times, and competed in the Commonwealth Games in Vancouver in 1954 and in Wales in 1958, and in 1954 was placed third in 'Mr. Wales'.

With regard to weight-lifters Percy was inclined to view their exploits as extravagant routines of grunting and groaning, and once made an oblique remark about them. 'They eat iron pills like mad; it's a wonder they don't rust!'

1954 – April 29th - Monmouthshire WL championships held recently at Pengam, under the auspices of the newly formed Britania WL Club, were a definite success, in that they have paved the way for a revival of lifting in the county. Though the totals were not in world class, enthusiasm was very high, and a most enjoyable supporting programme left pleasant memories. **Percy Hunt's** demonstration of all-round fitness was the best I have ever seen. The Imperials gave a preview of their TV balancing act, **Alban Jones** intrigued the audience with his stretching contest, and **George Davies** and **Edith Leader** did well. Personal appearance by **Alwyn Evans** and judo display with **Norman Blackmore** completed the programme. Well done Britannia, and thanks a lot **Pat Malone**, chairman, and **Gordon Newman**, secretary.

Apart from Alban Jones's stretching contest in which wooden blocks were built higher and higher off the stage so that each contestant had to stretch lower and lower, Percy's only recollection of the main event of weight-lifting was in the heavyweight class where Colin Thomas won his contest because he was the lighter man by 6 lb.

1955 – October 15th - Mr. and Miss West Wales contests, The Drill Hall, Carmarthen, at 2 p.m. Open to those living in all districts West of Neath. Programme to include gymnastics, club swinging, balancing, muscle control, weight-lifting and **'The Great Mavello'**. Also demonstrations by **Oscar Heidenstam** and **Hubert Thomas** - Judging 12.30 p.m. Tickets (2/6, 3/6, 5/–) and entry forms obtainable from **Myrddin John**, 209 Cwmamman Road, Glanamman, Carms. Memories there are plenty. **Oscar Heidenstam's** great hit as the star of the show - **Walter Wals** and his top-line gymnastic teams from Swansea YMCA, the fine ovation earned by the inimitable **Percy Hunt**, the two fine lifting matches refereed by **Tom George**. The

116

return to form of **Hubert Thomas**, club swinging by **Brynley Harries**, and muscle dancing by **Teify Jones**.

Percy's reflections in the gym of the contest were of an enthusiastic, supportive and captive audience, even though the event itself was not a complete success with only the 'Mr. West Wales' title being decided - the ladies' section was lacking in numbers for a winner to be selected. With an evident gender imbalance in the physical excellence competitions, despite a good showing in the 'Mr' title won by Edward Williams (Llanelly), runner-up Leighton Price (Gorseinon), with Eric Dezulian (Swansea), third, the only real interest for Percy was the thrilling duel between display organiser Myrddin John (Penygroes) and Tom Pearce (Glynneath). In a resulting close win for the Penygroes lifter by 5 lb. in a 515 total, Percy was to say of the match that as a traditional lifter in the all-round 42 category, Tom Pearce tended to be uneasy in the Olympic set, his record-breaking abilities being found in the 'Pull-over and Press on Bench'.

Who is the Fittest Old Age Pensioner in Wales?
When the Welsh National Physical Culture Association, supported by Health & Strength, decided to include an extra competition in the 'Mr. and Miss Wales Display' of 1957 to find the 'Fittest OAP in Wales', there was little doubt that the contest was custom-made for Percy. It is possible that he had an influence in the competition's emergence, having reached retirement age in fine fettle. Whatever the facts, Percy considered himself a professional, with ambition still evident.

The conditions for the competition, printed in the 'Welsh Window' column of *Health & Strength* magazine, are as follows:

Each man will be given two minutes to demonstrate his fitness in any way he chooses and using any apparatus he likes. A panel of knowledgeable persons will assess the quality of each performance and the finalists will appear at Parc and Dare Hall, Treorchy, on Saturday May 25.

Front Stalls 5/-, Back Stalls 4/-, Side Stalls 4/6. Royal Circle 5/- and 4/6, Balcony 3/-, 2/6 and 2/-. All seats reserved.

The venue for the 10th Annual 'Mr. and Miss display was not only a return of the event of the previous year to one of the finest examples of miners' and workmen's halls in South Wales, but a coming home for Percy to distinct memories of past performances in the years of industrial depression.

Sifting dozens of applications, Emlyn Jenkins decided on three finalists, one of them, unexpectedly, a woman competitor, alongside the Port Talbot physical culturist. The lady herself was a local resident of the steel town and an arch-rival of the 'Great Mavello' with his claimed and coveted position as 'World's Undefeated Versatile Athlete'. A year older than Percy Cardwell Hunt, 66 year old contortionist-cum-keep-fit exponent Mrs. Honora Jones was also small in build and her complexion and features were said to have been of a 'Romany' appearance with thick lenses to her spectacles to rectify her myopia.

The third candidate was described as 'high-spirited'; a commendable state in middle-age let alone for 78 year old Josiah Jones of Newport, who still worked as a hedger and ditcher for Newport Borough Council. Here was a rugged old hand with still a lot to prove.

Although both of his rivals gave fine displays, the result of the competition was said to be never in doubt with a win for 65 year old Percy Hunt, who gave an all-round exhibition of fancy skipping and gymnastics.

The Thomas and Catherine Davies Memorial Cup, which he received for winning the event, was donated by physical culture enthusiast and National Eisteddfod Bardic Crown winner Rev. Rhydwen Williams and by Mrs. Margaret Williams, of Rhyl. The small silver cup and a donation to an OAP group in Port Talbot, were presented to Percy by the Rt. Hon. the Lord Mayor of Cardiff, Alderman D.T. Williams, OBE, JP, who duly complimented him on his fine display and said his '...demonstration of physical fitness for an old age person was quite remarkable'.

Runner-up was Mrs. Honora Jones, mother of six children and grandmother to 14, who produced a performance that made the audience wince at her splits and spine twisting routines.

Third was Josiah Jones who put on a pair of boxing gloves and threw down the gauntlet to any man in the audience. Sure enough a man accepted the challenge and it was said that Josiah ducked, pranced, weaved and punched in an entertaining and professional style. In another act he dropped from a standing position to the floor and picked up in his teeth a handkerchief with a ten shilling note inside, before standing up again.

On a day of triumph most events and personalities in the display were of interest to 'The Great Mavello'. He was certainly in fine receptive and courteous mood to the star attraction, Hazel Cleaver (Miss Britain 1956), supported by Tom Wheeler, whom Percy discovered was a relative of one-time

31. On Stage before the Fittest OAP in Wales Competition
(Press photo)

knuckle champion Tom Spring; the Welsh Gymnaestrada Junior Girls' Team; acrobatics by Alma Smith and young Leslie; magic items by Randall Pinney; archery by the Pentref Bowmen; and the 'Thomas Inch Middleweight Challenge Dumbbell Contest'. The newly crowned 'Fittest OAP in Wales' was not however impressed with Oscar Heidenstam (Mr. Physical Culture), who some regarded as an inspiration to all competitors, considering him to be over-blown in stature and condescending in manner.

With the event providing the opportunity for presentation of WNPCA 'Standard' awards to athletes in their respective disciplines - Dorothy Summers (1957 British gymnastic champion), Bert Davies (six times Senior Mr. Wales), Joan English (thrice Miss Wales) and Frank Baldwin (judo black belt) - Percy believed that he too, as a veteran athlete with a pioneering attitude, would receive such an award if he repeatedly won the OAP contest. The opportunity was there provided the competition continued long enough; certainly Emlyn Jenkins believed that the Welsh association had '...started a project which will go a long way and do much good'.

The full results of the display Percy put up in the gym were as follows:

Mr. Wales ('City of Cardiff Cup' 18 - 40)
First	Trevor Edwards	Blaenewm, Rhondda
Second	Tony Chandler	Barry
Third	Albert Williams	Ebbw Vale
Fourth	Ron Gillam	Ystrad, Rhondda

Miss Wales ('Borough of Newport Cup')
First	Pamela Chandler	Barry
Second	Barbara Gibson	Llanhilleth
Third	Marlene Biss	Ebbw Vale
Fourth	Pamela Watkins	Ebbw Vale

Junior Mr. Wales ('Borough of Rhondda Cup')
First	Michael Bowden	RAF St. Athan
Second	Paul Blake	Treorchy
Third	Vivian Williams	Porth
Fourth	Alan Thomas	Bargoed

Junior Miss Wales

First	Julia Moore	Risca, Mon
Second	Jean Williams	Ebbw Vale
Third	Irene Kirby	Ebbw Vale
Fourth	Vivian Langford	Treorchy

Senior Mr. Wales (over 40)

First	Hubert Davies	Griffithston, Mon
Second	Terence Watkins	Cardiff

Weight-lifting Match

Myrddin John (Wales) (Welsh Bantam Champ.)	160 170 210 - 540
Alan Davies (Margate) (S.E. Counties (Bantam Champ.)	150 140 190 - 480

Fittest Old Age Pensioner in Wales

First	Percy Hunt Port Talbot	Aged 65
Second	Mrs. Honora Jones Margam, Glamorgan	Aged 66
Third	Josiah Jones Newport	Aged 78

Thomas Inch Middleweight Challenge Dumbbell Contest
Winner: George Davies of Ebbw Vale (Best attempt)
Referee: George Kirkley, London

Percy also listed the officials involved:

George Kirkley (Editor, H. & S. International Physique Judge); Oscar Heidenstam, London (Secretary, National Amateur Body-Builders' Association International Physique Judge); Dr. Jack Matthews, Cardiff (Welsh rugby International, NABBA Judge, and Hon. Medical Adviser to the WNPCA); Alban H. Jones, Cardiff (NABBA Judge); Flight Lieutenant T.E. Brock (Station Physical Fitness Officer, RAF St. Athan); Flying Officer J. Rosendale (Station Weight-Training Officer, RAF St. Athan); Amayas

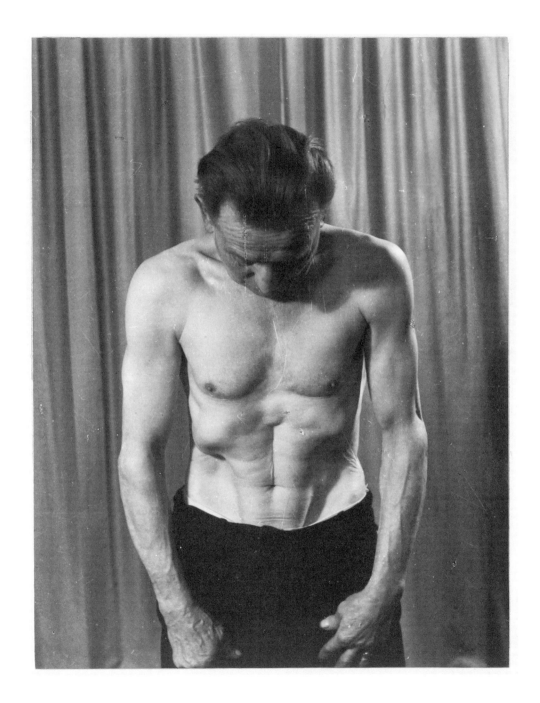

32. 'My muscles are supple, that's why I am the fittest OAP in Wales.'
(Press photo)

Thomas (PE Organiser for the Rhondda); Rhydwen Williams, Rhyl; Eddie Kelly, Cwmbran; Tom Wheeler, Birmingham; Mrs. Carol Evans, Cardiff; Mrs. Jack Matthews, Cardiff; Mrs. M. Whittall-Evans.

Percy was to find that the display was again not without controversy over the true nationality of athletes from RAF St. Athan when an official objection lodged by the Atlas Barbell Club, Treorchy, against the holder of the 'Junior Mr. Wales' title Michael Bowden, was upheld and second placed Paul Blake was awarded the first prize.

There was also something of a hiccup in the Thomas Inch dumb-bell contest with the failure of several competitors even to move the gleaming, solid cast, iron dumb-bell, let alone lift the weight of about 140lb. in a 'One Hand Bent Press', loaned by Tom Fenton of Cardiff. Other challengers had managed to lift the weight off the ground, but it came as no surprise to Percy that the verdict was awarded for the best attempt, with even the mighty efforts of George Kirkley, *H. & S.* Editor and League Organiser, not succeeding. Having met Thomas Inch at H. & S. League shows, the Port Talbot versatile athlete had known of the weight (one of three cast) custom-made with a narrow handle and wide diameter to fit exactly the grip of the famous weight-lifter.

Back home Percy had as usual responded to the local press, reporting, 'This is the finest honour I have had for years.' Later in the year they referred to Percy playfully as 'The Peter Pan athlete of British sport', with its dual implications of being youthful and having not grown up.

Gaining further celebrity status in town and in the work-place, a surprise challenge to Percy's athletic expertise came from a fellow worker goaded on by mischievous comrades. Built like an ox, but said to be two pence short of a shilling, he challenged 'The Great Mavello' to a series of feats climaxing with a boxing match, the solo singing element not appealing to a man who was tone deaf. Taking on the biblical proportions of a David and Goliath contest, Percy was no easy fodder for any giant and readily invited the challenger to the gym one evening, which the man accepted. Well prepared on home ground, Percy decided upon the psychology of fear and gave a pre-match demonstration of what he was still capable of in terms of strength, agility, speed of hand and fleetness of foot. It was said by pupils present that the opponent was so unnerved with Percy's telling touches of dramatic emphasis in technique and outbursts of aggression, he could do no more than shake his hand and be grateful that his submission was accepted cordially.

A diary event in England is accompanied in a later issue of Health & Strength by an appraisal of Percy's performance in the display:

1957 – **September 21 - Health, Strength and Beauty Show** at the Corn Exchange, Loughborough, at 3 p.m. Mr. and Miss Central England contests, Reg Park, Great Mavello (Percy Hunt), Edgar Jankovskis, free style wrestling (Ivann Nuthall, England, v Count Eley, Italy), Two Supermen (balance/strength), Loughborough College Gymnasts. Entry Forms for PE contests and tickets at 6/6, 5/-, 3/6 and 2/- from G/LDO Jack Taylor, Sports and Social Officer, Herbert Morris Ltd., Loughborough, Leicestershire.

Midlands and North from Wally Wright

...and from Port Talbot, Percy Hunt, the 'Great Mavello' proved the benefits to derive from following a long life of physical culture with an amazing demonstration of suppleness and fitness which would have done credit to anyone at least a third of his sixty-six years of age.

The show was a disappointment for G/LDO Jack Taylor, a well known free-style wrestler, with the hall only half full of spectators. The lack of support is believed to have been the reason why Percy never sought to take part in another display in Loughborough.

Adonis and Venus

Engaged for a Physical Culture Display staged by the Neath YMCA Weight-Lifting Club and held in the Gwyn Hall, Neath, on 27 March 1958, Percy declared that he was in fine fettle awaiting the return contest in May of the 'Fittest OAP in Wales'. League Organiser George Kirkley was present and took on MC duties in the show, in which the man event was an 'Adonis and Venus' contest.

Despite the hot conditions on stage for the athletes, Percy did his routine comfortably and enjoyed a good programme of events. Hubert Thomas, NABBA Sportsman of the Year, won the 180lb. dumb-bell challenge, Albert Williams (Ebbw Vale) took the 'Mr. Adonis' title - runners up were Brian Brawn (RAF Cirencester) and Domic Avo (Caerphilly). Pamela Chandler (Barry) (Miss Wales 1957), won 'Miss Venus', followed by Pat Brettle, Lynette Griffiths, Beryl Griffiths, and Jean Roberts.

With tropical conditions on stage worsening, the weight-lifters in the contest were said by Percy to sweat steadily, forming pools on the stage which had to be frequently wiped dry. The results of the two lifting matches seemed to him as much about the amount of fluid the body had left as the competitors' muscular strength. The matches ended with victories by Ron Jenkins over Alan Watts and by Gordon Newman over Peter Arthur.

Without doubt the star of the show was Reg Park, so much so that Percy thought it opportune to offer 'Mr. World' and 'Mr. Universe' (Class 1 amateur and professional) the services of his velvet-lined posing box. Fitted with a light source above for dramatic highlighting of Percy's physique, which was now richly pigmented in a gold colour, the posing box idea had been used in the early years by Macfadden and Sandow and the painting of the physique in an act attributed to Monte Saldo. So here again the posing box was revived in Wales by 'The Great Mavello', with the intense desire by him to associate Reg Park within his construction, quite forgetting the physical differences between them; the Englishman weighed 16 stone and stood 6'2" in height. It was said by former pupil Jim Hegarty, who was present offstage when Percy approached Park, that if a few lengths of timber and a few yards of black velvet had been magically available there and then, Percy would surely have added an immediate extension to his posing box to accommodate the idol of British physical excellence.

Recognised as a colossus of his time, most of the St. Mary's Street gym pupils idolised Reg Park and were eager for any new insights into their hero's methods of training from Percy's offstage acquaintance with him, for he had already met the body-builder in a display the previous year. Back home in the gym a couple of days later his description of the encounter with Park was without reference to the posing box episode and came in a critical appraisal tempered by the fact that he had again found the man modest and likeable despite what he always viewed as his quite repulsive muscular development. He went further in his critique and revealed that by the athlete's own admission he was racked with spasms affecting every muscle after warming-up before he took the stage, interspersed by a few well-chosen curses. Percy thus concluded to us, his pupils, that no further evidence was needed to convince anyone of what he already believed and condemned, namely that such muscular excesses were completely unhealthy. I don't believe many of his pupils heeded his advice for we were all eager to develop large muscles, even though the results would be somewhat painful.

Whatever his reservations concerning the body-builder's physique and supposedly drug-free method of training, his inclusion on the same billing Percy believed in keeping with his position as a respected all-round athlete of the old school. Their coming together provided the opportunity not only for mutual acquaintance but, for reflective spectators, an opportunity to compare physical culturists of quite different training principles and periods. As a man said to be not over-awed by the physical culture hierarchy and athletic greats of the modern movement, the presence of the English Body-builder therefore held no conceivable perils even though Reg Park's physical culture was quite different from Percy's traditional athleticism.

Where's Garnant? That's the question everybody's asking for the eleventh **Mr. and Miss Wales Display** will be held there next Wednesday, May 14, at 7 p.m...

So wrote Emlyn Jenkins for those athletes and members of the public unfamiliar with the venue, and continued with detailed instructions as to how to arrive at the venue by road:

...Buses will be running every half hour from Neath to Carmarthen and Ammanford and display passengers should alight at the Half Moon stop. Other road users should head for Pontardawe G.C.G. and Garnant Workmen's Hall.

...Topping the bill will be Mr. Universe 1957, John Lees, who needs no introduction to readers, and he will make two appearances. The wonder balancer, Clive Purnell, Bristol, will present his unique item, direct from the London Scala, and there will be supporting items covering gymnastics (don't miss Margaret Neale, British champion), muscle control and yoga, folk dancing, and a spot of magic. The Peter Pan of Port Talbot, Percy Hunt, will be defending his title of Fittest Old Age Pensioner in Wales, and entries for this contest will be accepted up to the day.

Tickets at 4/-, 3/6 and 2/6 are obtainable from Myrddin at 5 Bryn Road, Penygroes, Nr. Llanelly.

Ready, eager and able to defend his Old Age Pensioner title, Percy himself was unsure of the Wednesday destination for he had never given a performance in Garnant Workmen's Hall and arrived at the show in a car driven by the father of one of his pupils who accompanied him.

With Emlyn Jenkins in control of weight-lifting for the 1958 VI British Empire and Commonwealth Games in Cardiff, the organising of the physical culture displays was left to Bantamweight lifter Myrddin John, who had taken over as secretary of the Welsh National Physical Culture Association.

Although he missed the familiar presence of Emlyn Jenkins, the Garnant event for Percy was not so much remembered for the appearance of English body-building star John Lees, but the collective triumphs of Gwent athletes winning four out of five physical excellence titles; 'Mr. and Miss Wales' - Albert Williams and Barbara Gibson, 'Junior Miss Wales' - Julie Moore, 'Senior Mr. Wales' - Len Browning, and, of course, his retention of the 'Fittest OAP in Wales', Emlyn Jenkins reporting him to be 'a clear winner'. Besides his success against the same finalists as in the previous year's event, Mrs. Honora Jones and Josiah Jones, Percy, when asked by a reporter for show comments, said that he found the display a good first for organiser Myrddin John. Of the events in the display of folk-dancing by Llandybie Youth Club, magic moments by Randal Piney, balancing with Clive Purnell, and muscle control and yoga by Tom Fenton, Percy was most impressed with gymnast Margaret Neale, the 1958 British champion, and the routines of the Cardiff Youth Club who presented the athlete. Then there were the novelty gym routines of Myrddin John's own pupils from Llandybie Secondary Modern School dressed in pyjamas.

Back in the gym Percy curiously declared that he would have liked to have seen Myrddin John's pupils holding lighted candles in some of their gym routines. The candle effect addition might have been a harkening back to the muse-like figures with lighted lamps, ensconced in niches on the Palace facade in Water Street, Aberavon. Who knows?

With another triumph in the OAP category, excerpts of the display recorded by BBC Television for transmission the following week also added to the occasion, although Percy was quite blasé about it all. The Thomas and Catherine Davies Memorial Cup presentation was made by Dr. Powell of Garnant, who also gave the teetotal winner a bottle of champagne to celebrate. Besides the problem of the alcoholic content, Percy was not even inclined to consume fizzy drinks due to the gaseous content collecting in the stomach, so the champagne was donated as a raffle item to members of an OAP group in Port Talbot. It was rumoured that the winner had a house party with neighbours and toasted the success of Percy's second award until late in the evening.

The joy of success in the Garnant display was to be overshadowed for Percy by the adverse effect upon the health of Emlyn Jenkins of organising weight-lifting events in the Empire Games. The last 'Welsh Window' of the WNPCA secretary for *H. & S.* reflects not only the close of a bravura period for the Welsh association of the 1950's, in which Percy Hunt had been very much a part, but a resignation and finality that was to pierce even the tempered resolve of 'The Great Mavello'.

In the account he pinned up in the gym for pupils to hopefully take note of those personalities who made their mark in Welsh and British physical culture, special mention is given to Percy which he underlined in the last two paragraphs:

> ...Evergreen Percy Hunt, Fittest OAP in Wales, still giving his unique demonstrations all over the district... always ready to help a worthy cause. Percy's ambition now is to be the Fittest OAP in Britain and I hope he succeeds.

It is certain he never held such a title, otherwise we would have known post haste, and there is no evidence to suggest that there ever was a 'Fittest OAP in Britain' competition.

> And so the new faces come and carry on the tradition. Value your heritage. The physical culturists of forty years ago struggled on alone. Today, organisations like NABBA, the H. & S. League, WNPCA and others are the Open Sesame to all with the will to work.
>
> The prestige of PC in Wales was won by toil, tears and sweat. Public opinion has now veered in our favour and we all have a great responsibility to act as worthy apostles of the PC way of life. See you around, then. Many thanks for your help and interest over years. It has been nice knowing you.

With the passing of 1958, Percy declared that he was in strict training, determined to make it three consecutive Welsh title wins in the Old Age Pensioner competition. With Myrddin John moving away from his usual role of organising physical excellence events to become secretary of the Welsh Amateur Weight-Lifters' Association, the veteran athlete found that Dennis Stallard was replacing the West Walian and also taking over the penmanship of 'Welsh Window'. Although it was evident among colleagues that Stallard had never taken to 'The Great Mavello', he dutifully, in the first year as an organiser, sought to arouse opposition against the reigning champion when he wrote, 'Let's see other 65 year old "youngsters" give him a run for his money'.

So the stage was set for the third 'Fittest OAP in Wales' contest of the 12th Annual 'Mr. and Miss Wales' Display, to be held on Saturday, 30 May, at Parc and Dare Hall, Treorchy, which was a return to the venue of his first success. Dennis Stallard, however, claimed that there seemed to be an unwillingness to compete and challenge the Port Talbot all-rounder and the event was cancelled. Rumour had it that a number of challengers appeared ready and able to compete, but were said to be deemed unconvincing enough for Dennis Stallard to allow the competition to take place. Any hope of Percy attaining a WNPCA Standard award disappeared with the decision to end the 'Fittest OAP in Wales' event Emlyn Jenkins had believed would do so much good.

Although disappointed at the outcome, the veteran athlete, later in the year, decided as of old to fling down the 'Knightly' gauntlet and issued a public challenge in *Health & Strength* magazine of 3 December, to all old age pensioners living in Wales to compete against him. The repertoire he set for the challenge was of course varied, with 'Hand and head balancing; Body feat of Strength; Barbell manipulation; Skipping; Novel Club Swinging; Muscle Control; to end with a Tenor Solo. Extra feats: Exhibition of Boxing; Wrestling; Running; Walking; Cycling; Dancing or Swimming.'

Among the older physical culturists, Swansea's Arthur Goss seemed to emerge as a possible challenger, acclaimed by supporters as the uncrowned King of versatile athletes in Wales. However, as Dennis Stallard pointed out in 'Welsh Window', any challenge between Percy Hunt and Arthur Goss - essentially a swimmer - would have to be in the over 40 category, as the Swansea man had not reached retirement age. As a one-time professional stage strongman, Percy never went in to a challenge without due care and planning in the expectation of winning. With the age difference greater than he would have wished for a fair contest the event was never resolved between them, nor did any old age pensioner of athletic ability rise to 'The Great Mavello' public challenge, and he remained the undisputed, 'Undefeated Fittest OAP in Wales'.

33. Head-Stand in Celebration of Percy's 76th Birthday
(Press photo)

Chapter 6

Later Years: Rounds on Shanks' Pony

'Fit 70- year-old retires- but not from gymnastics'. 'Percy, petite, powerful and popular...' alliterated *Guardian* reporter Malcome Rees, in a punchy journalistic and comprehensive tribute to the versatile athlete upon his belated retirement in August 1961 at the age of 70 from being a council road sweeper. Not expected to take things leisurely, Percy declared in the write-up, 'I am hoping to be able to travel around giving lectures to schools and other associations on the value of clean living.'

In the so-called permissive, fun-loving 1960's 'clean living', which, with its relevance to moderation in all things, Percy regarded as essential to fitness, was now akin to a kind of medieval asceticism in a town growing prosperous with revenue received from one of the largest steel-making complexes in Europe - The Steel Company of Wales Ltd., 'Abbey Works', Port Talbot Division, spread out on Margam Moors like a leviathan. It was therefore not surprising in the steel boom-town of the 1960's, that any kind of Spartan-like doctrine of restraint did not find many converts in the flow of indulgence, and sense of importance, that prevailed in the clime of further industrial expansion with the siting of BP Chemicals (UK) Ltd. on Baglan Bay. A wag declared to Percy that his 'clean living' philosophy was impossible in such a polluted atmosphere.

Industrial domination of the borough was somewhat counterbalanced by bold ambitions of developing Aberavon Beach into a hoped-for Blackpool of South Wales, a project encouraging to Percy Hunt with his hopes of appearances on stage in summer shows. Further transformations to obliterate the old town centre and replace it with a modern shopping complex in the 1970's were not, however, to his liking. Neither was the building of a motorway by-pass fly-over, extending four miles from the A48 at Pentyla to the A48 at Groes in Margam, razing the old village in its construction.

Along with the continued destruction of areas of a once familiar town, stone by stone and brick by brick, the Welsh physical culture movement as Percy knew it was also in the process of conversion, hastened by the untimely death in 1960 of founder Emlyn Jenkins, at 49 years of age; his demise effectively ended the Great Mavello's engagements in the WNPCA's displays.

The change of attitude which replaced Emlyn Jenkin's guiding idealism had now become hard-edged, self-centred, and Joe Weider-inspired. In this clime Percy did make one final appearance at the 1960 premier physical excellence event, now called 'The All-Wales Physical Display'. In the display former pupils of Percy's, body-builders Ronald Bradford and Donald Radnige, won 'Mr. Wales' and the junior title respectively. Not in tune with the veteran athlete's idiosyncrasies concerning muscle enhancement, their stay in the St. Mary's Street gym had been short-lived in the extreme.

Running parallel with changes taking place in Welsh physical culture there was, apart from the proliferation of private gyms, the growth of community sports facilities. Both former pupils of Percy, Welsh champion lifters Mike Brown and Phil Robinson, opened up training schools - Mike Brown operating both privately in his back garden gym and in the Taibach County Youth Club, with brothers David and Alan, and Phil Robinson as a council appointed weight-training coach in the eventual Sports Centre on Aberavon Beach. With the changes fewer pupils arrived at the St. Mary's Street Health & Strength gym, the place becoming a back-water for the continuation of old physical culture faiths and out-moded idealism.

The decline in the status of Percy Hunt's gym was also attributed to the gradual fall in popularity of the League as a main-stream movement, the whole dilemma turning him inwards to re-evaluate his position as a local personality. This was achieved with a degree of success by cultivating his image in town on what he termed his daily 'rounds on shanks' pony'.

When the Port Talbot veteran athlete took to his 'rounds' anyone and everyone were potential targets (some softer than others) for varying doses of recollections regarding physical culture and his part in the Health & Strength League movement. Although the subject matter might have been familiar he had an entertaining and fine sense of history about himself, as befitting a local legend, and would, if the mood took him or the right cue was given, encompass decades in a chronological mix of well-honed anecdotes.

The recollective mix was usually accompanied by information about his remedial exercise and advice on ailments affecting both nervous and digestive systems, lungs, and rheumatic and arthritic aches and pains of muscles and joints. People who accepted medical treatment from general practitioners were alienated from what they considered unorthodox, dubious practices, and quickly dismissed to their cost the therapeutic value they held. The athlete's practitioner, Dr. Donald Isaac, proved more enlightened and sent young patients with asthmatic and rheumatic complaints to him for curative and preventive treatment.

Percy's crusading routine also provided the opportunity to not only voice claims for remedial treatment but employ playful intimidation regarding the general apathy of townsfolk lacking physical conditioning. In this situation he came into his own with admonishing remarks like 'People have become too lazy! They are afraid to walk two yards. They have to jump into a bus or car wherever they go!' Even if he was for some town residents a continual and uncomfortable reminder of their excessive and inactive life-styles, his presence in town was on the whole a most welcome feature.

Having made it known that in twenty years as a road sweeper he had never lost a minute's work through illness and never once slept late, his fitness levels in retirement were intended to be celebrated as an event on his birthday, 5 August, with a press-covered engagement or at least a photograph of an item of balance in the *Guardian*, the *Gazette* or *South Wales Evening Post*. Opportunities in both instances for the 'Might Atom', as he was now referred to in the press and on the lips of wags in town, were almost non-existent at a time when peak August holiday activities on the unfinished development of Aberavon Beach, and Talbot Road YMCA shows, tended to dominate everything else. Nevertheless with social clubs on the Sandfields Housing Estate also focal points for large summer crowds, his second birthday in retirement was celebrated with an invitation in 1962 to prove his fitness in a display at the Bay View Social Club, facing the salty breezes on Aberavon seafront.

Percy's comments of the display in the *Guardian* were as usual quite unstinting in the praise he gave his performances, although the occasion seems to have been exceptional in terms of audience reception. 'I give them my complete workout,' said Percy, 'and when I told them my age they just wouldn't believe it. They gave me one of the finest receptions I've received in my whole 71 years.'[1]

In keeping with his birthday celebrations in August of the same year, the Plaza Cinema showing of 'Hercules Conquers Atlantis' provided the cinema management with the opportunity of inviting the town's own pocket Hercules to view his famous stage colleague Reg Park, who was the star in the muscle-rippling saga. Moving onto reflections of the body-builder, Percy mentioned to a *Guardian* reporter, 'One of the greatest compliments I ever had paid to me was by Reg Park when he told me that he wished he would be as fit as me when he reaches my age.' Percy was then in his late sixties.

Although the local *Guardian* rarely allocated space in the month of August to celebrate his birthdays in retirement, due supposedly to the August holiday period, such reasons might well have been combined with Percy's inability to sustain editorial interest in his fitness and age ratio comparison against a background of novelty events in a summer season of light entertainment. As an idealistic loner of the old ways he never had enough contacts of local influence or with enough faith in his intuitive and idealistic ways of keeping fit, strong and healthy, for him to make any effective claims for a healthy mind in a healthy body philosophy. Idealism was not to be a motivating word of the 1960s'.

'Cavalcade of Sport and Midnight Cabaret' At a time when the Borough Council of Port Talbot had assumed a certain status of industrial worth from its neighbouring councils with the building of the Abbey Works, it was only proper, so it seemed, that there should be even more spectacular, star-studded shows to emphasise the success of a town which before its own industrial revolution had less to offer its residents in the economic sense, except cleaner air.

So it was that on Tuesday, 17 January 1963, a Freedom from Hunger Campaign 'Cavalcade of Sport and Midnight Cabaret' took place. Figure-headed by the Mayor of Port Talbot, Alderman Frederick Snook, the event was held in the Main Staff Dining Hall of the Abbey Works.

That Percy Hunt was uninvited was regarded by pupils past and present, colleagues and friends, as sadly amiss on the part of the organisers. The versatile veteran athlete's displeasure at his exclusion from the celebrations was obvious and they fully supported his argument that if sports in the Principality such as boxing, rugby, soccer, gymnastics, judo, speedway racing, sailing, bowls, golf, cycling, table tennis, lacrosse and hockey were represented by leading sportspeople why not Port Talbot's and Wales's pioneering physical culturist and renowned H. & S. Leaguer?

Amongst the parade of sporting stars, past and present, introduced to the audience, many of whom were familiar with the all-round athlete, he would no doubt have taken delight, as a reputed Paper-weight boxing champion of Wales, in mingling with boxers Brian and Cliff Curvis, Lennie (The Lion) Williams, Benny Jacobs and Jack Peterson; then there was Ned Jenkins and Wilfred Wooler (both rugby and cricket), Dr. Jack Matthews, Ken Jones, Len Cunningham, Roger Michaelson (ex-pupil), and Dr. Tony O'Conner (rugby); Ivor Allchurch and Allan Durban (soccer); Trevor Bailey, Douglas Insole, Terry Lewis, Gilbert Parkhouse and Ossie Wheatley (cricket); Freddie Williams (World Speedway Champion), Kitty Nash Davies (swimming), Paul Davies and Val Howells (sailing), Mel Davies (cycling), Len Hill and Elizabeth Howells (bowls), David Thomas and John Povall (golf), Audrey Bates and Mair Evans (hockey).

Although past his bedtime, given his routine of early to bed and early to rise, Percy would no doubt have re-arranged his time-table to be at the cabaret on the stroke of midnight when the 'star-studded' event began. Arranged by TWW (Independent Television for South Wales and West of England) and Teledu Cymru, and compered by Alan Taylor, the stars he would have seen and met (if he had not already done so on other occasions) were Stan Stennett and singers Ivor Emmanuel, Patricia Bredin and Marian Davies, with stage and film star Donald Houston taking the place of Richard Burton who was at his sister Edith's funeral.

Among the fine assembly of prominent citizens of officers and working committee,[2] Percy was known to local businessman D. Bryn Thomas, appointed as one of two masters of ceremonies drafted in from the main body of officers. Having long recognised Percy's athletic versatility in write-ups in his weekly *Guardian* column 'Bryn Thomas's Sporting Chatter', the former St. Athan (Sergeant) PTI and all-round sportsman had once observed, 'It is a curious fact that great men are rarely recognised in their own countries, and this is unfortunately the case with Percy Hunt.' At first flattered by the re-constructed old adage of discrimination against the prophet within the boundaries of his homeland while accoladed abroad, he had thus looked to Bryn Thomas for his inclusion in the sporting event. Many years the Great Mavello's junior, with a BEM, preceded by a 'Certificate of Merit' for devotion to duty in the Second World War, Percy decided to confront Bryn Thomas as to why he was omitted from the celebrations. Possessed of a fluid verbosity in attack or defence that Percy never had, Mr. Thomas was said to have told him in so many words that he did not fit easily into any sporting category for such a prestigious occasion. Whether he was wary that, if invited, Percy might take the opportunity to give the assembled guests and audience a quick resumé of the benefits of his life style is unknown. Whatever, Percy's reply was just to remind Mr. Thomas of what he had written about how unfortunate it was that his (Percy's) greatness remained unrecognised in Wales, only now he was not even recognised in his home-town when it came to a special celebration of Welsh sportspeople in aid of charity, which he had always supported with his versatile athletic act. If there was a reply from Mr. Thomas, Percy did not elaborate further.

That Percy did not fit easily into a particular category in a show seen as an important occasion was not regarded by his supporters or any unbiased person as an excuse for excluding the veteran versatile athlete from the charity campaign; there was, however, in general, a confused, petty disregard on the

135

sports-scene for the disciplines of weight-lifting and body-building which remained unresolved by those persons organising the local charity event.

The Port Talbot Guardian came post-haste to Percy's defence while seizing the opportunity for a good local story of the injustice done to the town's 'sound mind in a sound body' advocate, with a retaliatory article a week later. The article was inserted for clashing, critical effect alongside the continuing 'Cavalcade of Sport and Midnight Cabaret' coverage:

No Invitation for 'Grand Old Man'

Port Talbot's sporting event to end sporting events, 'The Cavalcade of Sport', is over. It was undoubtedly a crowning success for everyone concerned, and reflects great credit on the organisers. Naturally, as the grand function was held in Port Talbot and organised by local people for a local hunger campaign, those Port Talbot-born sportsmen who had brought credit to the town in small or large measures were invited. But one sportsman who for a great many years has been performing for charity and flying the Port Talbot flag over Great Britain and America was not at the function. The sportsman was Percy Hunt, Port Talbot's 71 year old 'Grand old man' of physical culture, the mere holder of... The reason for his absence from this local extravaganza is simple. He was just not invited.

TV Shows and Tripper's Paradise

Just over a year later after the let-down of his exclusion from the '...magnificent spectacle the like of which had never before been witnessed in the locality', Percy appeared as guest artist on the TWW 'Here Today' programme on Tuesday, 28 January 1964. For his act he received the then princely sum of eight guineas plus the First Class return rail fare from Port Talbot to Cardiff of £1.4s.10d. Approximately two years later Percy appeared on BBC Television and noted with some dismay the Corporation's disappointing payment compared to TWW's. He was after all a professional and no such person takes kindly to a lesser fee for the same quality of performance.

His television engagements occurred in the period when the transformation of Aberavon Beach into a so-called 'tripper's paradise' was taking place in a miscellany of entertainment. Here, the prestigious Afan Lido opened by Her Majesty Queen Elizabeth on 25 June 1965 (the adjoining Sports Centre opened the following year by Dennis Howell, Esq., MP, Minister of Sport) had appeared an inspired although costly venture, but in keeping with the town's sense of success. Indeed, for some years, Percy felt there was a pretentious attitude taking over a number of the Afan Lido's personnel in the brave new world of keeping fit and partaking of leisure activities. Within easy reach of his home at 74 Morland

Road, and later 6 Romsey Road, Sandfields, daily visits to the Afan Lido's sports complex, particularly in the summer season, which extended Percy's 'rounds' in town to more regular jaunts to the seaside, were full of hope that those in authority would make use of his experience as a stage athlete in seaside shows.

Graham Jenkins, brother and look-alike of stage and film star Richard Burton, the Entertainment Officer and General Manager of the Afan Lido, among other duties, was quite familiar with the ubiquitous Percy Hunt, as was another personality, Bryn Thomas, now full-time Sports and unofficial Entertainments Officer in the Afan Lido complex.

Come the seaside summer season, Graham Jenkins recalled, Percy was '...always making himself available for various entertainment at the Afan Lido and Seafront Bandstand, particularly so if there was a body-building competition. In fact he did not require an invitation, it was difficult to keep him away.' Mr. Jenkins also observed '... that although in later life his body was of a young man, his mind had been besotted so much by his paranoia of keeping himself absolutely fit (he was forever climbing an Everest of fitness) that in the end his mind could no longer cope with the fight for fitness. He could not and did not understand why everyone did not do the same.'

Certainly, Percy pursued the 'blue-bird of youth'; certainly, there was an urgency if not desperation at times to keep proving that physical culture as a panacea was manifest in him. In so doing his behaviour did at times tend towards flourishes of exaggeration. As colleague and friend Will James said of the athlete in his years of retirement, 'He wouldn't tell lies but his imagination used to run riot at times.' These flights of fancy became a distinctive part of Percy's nature in selling the idea of a replenished state of well-being to what he still believed as an apathetic public. If that means delusions of grandeur then so be it.

Without doubt Bryn Thomas bore the brunt of Percy's persistent impromptu approaches for engagements, the '...making himself available for various entertainment...' referred to by Graham Jenkins, being nothing more than occasional perfunctory introductions as to his worth as a veteran athlete of Health & Strength before crowds and audiences. The proof of acclaim, Percy argued, was in performance.

Gordon Davies, an amateur thespian, richly-voiced, who had taken over from Graham Jenkins upon his departure to fresh pastures in Jersey, was also unable to help. His inability to assist Percy in his endeavours was probably due to the free rein given to Bryn Thomas to do almost what he liked in terms of entertainment. It was said by those close to the Sports Officer that to have given the veteran physical culturist a foot-hold in such proceedings would have seriously hampered his baton-waving control.

The main proposition made by Percy was not to be taken lightly in that he wanted to establish a summer season act involving his undefeated 'Fittest Old Age Pensioner in Wales' challenge to any persons (men or women) over the age of 65 - Percy was then in his 70's. Certainly the idea had crowd-pulling potential if enough candidates could be encouraged to challenge him. With the possibility of challenges extending the whole range of Percy's 21 feats, which would have meant bringing out of retirement his world title series of weight-lifting, boxing, wrestling, swimming, cycling, etc., the outcome might well have been worth staging, given the increasing popularity of keeping fit and the novelty value in a variety of disciplines.

His inability to acquire even one legitimate seaside engagement was, he announced, in direct contrast to The Steel Company of Wales Ltd., 'Abbey Works', Port Talbot Division, who employed his skills (as of old in the 'Puby' Hall) between boxing bouts at an exhibition given by Swansea's Cliff Curvis (British Welterweight Champion) and Eric Thomas of Cwmtwrch, in an open-air event celebrating Coronation Day, 7 June 1953. Percy did not allow distance of years to exclude a point of comparison when the need arose.

Percy never gave up trying to manufacture engagements and so persistently did he pursue Bryn Thomas that the Sports Officer often resorted, or so it seemed to staff at the Afan Lido, to appointing his assistant, Percy's former schoolboy star pupil Alan Rees, to handle the delicate situation, but this only compounded the problem. When Percy approached Alan Rees for support it all became a matter of hide and seek, and most unfortunate was the nuisance label applied to 'The Great Mavello'.

It was inevitable that such procedures would open old wounds inflicted in clashing resonances of past situations in Talbot Road YMCA days, where actor-to-be Sir Anthony Hopkins came to know of Percy Hunt. It was here that the H. & S. Leaguer had carried on supporting shows with exhibitions and held free training sessions. Here, in the YMCA, he had taught members of the Port Talbot Harriers weight-training in the 1930's, before Bryn Thomas took over the now paid position of PTI that he had sought.

Bryn Thomas was indeed suitably qualified as a Royal Air Force Physical Training Instructor to take on the position in the YMCA, with a Wycliff College, Gloucester, background compared to Percy's elementary education. Despite such sound achievements, Life Vice-President of the Welsh Amateur Athletic

Association, Arthur Williams, wrote in the local Guardian, in response to what he knew as Bryn Thomas's plug for the Harriers' adoption of weight-training as a new method in the 1952 season, '...Our old friend, Percy Hunt, may sniff when he reads this, and at what is now termed a 'new discovery' in training. He can truthfully say he used it himself for years, and it was by this method that he got Roy Williams fit when the YMCA Harrier won the Welsh 220yds in 1938.'

Rivalry had therefore long been apparent between 'The Great Mavello' and 'Uncle Bryn' - as he was popularly known in YMCA extravaganzas, 'Gang' shows, and 'Bryn's a-poppin' events - the younger man seeking to establish himself as the 'King' of town personalities, a regal position which Percy claimed he had long held and was not contemplating abdicating.

Clashes of personality and rivalry were to gain momentum with Aberavon Beach increasing in popularity as a venue for sporting events, beauty contests and variety shows. Arthur Williams officially organised seaside Welsh AAA races with calm authority in contrast to the almost frenetic gusto of Sports Officer, Bryn Thomas, while Percy unofficially circulated the holiday-spirited crowds, the shows and competitions, recharging his ego and displaying youthfulness in spontaneous demonstrations of balance and acrobatics in the increasingly futile hope of securing an engagement.

The only lasting consolation left for the veteran all-rounder, apart from the friendship of close colleagues, seems to have been the interest shown by stage and film star Richard Burton. Having first met Percy in a demonstration the athlete gave in the Taibach County Youth Club, the film star celebrity was sufficiently impressed to thereafter frequently enquire of the H. & S. Leaguer and he even visited him at his home. Percy's recollection of the visit seems to have been suitably reserved, as if it was only right and proper and even inevitable that Richard Burton would recognise a fellow celebrity and realise what he was about.

King Lear v The Great Mavello
On his daily 'rounds' in town, Percy was ever ready to unsheath a rapier-like tongue in the defence of keeping fit and healthy. He would thus often illuminate a point of disbelief with a demonstration such as a 'handstand' or similar balancing item, but Percy was now more careful whom he approached when declaring the benefits of healthy living for he had overmatched himself with a gentleman named Les. Les, at the time, happened to be on release from Bridgend Psychiatric Hospital as an out-patient, having already dispersed, through most peculiar but harmless behaviour, the lady members of the 'Port

Talbot Painters' Guild' in 1969. In this man 'The Great Mavello' found a complex and unnerving character.

Les Davies, a former Metropolitan policeman (Sergeant?), was a wiry giant of a man in his fifties who had suffered severe shell-shock during the London blitz. Gaunt and white of moustache and beard he often carried an impressive tome of world literature under his arm and was above all a formidable, verbal counter-puncher, enhanced by a rich, basso-profundo-like operatic voice. Whenever he went into verbal over-drive and his large, long-fingered, expressive hands soared upwards, bird-like, in dramatic gestures counter-pointing prophetic exclamations on the plight of the world and Port Talbot, Percy for one almost half-expected Les to orchestrate a natural elemental disaster. Knowing the man, I suppose Les (nickname 'hairpin') would have been an admirable 'hamming' King Lear.

Their first meeting took place in unusual circumstances for Percy, but not so for the culture-minded Les - the opening day of the first Art Exhibition of the painters' guild. Percy was there on his 'rounds', strolling into the exhibition, held as part of 'Croeso '69' celebrations, in a large, dusty building in Station Road, once occupied by a well known firm of wholesale and retail fruit and potato merchants managed by Major Wally Chidzoy.[3]

A guild member myself, I introduced Les to Percy in a somewhat frantic situation arising from the theft of a portrait in the exhibition of 'Rolling Stones' pop idol Brian Jones. Casting an eye in amusement from his great height of about 6'-5" upon the 4'10" form of the all-round athlete, he immediately pursued a jargonised nonsense lecture on aspects of French Impressionism, inflecting his voice in an exaggerated manner with a few French-sounding words thrown in, to a smiling 'Great Mavello'. Before Les could warm to his sense of the absurd Percy seized the initiative and matched, more or less, Les's efforts with a loud rendition of 'Italian Salad', upon which he responded by bursting forth in theatrical laughter and intoned something about a 'flea'. 'Ha-Ha—Ha—-Ha——Ha———a—F—-l—ea—-!' When Les made a mock movement, as if to make a quick grab at Percy, the athlete slipped below his outstretched hands, did a sharp shuffle with his feet, and escaped quickly into the crowd outside.

After their first meeting and comic encounter, it was apparent that Les Davies was not the kind of sympathetic listener to whom Percy could happily expound his physical culture theories. Les himself was full of theories, theories metaphysical, adorned with quotations from Plato, Aristotle, Voltaire, Shakespeare, Wordsworth, Keats and, inevitably, Dylan Thomas; far too rich a mixture for most townsfolk let alone Percy Hunt. From that moment whenever they met, which was not often as the veteran athlete went out of his way to avoid him, a mock battle would ensue with Les abusively roaring 'Let me have the little ....!', and Percy, it is said, reacting in mute response and animating his way out of the situation by skipping and side-stepping around him before feigning to hit him with a flurry of punches in space. He would then speed away into the distance, this being likened by onlookers to the conclusion of a Charlie Chaplin silent film escapade.

I suspect that Percy never quite forgave me for introducing Les Davies to him, although it was inevitable they would meet while 'hairpin' was in the community intent on achieving his own particular cocktail of cultural credibility. To this end he was greatly encouraged by a free-wheeling local deputy head librarian, who threw in his lot to become a salesman with a reputable double-glazing company.

Mr. and Miss Great Britain

Of the competitive activities held in the Afan Lido, the first ever staging in Wales of 'Mr. and Miss Great Britain', on Saturday, 9 October 1971, in conjunction with the British Amateur Body-Builders' Federation and its Welsh equivalent, was a physique poseur contest Percy had looked forward to with anticipation. The star attraction in the display would be IFBB and NABBA (Pro.) 'Mr. Universe' 1970 and current IFBB 'Mr. Olympia' 1971, Arnold Strong (Schwarzenegger), and among those in the audience by invitation was Sergio Oliva, his closest rival.

With Dennis Stallard the principal motivating force behind the bringing of the competition to Wales and the event compered by Percy's former pupil Donald Dennis, the versatile athlete believed, despite his past differences with them both, that admittance on the night was assured even though officials of the show failed to send him an invitation. How could it be otherwise in his home-town, with him in his 80th year and arguably one of the finest, if not greatest, of early Welsh H. & S. Leaguers and versatile athletes? To deny him an invitation to a premier event would have lacked grace and been an unbecoming arrogance by the organisers.

Although alienated by a new set-up, without the camaraderie once a natural part of the League and the WNPCA, Percy arrived in good time outside the Afan Lido and Sports Complex. Donald Dennis, recollecting his arrival, clarified his position in the scheme of things in a letter to me:

...Dear old Percy wanted to see the show and, although I was the compere, I was unable to find a complimentary ticket. It was terrible for me because Percy was such an old guy, and it wouldn't have done any harm for the organisers to have given him a complimentary ticket. My wife and I sat him down and we bought him a cup of tea and had a long chat about the old days.

Sallying Forth as Usual

Percy sallied forth as usual after a hurt to his pride, continuing his daily trek to town with a resurgent attitude. Ever mindful of his lineage within the historical perspective of the Health & Strength movement, his walkabouts and pep-talks now began to become more photograph orientated. These images by town photographer Newark Lewis showed what Percy considered his best posing prints, which had also led him to seek to exploit them in the late 1930's and late 1940's, by linking photographs to a particular product beneficial to health.

So here he was again attempting to revamp his attempts to advertise a healthy way of life, which had resulted in low key commercial benefits when the manufacturers of 'Horlicks' instructed Mr. Belli, the Italian owner of Belli's Cafe, Station Road, to give Percy Hunt a free cup of the beverage for as long as the athlete wished to consume their product. This free cup of the nourishing liquid was due to his enterprise in showing, and on occasion distributing among the general public on his 'rounds', selected photographs, on the back of which were printed the product name 'Horlicks' and the cafe 'Belli's'. Although none of the captioned prints seem to have survived, the implication was obviously that if you drink 'Horlicks' you too can become a versatile athlete like Percy Hunt.

While showing the photographs, without any intention now of financial gain, he would sometimes reminisce about his second advert promoting the product 'Bovril'. More in keeping with the competitive world of commercial enterprise than his previous effort, he was, as he had reminded the manufacturer back in the 1940s, and did again with the general public on his walkabouts after retirement, a 'Bovril' silver medal winner in the 1930's for all-round athleticism. However, as a convincing advert for 'Bovril' it completely lacks the necessary impact, taken up as it is by the dominant motto of the H. & S. League[4] (Plate. 27). Nevertheless the manufacturer rewarded Percy's resourcefulness not with a hope-for cheque, but with three large crates of the product. The main problem, he admitted, had been storage with the bulk, it was said, of about 1,500 jars. In order to deplete the stock every one of his pupils at the time was introduced to the nutritious value of 'Bovril', whether they enjoyed the product or not, Percy freely and happily giving them a jar each week for some time to come before the supply was finally exhausted.

Apart from the commercial aspects of 'Horlicks' and 'Bovril' depicted in the 'Mavello' montage and other prints, the personification of the H. & S. League maxim 'Sacred the body even as thy Soul' photograph of the 1920's, captioned 'Percy and the Angels'[5] (Plate 10), was to be controversial among some of the town's citizens. This dislike of the image arose mainly among the elders of church and chapel, who found Percy's half-nude pose between angels a profane image. He defended the composition as a right and proper statement to make for a crusading H. & S. Leaguer intent on 'clean living', who castigated the evils of alcohol and smoking. He was, however, as the years elapsed, to relent on his resistance towards moderate alcoholic intake himself, which in turn was seen by those of a pious nature to weaken the purpose behind the composition of 'Percy and the Angels'.

The departure from previous abstinence was said to have occurred about the same time that he was made a life member of the Port Talbot Branch of the British Legion Club, stimulated by a complimentary dram of spirits or glass of ale, taken for 'medicinal' purposes of thinning the blood, which became a weekly habit. Smoking, however, was a life-long dislike even though it was written into the League constitution that limited use of the weed was permitted to leaguers in mid-to-late life. He declared, 'I do not smoke because I wasn't made to be a chimney.'

Often applied in his pre-display pep-talk and on his walkabouts in town, the anti-smoking one-liner introduced recollections of Health & Strength celebration dinners in London of the 1920's and the 1930's, when he was invited as a renowned Welsh G/LDO. Close observation of the greats of British physical culture at these functions made them vulnerable in Percy's view. Somewhat dismayed at the excess of alcohol consumed and the cigars and cigarettes smoked, the Welsh H. & S. Leaguer claimed he stood up at an event celebrating the great weight-lifter Thomas Inch and promptly denounced in so many words what he saw as a soirée to unbounded excess. On his 'rounds' in town and in the gym, he was to refer to Thomas Inch as 'Mr. Public House' after he had bloated himself up from middleweight to heavy-weight by drinking large quantities of beer.

While on critical recollections of the famous Thomas Inch's rival in the commercial field of physical culture and remedial work, lifter and one-time boxer, W.A. Pullum, also came in for criticism after Percy's post-war 1940-45 visit to his Camberwell gym, 5 Church Street, London. Here the Welsh athlete saw Pullum apply double standards as a BAWLA technical adviser by including a cheating, double heave in a 'Military' Press lift. If such cheating did occur, and we have no reason to doubt Percy, then we are probably seeing early on experimental techniques first applied and then introduced by American athletes.

Such grievances came in limited clusters or recollections and were often dispersed among items in a lighter vein when he discerned a falling away of interest by townsfolk. He would, for instance, elevate the status of Welsh physical culturists who, like himself, gained health and strength after physical disability by judicious exercise with weights. One example of a number quoted was Gerald Foxwell of Ebbw Vale. Building his own gym with his father's assistance, the young man became a competent athlete and noted weight-lifting referee in the 1950's.

If in later years Percy was more subdued in promoting physical culture as a way of life or critical of famous athletes, he was a vociferous supporter of Aberavon Rugby Football Club. Indeed, despite his shouting the top notes in tenor praise of the 'Wizards of the West', he was no match for the much younger chief supporter, Mrs. Mainwaring, her Wagnarian-like call to arms, 'Come on Aberavon!' or 'Come on the Wizards!, bellowing loud and clear above Percy's trumpeting top notes from the Grandstand. Only when the visiting enemy was Neath did these impromptu duets become operatic with Percy and then 'Madam' Mainwaring, as he called her, sounding like lovers in torment above the Grandstand chorus.

Appropriately in the rugby season Percy would mention on his walkabouts, as a 'Derby' game approached, the success of four former pupils in playing for Aberavon RFC and Wales. Sometimes his cousin Dai Hunt Davies headed the honours from post-war years of 1914-1918, before current players - wing three-quarter John Collins (who had trained only briefly as a youth in Percy's gym), outside-half Alan Rees and wing forwards Roger Michaelson and Bobby Wanbon - came up for airing.

Acclaim in later life thus became not so much realised in Percy's now diminishing opportunities for achievement, but in association with sporting abilities of former pupils. Retrospection laced with such references no doubt brightened his advancing years. Apart from pupils who found fame on the rugby field Phillip Wells - one of his latter-day nursery pupils - won the nine stone Welsh Strength Set Championship in the early 1960's, the triumph proving to be a remarkable feat after some years before Percy had cured him of a spinal defect with physicultopathic treatment.

Percy too was to apply physio techniques to himself after sustaining a leg injury in a car accident near home, the shock of which his wife believed was the root cause of what she later correctly diagnosed as diabetes. Shrugging off assistance, he jumped up almost immediately, so he said, in a reflex action against the hurt, leaving the scene of the accident without ever seeking medical help.

It was evident the leg injury did not heal the way Percy had hoped, even though he daily treated with massage a large protrusion of muscle on the front of his left thigh. He was now not quite the same sprightly figure striding forth with his usual welcoming smile and greeting, but one who attempted with difficulty to disguise the injury evident from his painful limping walk. The sight of the veteran athlete moving slowly and purposefully along the uneven broken pavement at the side of the partially demolished Market, when the commercial area of the Ancient Borough had already been razed to make way for the Aberafan Shopping Centre in the mid-1970's, remains to me unforgettable. It was an image not of sentiment but of heroic dimension, symbolic of past traditions locked up in the rubble and torn fabric of demolition, yet held young and championed in the unbowed figure of 'The Great Mavello'.

For a number of the more senior townsfolk the passing away of familiar streets, lanes, alleys and buildings to be replaced by a new covered shopping complex probably induced an identity crisis, even though possibly not every aspect of what had gone was a profound loss to them. Percy himself missed the bustle of activity in Water Street and High Street, the Market and the Arcade and the friendliness of people he met even though, in the undisclosed diabetes of latter years, he was vulnerable to the wag who reminded him of the greater strengths of rivals. In a healthier state he would have dismissed the inference of inferiority with a humorous response instead of now registering annoyance.

The main rival offered was Swansea stage and circus strongman Jack Lemm (real name Lamnea). Taller and heavier at about 12 stone and a couple of years Percy's senior, Jack Lemm (also known as Swansea Jack) toured South Wales with his show, which included 'ladies' boxing' as well as his feats of arm-wrestling and weight-lifting. His act was highlighted by a spectacular show-stopper that entailed whirling round a motor cycle and rider attached by a rope encircling his neck until they were air-borne. Although he admired the Swansea athlete's enterprise, Percy did not take his claim to the title of the most perfectly developed man in the world seriously as his angular close-fibred muscled build may not have been aesthetically pleasing; his strength was a different matter.

Despite the worsening condition of Percy's untreated illness which he

**34. 'I have helped charity and good causes all my life and what have I had?
A kick in the pants!'**
The Municipal Buildings under demolition.
(Photo montage by the author)

believed as a Health & Strength athlete could be cured with exercise and diet, he carried on his 'rounds' dutifully as usual taking in 'Mor Awelon' old people's home situated near the Aberavon Beach. Here, in the home, where he was a welcome visitor, he would chat and give impromptu performances of fun and athletic antics that put the residents in a good mood for the rest of the day. He was after all one of their own as a senior citizen and living proof of the value of 'a sound mind in a sound body'. However, on one particular visit it came about that a female resident took offence to his remarks concerning the 'Churchillian' face formed in his abdominal muscles, minus the cigar! The cigar inference had unfortunately taken on exaggerated phallic proportions from suggestions made by a chorus of female old age pensioners at one of his displays many of whom, ironically, resided in 'Mor Awelon'. Not a part of such events, but having heard from her sister residents at the home suggestions of a lewd nature, the lady in question vented her anger on Percy Hunt, who was thereafter refused further visits. He responded to the incident with his not uncommon reaction to a hurt, 'I have helped charity and good causes all my life and what have I had? A kick in the pants!'

His muscle control display had also posed problems to an ex-Mayoress of the borough convalescing one Christmas in Port Talbot General Hospital, who complained to a visiting, local, retired pedagogue and lay preacher about Percy's act. 'Dear me, Mr. Rees', said the old lady and former Mayoress, 'it was rude of him to do that in the women's ward!'

The therapy of physical exercise Percy held sacred and he could see no offence whatsoever in revealing muscular areas of his body in dynamic mobility, whatever the venue or whoever the audience. Any overt sexual inferences he took in good humour and, perhaps naively, expected everyone to do the same.

His friend and former gym colleague Will James recalled, 'The last time I saw Percy on his rounds was on Aberavon Beach, and old Perce had suffered a stroke. He was shuffling along, shuffling along. "Hello, Will," he said. "Hello, Perce," I replied. "How are you feeling, Perce?" "Great! Fit as a fiddle! Fit as a fiddle! Physical culture makes you beautiful and keeps you young." '

It was typical and expected of the man to put on a brave face. In the latter period of his illness, when no general hospital bed was available, he was sent to Bridgend Psychiatric Hospital to convalesce - not the best possible place to recover from a stroke.

I visited Percy one night in January 1977 and entered the leafy grounds of the hospital where the shuffling, bowed, shadowy figures of inmates out for a winter stroll could be seen as they muttered their jumbled meanings, as if speaking in tongues to the cold starry night. Having found the ward I stood outside the darkened area where inmates on medication either sat motionless on the edges of their beds or collected in huddles and whispered before pacing a short distance to return and regroup. A female nurse approached from the semi-darkness of the ward and I was ushered to a waiting room. Here I awaited Percy's arrival, upon which fractured smiles and exaggerated gesticulations of patients seemed to mock his entry as 'The Great Mavello'. He was pushed before me seated uncomfortably in a shabby wheelchair with the right arm broken. Percy recognised me and, although unable to speak coherently after a second stroke had overtaken him, made it clear to me with almost pleading eyes that he was in an alien place and wanted to go home.

In a week or so, at his wife's insistence, Percy was brought home, arriving on an icy cold morning in what was described as a large van and not an ambulance, the roof white with frost, his cold body wrapped in a blanket unable to retain heat. Soon his condition worsened at the onset of pneumonia and he was transferred to Cimla Hospital, Neath. When the change of venue and his deteriorating health were made known to me I visited him again on the evening of Thursday, 27 January. Percy was asleep, the only patient in a small side ward with two seated silent young nurses in attendance, one each side of him like 'weepers' in reverence. In the heat of the ward, with the bed covers thrown down to his waist, he looked in the pink of condition against the sterile whiteness of the bed linen, only the strange transparency of skin and laboured heave of his chest, as if of a troubled sea, might have suggested otherwise. I almost expected that, with each caress of a nurse's hand upon his, 'The Great Mavello' would somehow awaken himself from his warrior sleep and arise to greet me as of old in a great sense of well-being.

He died the following morning of Friday, 28 January, at 8.30 a.m.; the death certificate recorded the causes of his demise as 'I (a) Broncho Pneumonia II Diabetes Mellitus', as certified by G. Kummar MB.

Percy Cardwell Hunt was interred at Holy Cross Churchyard, the resting place of his wife's parents and two of her younger brothers, on Tuesday, 1 February 1977 at 2.30 p.m. The officiating minister, Rev. Elfed Lloyd, JP, of Salem Chapel, Sandfields Road, a close friend of the deceased late in life, had expressed the wish to bury the H. & S. Leaguer whom he regarded as a prime

35. Percy aged 85 years
Outside his home at 6 Romney Road in the Autumn of 1976.
(Photo by the author)

example of a man given to the commendable pursuit of the finer qualities of physical development.

The day of the funeral was cold-canopied and sombre grey. The cluster of mature elm trees, bereft of summer foliage, which partly screened and crowned the elevation of the subdued Victorian Gothic Church with fine branch tracery, looked down upon the open grave among irregular rows of inclined headstones, ancient and modern. The singing of the burial hymn 'Abide with Me' by a small gathering of mourners floated faintly in the air, almost subdued by the discordant rush of nearby motorway traffic and the raucous din of rooks in the trees.

The athlete's passing brought to a close an era made even more focused and prematurely apparent with the gradual dismantling and disposal of his Health & Strength League gym and contents prior to his death. Against such a backdrop of dissolution, press tributes were comprehensive in local and county tabloids, as were recollective token appraisals by colleagues, pupils and family, but it was town 'rounds' acquaintance John Morgan who was moved enough to pen a eulogy for his own keeping.[6] An amateur artist of Parisian genre, given to literary flow when prompted by occasion, he believed himself to be perceptive of character and wrote:

> Percy Hunt was someone everybody in town seemed to have seen around forever. Physically he was small but he was a mini-bomb. His achievements were truly staggering but the colossal ego he was very much entitled to - was missing entirely from this quietly spoken, kindly, modest, very likeable man. I was always immensely impressed by him, a little man who exuded a truly and unmistakable quiet strength and force. He was not to earn the glories and rewards but I must be just one of a multitude who smiled to see him - stopped rushing to speak with him - and automatically straightened my back!

Triumphant in sentiment, the writing mirrors much of the myth and the legend of Percy Hunt, 'The Great Mavello'. It is a piece of penmanship he would no doubt have acclaimed as a curtain finale befitting his life and times.

THE END

Appendix 1

Percy Hunt's Awards

As a Health & Strength League athlete, the main awards achieved by Percy were the movement's 'Certificate of Merit', of which a portion of the feats were based upon the British Amateur Weight-Lifters' Association (BAWLA) 42 All-round strength lifts. These awards were the foundation of his maturity as a versatile athlete and stage performer. Although of less merit than BAWLA's lifting certificates, their overall excellence arose from award schemes designed to encourage membership from a variety of sports, as well as the original purpose of helping to improve the health, fitness and happiness of the Nation as a whole.

A retrospective study of such feats led immediately to 23 of the 'Certificate of Merit' awards, the earlier ones distinctly different in graphic design and age from the rest. Six in number and without date reference, the early certificates are believed to have been issued after the First World War, but before the mid-twenties, and have decorative border embellishments rich in Celtic design. Intricately interwoven in the design are legendary figures of St. George, Hercules, Wallace, Hygeia, Galahad and Chuchlin. The composition of the 17 later certificates is in part a return to the allegorical interpretations of the H. & S. League motto - 'Sacred thy body even as they Soul'. The athlete as usual stands before a new dawn while (in the design) holding at bay the fanged serpent of ignorance, not as yet quite slain. In so doing he also protects a comely, classically draped female figure of either Vestal Virgin or Muse-like origin, who, herself, proceeds to crush a smaller serpent with her dainty foot. Nearly all the certificate awards are dated from mid-twenties to the late thirties, and inscribed with Percy's LDO and medal distinctions - S/ and G/ -.

We find that both early and later certificates are in the main awarded for weight-lifting in BAWLA's 42 lifts category, with all-round disciplines included in separate awards. A number of the feats were also awarded medals and badges.

Early certificates as written are as follows:

8 stone class, lifted $88\frac{1}{2}$ lbs. in the
One Hand Snatch, this being a very high standard
of proficiency in weightlifting.
8 stone class, lifted 98 lbs. in the

36. Early Health & Strength Certificate

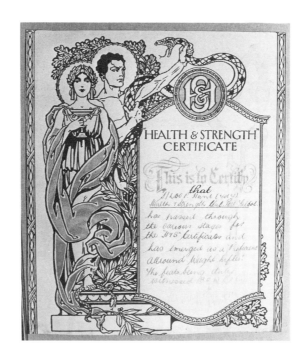

37. Later Certificate

Two Hands Snatch...

8 stone class, lifted 112 lbs. in the
One Hand Clean and Jerk...

8 stone class, lifted 112 lbs. in the
Two-Hands Military Press...

8 stone class, lifted 120 lbs. in the
One Hand Bent Press...

Qualified as an all-round Athlete by his
performance of Weightlifting, Trapeze,
Fancy and Trick Skipping, Balancing, Wrestling,
Boxing, Ball-punching and Club Swinging.

The later certificates as written are:

(8st.) Performed in Oct. 1925,
the feat of a Wrestler's Bridge
146 lbs. with a 10st. man on knees.

(8st.) Performed in Oct. 1925,
before several witnesses a
Two Hands Clean and Jerk
$155\frac{1}{2}$ lbs.

(8st.) Performed in January, 1926,
at the 'H. & S.' Club,
Aberavon a Rectangular Fix of
60 lbs.

(7st.12) Performed on 23rd Feb.,
1926 at Port Talbot
an Abdominal Raise of
$42\frac{1}{2}$ lbs.
(7st.12) Performed 23rd March,

1926 at Aberavon a Pull and Press
on Back with Bridge feat of
145 lbs.

(7st.13) Performed on April 28th,
1926 with a Chest Expander a
One Arm Press of
175 lbs.
and a Back Press of
175 lbs.

(7st.13) Performed on April 20th,
1926 at the above Gym a Two Hands
Clean and Push with a Barbell of
115 lbs.

(7st.12) Performed on May 18th,
1926 at Port Talbot Gym a Left
Hand Clean and Jerk of
90 lbs.

(8st.) Performed on June 15th,
1926 at the above Gym a
Right and Left Hand Snatch
80 lbs.

(7st.12) Performed in July 13th, 1926
at the above Gym a Two Hands Continental
Jerk with Dumbbells
122 lbs.

(7st.7) Performed on August 10th,
1926 at the above Gym
a Right Hand Clean and Bent Press of
112 lbs.

(7st.7) Performed on Sept. 7th, 1926,

a Two Hands Anyhow
with Dumbbells of
148 lbs.

Performed the feat of
Two Hands Dead Lift
$308\frac{1}{2}$ lbs.

(7st.7)... Passed through the
various stages for the
'H. & S.' Certificates and
has emerged as 'Proficient
All-round Weightlifter.'

Performed not only once
but at all P.C. Exhibitions
the Feat of Skipping,
Cross Hands and Double Skipping
100 times.

Has been successful in performing the twenty feats
detailed in the 'Health and Strength' Certificate of
Merit scheme for Strand Pulling. The feats have been
performed and duly witnessed on April 11th, 1938.

Qualified as an All-round Athlete by his
performance of Weightlifting, Trapeze,
Fancy & Trick Skipping, Balancing,
Wrestling, Boxing, Ball-punching and
Club Swinging. Performed in his Aberavon
Gym on Nov. 1938.

All feats were duly witnessed under BAWLA rules by principal H. & S.
Leaguers and by gym assistants Joe Manship and Will James; their own feats
were in return witnessed by Percy, and both assisted in assessment of pupils.
Successful feats were sent away to H. & S. and a certificate or certificates,

returned signed by a League official. It should be emphasised that G/LDO Percy Hunt was a disciplinarian and all feats would have been scrutinised with the expected integrity.

He received similar awards from H. & S.'s sister publication Health and Efficiency, with diplomas for 'All-Round Athletic Prowess' and 'Physical Development'.

He received a Maxalding 'Gold Medal' in the 1920's. It was one of the first of his medals to be sold in times of hardship.

With the popularity of physical culture, manufacturers of claimed health-assisting compounds were eager to link their product to the movement, the beverage 'Bovril' being a prime example.

On the 8 January 1931, upon the recommendation of a Bovril adviser, Percy Hunt received both their 'Diploma of Merit for outstanding "Body Control"'and a substantial solid silver medal. The large diploma boldly illustrates a typical classical reference to the athlete victorious, while embossed on the obverse side of the medal is Bovril's vigorous motif of a bull's head and on the reverse side is engraved the athlete's name. The medal is presented in a purple, velvet-lined, black case.

In recognition of Percy's renowned proficiency as an all-rounder and the successful operation of his gym, pupils at the time presented him with a commemorative rose bowl.

H. & S. - 'Britain's Best Developed Man in Great Britain over 40 years of Age', 1936.

American Strength and Health League. This is to Certify that Percy Hunt is a life member and honorary vice-president of the American Strength and Health League. George F. Jowett. Bob Hoffman. Feb. 17th., 1933.

American Continental Weightlifters Association. Percy Hunt is a life-member of this league and is entitled to enjoy all its privileges. President: Bob Hoffman. Alan Carse - International sec-treasurer. Jan.12th., 1937.
Certificate of Award. This certifies that Percy Hunt of the Henderson

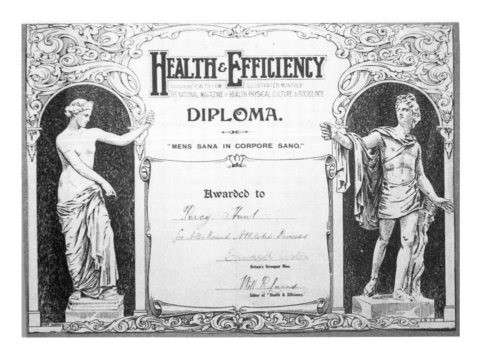

38

39

Y.M.C.A. has been awarded this certificate for participation in all athletic events and in recognition of his inspiration to athletes all over the world. Life membership. President: Boynton Merrill, Junior. General Secretary Bill Hicks. Henderson, K.Y. U.S.A. Feb.12th., 1962.

Correspondence with Matthew Brown, a leading member of the 'Mercury' WL Club, Henderson, Kentucky, also secured him life membership of the club.

He was without doubt proud of the American connection and recognition by a country he was never to visit. In his opinion, like many a prophet, he was without honour in his home-town and country. Percy made the most of this belief in verbal displays, fortified by his American Strength and Health 'Gold Badge'.

Appendix 2

Percy Hunt's
Mainstream Gym Athletes

The membership of the Aberavon St. Mary's Street gym was considerable, so I have limited the choice of pupils for mention to those who engaged in mainstream movements as athletes of substance or with potential, between 1920 and the 1950's.

Foremost athletes in the history of Percy's gym were assistant coaches Joe Manship and Will James. Employed in heavy industry, both came with natural ability and much energy at different beginnings to merge their efforts later in furthering the reputation of the gym as one of the leading schools of the Health & Strength League in Wales.

Joseph Manship

Nine years younger than Percy Hunt, Joe Manship joined the H. & S. League gym about 1920 upon the advice of a fellow weight-lifter, Thomas Saxton - an enthusiast who used his bedroom as a makeshift place of exercise - later becoming Percy's assistant coach. The partnership which followed proved a popular and agreeable combination, undertaking regular engagements in and around the industrial valleys of South Wales.

A weight-lifter by temperament with the capacity for exerting brute-like strength, Joe demonstrated such power gaining a 'Bovril' Silver Medal and Certificate award for the prodigious feat admirably entitled 'Tomb of Hercules'. It demanded that Joe Manship, at 8st. 8 lb. support a disc and block weight load of 1,138 lb. upon his raised frontal torso area, with arms and legs holding the position in a homage to the Greek Mythological hero of strength.

Around 1937 Joe also broke a number of Welsh weight-lifting records when Percy had taken a gym team to compete in the famed Llanelly YMCA. In the same competition pupil Ben Humphries took the 'Slow Curl' title.

Although Joe was to remain associated with Percy's gym it was decided that, with training demands of pupils unable to be met through lack of space, he should set up another H. & S. League gym to take the overflow. Having gained LDO status, Joe Manship opened up classes in weight-lifting, physical exercise and boxing in the hall of the old YMCA, situated near the General Railway Station, and later in the new YMCA, Talbot Road.

When Joe took over the training of the Port Talbot Harriers in the YMCA he called in Percy to assist him. His assistance provided the opportunity for the all-rounder to introduce weight-training to combat the need among runners for development from the hips down in disregard of upper body strength.

Joe Manship was to remain Percy's closest companion in the physical culture movement and, in his prime, before the cool, liquid amber of the 'hops' passed his lips in copious draughts, a powerful foil to the stage exploits of the 'Great Mavello'.

William John James

When Percy Hunt, upon Joe Manship's recommendation, invited Will James to join them both in 1929 - Percy was then 38 years of age, Joe 29, and Will 19 - it completed a triumvirate, a triple force, which by their influence and endeavours raised the Aberavon Health & Strength League gym to a focal point for everyone from the natural athlete to the 7st. weakling.

Following all-round tradition, Will James gained medals in rugby (he played for Aberavon RFC), soccer, cricket, cross-country running, weight-lifting, strand-pulling and physical development. He also achieved 20 special H. & S. certificates for weight-lifting and strand-pulling, with another certificate for a skipping performance. His physique excellence titles are: Runner-up 'Best Developed Man in Wales' 1938; won 'Mr. Port Talbot' 1948, and 'Senior Mr. Wales' 1951.

Unlike Joe Manship, Will James was only an occasional assistant in Percy's displays. The two used different methods in the novel bodily lifting of the versatile athlete by his hair. While Joe used the strength of his fingers and forearm to lift him a couple of feet off the ground, Will whirled Percy by holding the athlete's plaited hair between his teeth in a leather bit.

Will James was resolute in support of the League and can be viewed as one of the most dynamic of the early-to-mid-stage generation of physical culturists in the St. Mary's Street gym and arguably one of Wales's finest all-round athletes in the H. & S. mould of the day.

Isaac (Iki) Davies

Not long after Joe Manship came upon the scene, a young miner arrived in the gym from the village of Bryn. Quick to learn the various systems of exercise, he became an accomplished physical culturist in his own right, leaving Percy's gym to run a well-equipped place of exercise in the back garden of his parents' home at 6 Maesteg Road, Bryn. His early recollections of Percy Hunt were printed in the *Port Talbot Guardian* of 6 July 1973:

Percy Gave Us Strength

I can remember when I was a young lad going from our village of Bryn, riding my old push-bike to Aberavon, to Mr. Hunt's gym in about 1920. He had opened a gym in St. Mary's Street, not long before having come home from the 1914-18 war. He had several pupils training with him and I was very pleased when he took me as one of them. He was very kind and understanding and in a few months I felt a lot stronger and was riding the old bike a lot faster, and in due course a few of my friends came to Percy's.

In about 1926, we miners came out on strike and had a lot of spare time on our hands, and Percy came to the Miners' Hall and gave many a good physical culture show, which helped a great deal to keep the dark days sunny.

Ike Davies's contact with Percy and his pupils was to be sustained for some years in friendly rivalry when Ike's establishment became a favourite venue for weight-lifting matches between lifters from both gyms.

Apart from his involvement with his own gym, he also became secretary of the Physical Culture School, Ewenny Road, Maesteg, where the brother of Ike Dupplaw, the other half of the talented Maesteg all-round athletic duo, William James Dupplaw, served as Instructor.

In keeping with the athletic all-rounder, Ike Davies was a keen amateur flyweight boxer and in the early days when Welsh and later British and Commonwealth Heavyweight Boxing Champion Tommy Farr toured the valleys taking on all-comers - particularly those of a lighter weight and greater speed - for practice in preparation for professional contests, he sparred with Farr in the back room of the Full Moon Hotel, Cwmfelin, Maesteg.

Ike Davies was also a genuine strongman with a BAWLA certificate for a 'Squat Lift' of 350 lb., at 9st. 6 lb., accomplished in the early 1930's when he was about 22 years of age.

As an SG/LDO, Ike Davies was to faithfully adhere to the H. & S. League movement, sustaining and progressing its aims and beliefs in a quiet unassuming manner.

David Henry Davies

Among the early pupils after the First World War, David Henry Davies was to achieve considerable fame as an athlete in the conventionally-accepted Welsh National game of rugby union football. Five years younger than his cousin Percy Hunt, he was the elder son of Thomas Hunt's sister Mary (Annie) Davies, adding his mother's maiden name to become known in rugby circles as Dai Hunt Davies.

Invalided out of the First World War, with part of one of his heels shot away, the war injury left Dai Hunt Davies with ankle ligament damage and considerable calf muscle wastage. Using physicultopathic techniques his injuries were quickly and successfully treated by cousin Percy, the inevitable limp affecting movement being compensated for on the field of play by building up the inside heel area of the particular rugby boot. Assisted by the balancing effect of the adjusted footwear, Dai Hunt Davies was considered one of the fastest centre three-quarters on the burst to play for Aberavon RFC and other clubs in Wales. He also became a master of selling the 'dummy' pass, effectively accomplished by a slight jink movement, which Percy put down to the considerable strengthening of calf and ankle area of the damaged heel.

He played for Aberavon Harlequins RFC and graduated to the senior Aberavon side in the same season of 1919 to 1920. In the 1923-24 season he possibly won more than a single cap for Glamorgan County and made his International debut against England in what was to be his one and only game, the Welsh side losing the match in a bleak period when defeat was the norm against the home countries. In such a situation, as Percy was to say, 'If you did not click immediately, you never had a second chance.'

William (Bulldog) Garnon

In the late 1920's there came to the gym a strongly built young man who really fancied himself as a wrestler and would openly declare this fact to the predominantly all-round athletic fraternity training there. This emphatic announcement was to be no empty boast by Bill Garnon for he eventually held not only the Welsh professional heavyweight title for fifteen years but took the British crown in a 'blistering' 15 rounds against champion Atholl Oakley in 1934. He also fought twice without success, but with typical courage, for the world title against the renowned Jack Sherry.

Born in Fishguard, West Wales, Bill Garnon moved to Swansea in his teens and from there obtained manual employment at Dyffryn Engine Sheds, Port

Talbot. It was not long before he located Percy Hunt's gym and here he displayed an impressive lower back strength with a 'Dead Lift' of 500 lb. Eager to enter the professional wrestling arena, he was encouraged by everyone in the gym to take up the challenge in an advertisement by British heavyweight wrestling champion Atholl Oakley, requesting the services of a young wrestler. This unanimous movement seems to have stemmed from the need to rid themselves of this immensely strong young man, for not only did his strength threaten the stability of the wooden gym floor but also inflicted on everyone the ordeal of inactivity, which broke the necessary continuity of exercise, during the wait for him to finish the 'Dead lift', which used up all the usable poundage.

Certainly there were no recorded feelings of camaraderie by the rest of the school of athletes towards Bill Garnon, for he rapidly outgrew, as did others along the way, the restricted capabilities of a small gym. Such a situation often arose with strongmen and then for everyone else's sake they would move on.

On occasion Bill Garnon sent a letter to the gym relating briefly his progress, and correspondence held by Joe Manship records that in 1930 he had emigrated to America. There he wrestled against top adversaries Stanislaus Zbysko and the massive 6'6" George Godfrey. Another letter records he was also in demand as a film extra in a number of swashbuckling productions, 'Jamaica Inn' being the best of them.

As an itinerant wrestler Bill Garnon worked his way from Mexico through the USA, and in the lumbercamps of Canada took on all-comers under the guise of 'The Masked Marvel' - a possible link with Percy's stage name - his breadth of travel including a stay on the Continent.

At 5'8" in height and weighing 16st. in his prime and 18st. in later years, 'Bulldog' Bill Garnon was celebrated as a tenacious wrestler, hence his intimidating title.

Donald Dennis

From among the band of young athletes an ambitious lifter, and later body-builder, Donald Dennis, came to the fore after his return home from service at the close of the Second World War. Resuming training with friend Neville Williams, who later became Vice-chairman of the WNPCA, his early admiration for Percy's all-round athleticism was to be submerged under the influence of the superior body-building physiques of the American servicemen he encountered and the intensity and volume of work required in specialisation.

Although Donald was claimed to have achieved a number of unofficial Welsh

AWLA and BAWLA records, he never reached his full potential as a weight-lifter. He was regarded by colleagues as a moderate bantamweight lifter, but the sudden death of his father was to restrict his development and he never recovered from the loss.

Whether because of his unfulfilled ambition as a lifting athlete or not, he acquired copious knowledge of weight-lifting and body-building, gaining qualifications as a BAWLA Advanced Instructor; Certified Divisional and Fully Certified Referee; International Judge IFH; and membership of SMAE (Swedish Massage and Electrotherapy) Institute. His appointments were as an International WL Referee IFH; Senior Instructor FWAWL; National Coach WAWLA; Senior Referee and National Coach SAWL and Lecturer in PRT, becoming for a time Hon. Sec. of the Welsh AWLA.

His knowledge of the iron game in all its variations, and in particular the wider physical culture scene, was expressed with great self-confidence whether as a referee, instructor, noted compere at Welsh displays or a prolific writer in body-building magazines which culminated in the publication of his book *Progressive Resistance Training*.

Although Donald Dennis remained in Percy's view the most troublesome of pupils, Donald claimed that he turned away from the extremes of using drugs and began to re-evaluate and accept many of the clean-cut, unadulterated basic principles of training applied and championed by the versatile athlete.

Sidney Davies
Official Welsh record holder for pressing 170 lb. at 10st., which stood unbroken for some years.

Roy 'Bingo' Williams
Welsh 220 yd. champion in 1938 and 'Mr. Wales' physique excellence finalist in 1948. Essentially an all-round athlete.

Douglas Evans
One of the first genuine-looking body-builders when I first trained in the gym. A 'Mr. Wales' finalist 1948, 1949 and 1950.

Jack O'Neil
Although not regular as a member of the TBA or as a pupil in the gym, heavyweight Jack O'Neil proved to be a strong man of prodigious lower back

strength. It was found that he could 'Dead Lift' in excess of 600 lb., which possibly then, in the mid-to-late 1940's, was a British, if not a world, record, though an unofficial one without verification by qualified referees.

His use of disc poundage did not enamour him to colleagues or to Percy, whose nervous reaction of unusual facial twitches and limb movements accompanied the hope that the gym structure would once more survive another pupil's herculean prowess.

A somewhat isolated, cultured and reluctant pianist, with a most curious effeminate voice, whose strength Percy's gym was not designed to accommodate, Jack had a religious period when he avidly read the Bible. Seeking solace through solitary reading and simple worship, he would on fine summer days up-end a large rowing boat over his shoulders, like a West Walian 'coracle' fisherman, and with oars and Bible tucked under one arm carry his load to Aberavon Docks; there, it is said, Jack O'Neil would happily row around areas of the bay, sometimes for several days and nights, singing hymns and reading aloud extracts from the Bible to the ebb and flow of the tide, the sun, the moon and stars in high heaven.

James Hegarty

Although Jim Hegarty as a specialist body-builder trained with the TBA in Percy's gym, this was as a result of convenience and the inevitable attraction of the group's uncompromising approach to new techniques and principles in weight-lifting and body-building.

During the period from the late 1940's to 1950 Jim Hegarty achieved the H. & S. League 'Star Gallery' silver medal, November, 1949; 'Body-builder of the Month', silver medal, 1950; Book award for poseur - September and November, 1950; 'Mr. Port Talbot' and 'Mr. Glamorgan' titles, September and November, 1950, for which he received silver medals from both H. & S. and NABBA; the association's 'Most Highly Awarded Member of 1950' and in April the League World Wide competition 'Glory Plaque'.

The winning of 'Mr. Glamorgan', on Monday, 27 November 1950, at the Central Boys' Cub, Cardiff, with Peter Heale (former Mr. Glam. 1949) second, and Londoner Henry Downs, who went on to win the 'Mr. Wales' 1951 contest and 'Mr. Britain' 1956, third, prompted English bodybuilder Don Dorans to offer Jim Hegarty a free Don Doran's training system, which he accepted.

Don Doran, who had reached 'Mr. Universe' Class 4 standard in 1950, shrewdly advertised Jim Hegarty as another example of his methods, which up to that time was not strictly true, and Percy was said to be furious with Doran's claim.

When Jim Hegarty entered the 'Mr. Wales' contest in 1951, Percy believed that over-development of the lower limbs, due to the influence of Doran's claim for heavy poundage in exercise, compounded by his pupil's belief in the need to build up his legs with 'Squat' thrusts at the expense of upper body development, cost him at least a placing.

In a series of pen-portraits of H. & S. and NABBA athletes in the local tabloid, entitled 'Health is their Hobby', written by Donald Dennis, Jim Hegarty elevated body-building as being superior to '...ordinary Physical Training because Bodybuilding improves your physique whereas Physical Training just keeps you fit.'

A reader in a letter to the editor of the *Guardian*, 11 May, quickly took offence at Hegarty's claim, denouncing body-building in a damning, lengthy critique involving Plato's concept of physical education, which was essentially in part gymnastic. He went on to conclude that 'The very word 'bodybuilding' smells of exhibitionism' and that 'In Mr. Hegarty's case, the basic truths are being flouted and debased. The body is being developed at the expense of the soul - Yours etc. - "Bartel"'.

The very word 'soul' was like a barb to the body-builder and he responded in an article in which he suggested that his character and his soul are well catered for as he is '...a regular churchgoer, and a God-fearing person.' At Percy's prompting, his pupil added that for him body-building was not just an end in itself, but an activity which improved his strength and therefore his performance in a number of sports he participated in, namely rugby, cycling and athletics.

Whether the criticism affected Jim Hegarty's confidence is unknown for he was never to win the Welsh physique title, having thrice reached the finals in 1949, 1950 and 1951. He remains, however, the most successful of specialist body-builders in terms of awards in Percy's gym.

Alan Rees

Always searching for the potential prodigy from among his class of young schoolboys, Percy believed he had discovered a genuine talent in Alan Rees. There were many young pupils who showed promise, but he had the greatest all-round ability to be fashioned in Percy's own image.

Small in build, as was the structure of the terraced cottage in Richard Street where Alan Rees was born and brought up, the young athlete-to-be arrived at the gym as what he recollected as the original 7 stone weakling. It was not coincidental that promising schoolboys tended to be physically small for their age, appearing almost like clones of 'The Great Mavello'.

Nurtured in the rudiments of exercise with weights, Alan Rees was given every opportunity, during the mid-to-late 1940's and early 1950's, to cultivate the physical foundation necessary for any kind of athletic versatility. Assisting Percy in engagements also fostered a stage presence providing the pupil with early confidence and in a Guardian article describing two engagements he proudly presented Alan Rees '... as one who is following in his footsteps and has the makings of a champion.'

In the post-war awakening of sporting opportunity and athleticism, Alan Rees followed his own sporting inclinations, that were refined in County Grammar School days, emerging with talents generally appropriate to both rugby and cricket. The winning of a Welsh Secondary Schoolboy rugby cap became a preliminary to things to come. Alan Rees thus became skilled at senior level in both disciplines fostered at school to not only play rugby as an outside-half for Aberavon, Maesteg and ultimately Wales, turning later to rugby league when he joined Leeds in 1962, but as a professional cricket player with Glamorgan County. He was also a fine squash player of International standard.

Proud of his former pupil's success as a sportsman, there still remained with Percy the belief that his prodigy would have achieved even greater success had he continued building his physique and increasing fitness levels in the St. Mary's Street gym, the fountain-head of Health & Strength League ideals in Port Talbot.

Mike Brown
Competed for Wales in weight-lifting on 21 occasions and in his prime was chosen for the Commonwealth Games of 1974 in New Zealand and of 1978 in Canada, coming 5th and 4th respectively.

Roger Michaelson
Played rugby as a wing forward for Cambridge University, Aberavon, London Welsh and Wales.

Bobby Wanbon
Played rugby for the Green Stars, Aberavon and Wales also as a wing forward, before turning to rugby league playing for St. Helens and Warrington.

Ella Jones
Of the preponderance of males in Percy's place of exercise, in what was

167

regarded as a man's domain, only a few members of the opposite sex summoned up enough courage to flout prejudice locally against such a practice and use his gym; one such pupil was 16 year old Ella Jones, daughter of Abel Jones, a leading draper of the town. An accomplished gymnast and member of the formidable Swansea YMCA gymnastic team, the availability of Percy's H. & S. gym establishment proved sufficient to assist her development in the 1920's by providing light weights in conjunction with limited gymnastic facilities.

Controversy, prejudice and criticism inevitably followed a number of pupils of potential and ambition, whatever their gender, and there were always those who arrived and departed the gym like 'ships that pass in the night', journeying on to harbours and destinations of their own choosing.

Appendix 3

Gym Reflections

The prominence of the gym as I recall became evident in moments of easy respite between exercises when concentration gave way to a state where muscle relaxation seemed to engineer contemplation; then the gymnasium's proportion, colour, content and sense of atmosphere were readily absorbed. It was rectangular and comfortably small with a lingering odour of sweat and embrocation, an obtrusive stimulant to activity. Colours and textures were on the whole dominated by the two white-washed stone walls which acted as a source of reflected light, the remaining sides of timber frame being insulated with packaging cardboard. For the purpose of ventilation, two narrow, high-sighted windows were made along the timbered and packaging length. Both of these sides were faced with galvanised corrugated sheeting as indeed was the sky-lighted, saddle-back roof. Arrangements of exercising equipment filled various spaces, with barbells and dumb-bells (disc and globe weighted), kettle and block weights, pulley apparatus, parallel rings, Indian clubs, chest expanders and weighted shoes. Some equipment hung from rafters and a King Post beam or was hooked on fastenings screwed into a black-painted, wooden mantelpiece; other items leaned against the white-washed walls, in alcoves, in corners, on wooden shelves or were placed horizontal upon off-cuts of faded carpets of Persian design, which covered areas of creaking, silvered floorboards. With many devilish contrivances, the awaiting apparatus menaced and challenged all newcomers with the thought of muscular torments to come.

The fixation with developing herculean 'biceps', 'triceps', 'pectorals', 'deltoids', 'trapezius', 'latissimus dorsi', and many more muscles in repose needing dynamic tension, required an industrious input of energy, especially if a pupil intended to reach the ideal stage of physical development (which I for one never attained), said by Percy to involve equal circumferential dimensions of neck, biceps and calves.

Physical proportion and muscle size were thus often sought by ambitious pupils like the 'Holy Grail' and, as a relief from such crusading pursuits, Percy's stout, canvas kit-bag from the First World War, stuffed with a grand selection of clothing ranging from gentleman's 'pin-strip' trousers to ladies' 'corsets', proved an ideal punching bag. The 'old bag', as it was affectionately called - the usage of which immediately lent itself among pupils as a term for a woman of generous sexual favours well past her prime - was great for letting off steam in cardio-vascular invigoration, receiving a dreadful hammering over the years. One pupil commented once, well out of Percy's earshot, that the kit-bag had probably seen more action in the gym than it ever experienced throughout the 1914-18 War.

Whenever the bag was punched, and I hit the 'old bag' often enough, it sometimes had the annoying habit of retaliating to incorrect punching. It would either swing and spring suddenly towards you because of its multiple-stringed elastic hanging device or twist and spurt alarmingly at you at the same time. Such confusion usually inspired the novice with so great a pugilistic passion that the onslaught of misdirected blows upon the illusive 'old bag' showered everyone with autumnal-tinted rust particles from the shaken tin roof above.

Even Cambridge undergraduate-to-be Roger Michaelson, brought to the gym in vacation-time by his uncle and mature pupil Vince Thomas to train and eventually to win his boxing colours at Clifton College, Bristol, found a little difficulty in keeping rhythm, although another pupil, Bobby Wanbon, delighted in the unpredictability of the bag, as it swayed at all angles.

When pupils applied their pugilistic energy with wayward technique or in too exuberant a manner, Percy would give his display - a cultivated brand of stylish but lethal reserve. I suspect that the elastic attachments to the kit-bag were devised not so much out of the convenience of using that material for the job, but to test pupils' temperament and hopefully instil discipline.

The 'old bag' had a permanent position when in use, otherwise it was placed in a corner near the gym entrance, suspended from a hook tied to the King Post beam of the roof. The beam also supported two pulley exercises, both similar to the one bolted to a strengthened rafter just to the side of an old bureau for development of deltoid, trapezius and latissimus dorsi, and iron rings for gymnastic work. Percy always stressed the use of basic ring work as essential for muscle toning, although there was nothing fundamental in the 'dislocation' of the shoulders or the heroic magnificence and dramatic torture of the 'crucifix'.

Apart from Percy's execution of the 'crucifix, achieved either from a lowering above or a more concerted lift below the rings to the position, I have only ever seen one pupil, Cliff Webley, easily complete the more difficult elevation. The ease of performance resulted because, while his upper body development was wrought in the herculean mould, his legs had been laid waste through poliomyelitis, so there was little weight to hold in the lower limbs.

Besides pulley and parallel rings, with an iron bar inserted in the ring ropes that were double-folded for pull-ups, the King Post beam also supported, when two meat hooks were attached to the ring ropes, rather heavy loads whenever a promising pupil did the 'Squat'. One pupil of natural brute strength found quiet satisfaction in the lift. Squats by this youth were serialised episodes of dramatic expectancy as eventually nearly 400 lb. was put on the bar. The mathematical complexities of load and stress for Percy were always sublimely replaced by faith, hope and a few restraining ties tacked onto the problem. It was practical and had been on the whole effective in the past with men of great strength, but now the structure was older. With the considerable load each creaking, wooden support and slow grinding of the rusting tin roof caused Percy to look upwards furtively in nervous expectation. The ultimate question posed was not so much whether the athlete would succeed in lifting the weight but whether the old gym roof would collapse about our ears before he lifted it off the hooks onto his hunched shoulders. The crisis on hand was resolved when Percy hit a high note of alarm and uttered 'Too heavy!', motioning the offending pupil to drastically reduce the poundage, and, in the same week, sending him a formal letter informing the athlete that his presence was no longer required in the gym. It was this banishment from the St. Mary's Street gym which indirectly encouraged Mike Brown to succeed as a Welsh International Heavyweight and Super-heavyweight weight-lifter and 'Power' lifter.

Less stressful for Percy and the gym roof was the popular use among pupils of an 'In-Klein' style bench mainly for Abdominal raise and Bench press. Popular too were the wooden mantelpiece support of spring and pulley chest and triceps developer, 'kettle' weights, and wrist and forearm exerciser, situated on what was incorrectly referred to by some pupils as the 'East end' of the building, opposite the entrance. Here, in the near alcoved corner, were assembled the monopoly of miscellaneous exercises and poundage, notably the raised parallel wooden bar structure for shoulder press-ups or dips, two 56lb. block weights, the main disc loading barbell with the standard weight of 70 lb., and two stage strongman globe barbells, respectively weighing 60 lb and 90 lb.

While the majority of pupils lionised mighty explosions of breath and looseness of style, with a cheating heave to assist past the 'sticking point' in a lift, a number of us also followed aspects of what Percy believed to be essential to sound training. He would advise principles of a gentle warm-up of free-limb movements before using weight in a steady application over a full range of joint movement, with the need to work up to poundage in his favoured strict 'Military' technique, which limited the load when confronted by the 'sticking point'. The term became known among some pupils as the 'adhesive moment'.

Much of Percy's approach to training was based on what he termed 'Train, not strain' and had its primary function in the basic exercise of slowly breathing in and breathing out adopted in lifting the lighter weights. This practice he believed promoted health and strength in equal portions. It had roots in remedial work.

All exercises involved usually between five to ten 'reps' (repetitions), in 'sets' from three to six or more. Training methods were based upon manuals, ancient and modern, combined in all-round variations suitable to pupils' appetites and preferences, with little attention being given to the demanding and outmoded 'Military' style. Included in schedule systems of exercise were gymnastic ring work, Indian Club Swinging, Abdominal Raise, Two-Arm Curls with Barbell, 'Zottman' Curls (dumb-bells), Two-Hands Press, Two-Hands Clean and Jerk, Bench Press, Squat, Deep Knee Bend, 'Hack' Lift and Dead Lift, with a series of stamina-building exercises - Punching the 'Old Bag', use of Footweights, Skipping, and Running on the Spot.

With body-building taking the plaudits as the in-thing to follow, the word was for Multi-Sets, Muscle Priority, Split Work-Outs, Forced Reps, and Flushing, a few pupils specialising in growth of specific muscles as a means of acquiring distinct embellishments at the expense of the hoped-for symmetry of all-round development. Percy, not surprisingly, held no regard for such practices and often criticised them for their physical imbalance. The distinctive muscularity they produced involved either bulbous biceps and deflated pectorals, hulking deltoids or ridiculously starved calves and thighs, shrivelled biceps or knobbly trapezius, or vice versa. These contrasts in muscle size and emphasis were comparative, for even the seemingly undeveloped areas of their physiques had above average dimensions.

Pupil Bryn Bullpit was to display similar disproportionate deltoid and trapezius muscles, achieved by grasping a hanging bar from the King Post beam and with arms wide apart half pulling himself slowly upwards repeatedly, in front and behind the bar, to finally hang motionless on it for three to five minutes. For some time afterwards, with disc weights attached to his waist, his shoulders appeared broader and arms longer than before. As a result of continuing the exercise a degree of permanent shoulder width that was much treasured by the athlete became apparent.

Once when Bryn hung on the bar passively with eyes closed, his upper body glistening in sweat, a nearby gathering of fellow pupils was looking up at him from a restive crouch of exhaustion while others stood and it seemed to evoke a quite dramatic tableau in the Rembrandtesque feel for light and dark, effected by the single light source above and depth of shadow behind. It was not difficult to transpose and liken the image to aspects of the Dutch master's religious compositions, for when the pupil opened his eyes in a somewhat troubled far-away look the 'Ascension of Christ' emerged as a possible example. Such aesthetic indulgence was to be abruptly interrupted and transposed from the sublime to the absurd when Percy, impatient of pupil inactivity, gave a swift machine-gun rendition of the 'Italian Salad'. Bathos thankfully rarely featured in the general mood of sustained vigour in the gym although, from time-to-time, as in the Bryn Bullpit episode, it was a defuser of exalted visions.

Pinned to the white-washed longer wall, photographic icons of illustrious physical culturists, of more earthly intention, gave a fine historical continuity and perspective of different periods and purpose. Gazing at us with an air of muscular nonchalance were Macfadden, Sandow, Maxick and Monte Saldo, of the old school; John Grimek, Steve Reeves and Reg Park, of the new. Framed and placed in a position of honour amongst the collection of pin-ups were two celebratory composite images of Percy. On the opposite wall were two large framed and glazed sepia-stained 'Health & Efficiency' certificates, rather impressive in their pseudo classical design, awarded to Percy for 'All-Round Prowess' and 'Physical Development'. To make a point and emphasise current body-building practices for aspiring pupils, a life-size, fold-out magazine pin-up of the upper physique of Reg Park was brought by a pupil and fastened to the so-called 'West wall' of the gym, as a source of admiration and inspiration. Training schedules mingled with shop poster adverts displaying nourishing products such as 'Marmite' and 'Bovril', with a 'Five Boys Chocolate' illustration being given space possibly for its novelty aspect.

Important to all pupils were two old battered mirrors whose tarnished silvered areas reflected as faithfully as possible posing techniques and posture. If there was any sign of reflected imbalance, Percy would suggest stretching and weight-training exercises suitable to rectify the asymmetry. Inevitably, reflections of pupils at exercise before mirrors brought varied reactions, some undoubtedly nurturing narcissistic and machismo inclinations while others, with an acute sense of the ridiculous, having seen their grimaces, lost concentration to comedy.

The largest mirror hung horizontal on top of the mantelpiece, the smaller being partially inclined in an alcove flanked on either side by solid iron dumb-bells. Nearby stood a series of fixed wooden shelves whereon were placed a number of smaller weights, including a pair of Sandow spring grip dumb-bells. Among these weights, mainly used by Percy's class of junior schoolboys, stood footweights, referred to by Percy as his 'magic shoes', for improving fleetness-of-foot, which they did with surprising results even for the slow-moving pupil. Holding up the footweights dramatically like a trophy one winter evening when the wind in the East rattled the gym with its force, he declared that many a sprinter and marathon runner, rugby and soccer player, swimmer and boxer, triumphed in their sport with regular use of his magic shoes. When training sessions ended with their general use I, for one, felt compelled to race home to number 6 Sandfields Road, with what seemed to me effortless speed, as I chased, caught up, and chased again, my shadow in the ghost light of street lamps.

A run at the close of training sessions had long been a tradition for pupils of earlier years and although my homeward journey was a mere sigh compared to past pupils' lungfulls of distant miles from the gym to Briton Ferry and back again, I would on summer Sunday mornings follow Percy's footsteps and take mountain exercise, without any attempt to strengthen my vocal chords by shouting the top notes. While most of my fellow pupils would shy away from arduous runs of any kind, fearful of reducing prized upper body muscle size, I, without much in the way of herculean muscle to lose, had no such qualms. I would run up the central pathway of Mynydd Dinas, the serrated pattern of bracken but a blur in my race to the silent summit. Although reaching the mountain top always seemed in the triumphant mould of the H. & S. League athlete/warrior victorious before a new dawn of enlightenment, the exertion raised my heart beat and pumped my lungs to the limits of their endurance and the fluid filling my eyes distorted my view of the panorama spreading below me and outward to the sea.

Upon reflection, these energetic, perhaps masochistic, Sunday ascents of Mynydd Dinas were a revelation of the youthful spirit - the uninitiated might possibly rephrase it another way. From this height a finger or thumb could blot out the industrial scarring of the townscape with ease - a hand and the whole town vanished before my eyes. Although Percy had no time or inclination for this kind of playful town erasure, he would no doubt have recommended less polluted air to breathe for everyone, the culture of the physique in harmonious union with the mind being pre-eminent to him and apparent in his instruction to us all in the gym.

Exercise in the gym was understandably more invigorating in the frosty months of winter, summer on the whole being unbearably hot and stifling even with the door, skylight, and two cardboard-insulated narrow windows open. On winter evenings in the chilling air clouds of vapour swirled and eddied from the heat and movement of oxygenated, blood-gorged muscles, jets of steam spurted and dragon-hissed from flared nostrils and clenched teeth, and great metallic discordances of clashing iron and steel reverberated through training sessions.

Winter evenings of steam-hissing and metallic clashings appeared to encourage some pupils to increase further physical effort to enhance the already multitudinous ghostly vapours for the sake of visual effect. Such animation might not have come about entirely through aesthetic indulgence alone, frosty nights demanding complete exertion on the task or suffering the consequences of the infernal cold. Percy was a Spartan at heart and made sure the heating in the gym was never enough for pupils to rest too long. Indeed his Spartanism in winter frosts, however vigorously applied, was also influenced by wanting to reduce the costs of paraffin consumption for his almost unnoticeable little burner.

Toilet facilities were austere too with a bath of tepid water and cold shower provided in the kitchen in winter for cleansing the evening's sweat away, although a dilapidated self-made, leatherette, Turkish bath could be used at extra cost to pupils. Entrance to the kitchen was by way of a small door between mantelpiece and Percy's old bureau, the place even colder than the gym, and he accordingly advised us all to rub ourselves down vigorously with a rough towel before using a well-worn horse brush to quickly restore circulation. This was excellent advice under freezing circumstances, our bodies becoming bright red and tingling with great heat after application of towel and horse brush.

Compared with the stimulating shock of cold shower in winter, the location of the outside water-closet for pupils who required the facility was the scene of frequent episodes of comedy for those who did not. The WC was situated near the back garden door and, when Percy switched off the external light to save electricity, a torch was provided for finding one's way. There were, however, some adventurous pupils who refused the light, content to seek out their destination by the tactile sense of outstretched fingers and the not too difficult action of detecting the pungent odour of disinfectant. Often on such a venture one would hear the startled, choked shouts, and then the quick return, of men of strength but not courage, upon furry contact with the black, sharp-clawed, snarling, resident tom-cat. It was after all one of his haunts, with easy access beneath a gap at the bottom of the door, and for pupils without light the uncertainty of his residency added a curious edge to the release of bladder fluids.

Although the potential trauma of water-closet episodes produced comic relief from the toil and sweat of gym work, we were all at times the objects of a little mirth at our expense and none more so than Percy himself. For instance, his comment after taking part in a WNPCA display that he had again 'brought the house down', so good was his performance, effected quick response from a pupil that there simply cannot be many houses left in Wales. As folk-lore handed down from pupil to pupil would have it, whenever Percy arrived back from a long walk for the evening's session in the gym, he had like some intrepid explorer made a unique discovery - the sight and placement of a new muscle!

As a Maxalding Gold Medallist his control of major muscles, let alone ones found on long walks, was excellent. He was still able to display not only those highly prized ripples of muscle known as 'wash-board' abdominals, but central and single-sided isolations The central isolation was often demonstrated by Percy before pupils, its potentially dramatic effect being enhanced by standing beneath the harsh strong rays of the electric light. With legs slightly wide apart the control began by first retracting the abdominal muscles completely after exhalation to form a deep shadowy cavity beneath the rib cage. In this position he leaned forward, placed gentle pressure with hands on the front of the thighs and, by adjusting pressure, projected the rectus abdominus as either a rope of muscle in isolation or as a vertical roll of swell and ripple. With the abdominal isolations he formed with a flourish the striking resemblance of the bull-dog features of Winston Leonard Spencer Churchill.

This formation of the politician's face was practised with regularity before a mirror to keep perfect that popular image of patriotism, courage and defiance over adversity. We, his pupils at the time, always assured Percy - as others probably did - even if some of us seemed somewhat short-sighted at first, that the abdominal muscle formation did reveal a genuine likeness of the politician's face. This agreement nevertheless did not prevent pupils from asking him to tighten a muscle here or slacken one there when there was no good reason to do so other than through a little mischievous playfulness on our part. In the permissive and satirical 1960's we referred to Percy's faithfully muscled 'Churchillian' image, rather crudely perhaps, as 'flashing'.

Displays of 'Churchillian' abdominals and accompanying isolations became a cue for some pupils to bring up almost nonchalantly, aware of the all-round athlete's dislike for the heavily muscled, drugged-up-to-the-eyeballs body-builder and weight-lifter, the use of anabolic steroids. Seizing the bate - for that was the impression he gave at first - he would interrupt and exclaim, moderated with a line of humour and comic running action as if he knew what pupils were about, 'Look here, I do not believe in muscle-building drugs; they only make muscle monsters. A healthy mind and body with correct diet, garlic pills and weight-training are best. Look at me, I'm too fast to catch a cold!'

A natural performer, if Percy detected any lethargy among pupils in training he would stir things up with either a vocal burst of the 'Italian Salad' or 'On with the Motley' or put on a pair of boxing gloves and demonstrate his speed of hand and footwork. All three wake-up calls would work, but the most amusing and palatable was when he decided to prance and side-step up to a pupil to look him straight in the eye and smile, before suddenly swinging his gloved hand from behind his back to hit the athlete lightly in the solar plexus. The 'In-Klein' bench sometimes became a hurdle for hopping over to continue the movement in a flurry of punches in space, before Percy ended with a graceful bow and a wink.

Whatever method was used for restoring vigour in lethargic pupils, he would more often than not take from the gym bureau a battered album, which was a reference bible to pupils, so rich with his H. & S. certificates and letters from, and photographs of, famous American athletes. Swiftly from its pages a sixpenny paperback book entitled *Personality* was held aloft with a triumphant declaration - 'This is the reason why I am such a happy person!'

Apart from moments of playfulness, Percy's so-called happy nature kept a low profile in the gym, or so it seemed to me, to allow not only reflective recollections of past achievements to spring forth, but thoughtful excursions into the remedial side of his skills. A notable classic case history was his cure of the son of a local boot-maker and repairer unable to walk through serious spine and leg injury. For several months in three, half-hour, weekly sessions, Percy placed the boy alternately on his front and back upon a table, where he received physicultopathic treatment. When strong limb movement was achieved he used leather straps, fixed at convenient intervals and height, around the walls of the gym for the boy to grasp as he struggled at first from one strap to another. Repeated treatment with light weight exercise finally restored complete mobility. Enclosed among the memorabilia in the old bureau album, Percy brought out a sepia-stained letter from the grateful father, Grantley Golding, thanking him for helping his son walk again. Written on the craftsman's personal note paper, bordered with illustrations and captions advertising 'Paletine' make of sole he sold, he closed the note with a sure willingness to recommend to others in need Percy's remedial skills.

Once when in need of his massage, lubricated with lavish applications of his sovereign remedy for aches and pains of muscles and joints, 'Elliman's Universal Athletic Rub' (composed of turpentine, eggs and vinegar), I mentioned as he relaxed taut muscles that somehow I failed to see one of his public performances. Clearly taken aback by my revelation he promptly gave, before the arrival of further pupils, an abridged version of his stage act. His mini-display not only included the initial stripping of his silky, tatty, crimson dressing gown to reveal his oil-glistening upper body, but his pre-show pep-talk, which, at first, cloaked the comic overtones of his opening sentence:

'The first think I do in the morning is wake up! I then jump into a bath of cold water and finish with a cold shower and sponge down. I then do the cat-stretch five times.' Having said this he would again humorously recount to the accompanying demonstration the kinetic and therapeutic value of his favourite early morning feline exercise.

'You look up to heaven, and then look back down again to see if your trousers are still up,' he would announce throatily high when gazing roofwards, and with a decidedly deeper resonance when contemplating the floorboards and his plimsolls. The demonstration over his daily routine continued with an advertising plug for the nutritious food products he consumed:

'For breakfast I have a cup of Bovril and two slices of Hovis bread with Marmite and without butter, followed by opening my eyes in a bowl of cold water and finishing with a brisk rub down with a pair of horse brushes. I then not only clean my teeth (dentures when I knew Percy) with salt - using a chicken bone as a tooth-pick - but also my tongue. For dinner I have a little fish or meat with vegetables. A light meal for tea. In the gym until 8.30 p.m. I will now prove to you I am not muscle-bound by my performance.'

Beginning with a pose shown to good effect beneath the gym light, he turned to me with a grin and asked what he reputedly always enquired of audiences in later life - 'How old do you think I am?' I did not answer immediately but mulled over the usual droll comment said to arise from audiences that he was either two years old or a hundred, before playing the diplomatic game by replying that he must surely be in his 40th year. In his 70th year he proceeded to perform items of hand-balancing, weight-lifting and muscle control, with a passing comment as he wobbled biceps, 'You have got to eat plenty of jelly to do this,' followed by an ingenious light display before vocally ending with snatches from 'Somewhere a Voice is Calling' and 'Mother', the tonal quality firm and diction sure and clear.

Although Percy's act was incomplete the performance which for me brought out the essence of his showmanship in theatrical terms was without doubt the novelty strobe light effect.

So it was that on two lengths of rope were respectively fixed one small dental mirror, two large mirrors, a bicycle rear red light containing batteries, and a chrome-plated globe weighting each rope end. With the bicycle lights turned on and the gym light switched off, Percy held the rope lengths by hollowed, wooden domed handles, manipulating the light and reflection in fanciful, magical orbits in the close darkness. Trance-like in concentration he had gazed beyond me, so it seemed, with youthful intent through tracered red light outside the gym into the night. In rhythmic flow and with the sense of the miraculous in health and strength about him, he was in my imagination summoning acclaim from some cosmic audience already conversant with his athletic deeds, light years away, deep in the amphitheatres of space.

40. 'I challenge you to take on my 21 feats!'

Notes

Chapter 1

1. (a) One of the bells inscribed 'Borough of Aberavon', dated 1871, was used for official occasions while the undated bell was in general use.
   (b) A practice which originally gave its name to the term 'dumb bell'.

2. 'Maxalding means mind over muscle.' The 'Maxalding' philosophy of beginning with fitness of internal organs via abdominal control, followed by dynamic breathing and full spinal mobilisation for Nerve Strength and Height increase, Percy claimed extended his height by at least half an inch. Similar claims to height increase were made by other Maxalding pupils, just as a number of Percy's pupils claimed height improvement. No weights were needed in Maxalding combinations of isometric exercise and muscle control, but Percy agreed with the originator of the technique that each muscle could not be fully developed without mechanical help.

3. 'League' To launch the movement, a search for an appropriate badge was advertised with five pounds for the best design, won by Gloucestershire-born Fred Teckell, who also supplied the League motto. Both Percy and Fred Teckell (the first appointed H. & S. physical culture expert) were to meet cordially at League rallies and displays.

4. *H. & S.* Publications worked from a number of London premises, notably at Fetter Lane, 151 Fleet Street and 24 Store Street (Link House), the latter visited by the Welsh all-rounder a number of times.

5. Canon Kelly of St. Joseph's Church, Aberavon, was one religious leader who encouraged the setting up of an early H. & S. League Club in the Parish of Maesteg. In Aberavon Percy Hunt had already established himself as the voice of the League movement.

6. W. Newark Lewis worked at his craft from business premises he founded in 1902, at 5 Station Road - specialising in High class portraiture, engineering, marine and architectural photography. Named Hogarth Art Studios, presumably out of esteem for the 18th century English satirist

painter/engraver William Hogarth.   Although Newark Lewis found no good reason to use his camera as a vehicle for satirical comment - it would not have helped his living had he done so - the opportunity to at least deviate from the norm of formal portraiture presented itself with one sitter only - Percy Hunt.

Chapter 2

1.   Lies buried in Plot 11, Row C, Grave 36 in Caterpillar Valley Cemetery, France.

2.   Lies buried in Plot 4, Row A, Grave 32 in Bagneux British Cemetery, France.

3.   Pte. Percy Cardwell Hunt was not to know of restrictions on medal awards in lower ranks; recommendations for such honours were more or less granted on first come first served basis, which could be manipulated if so desired if a recommended recipient was preferred to another or if higher ranks were involved. Refused recommendations would not have been recorded.

Chapter 3

1.   From the 1920's to the 1930's most of these places for health and strength were to be found for example in:

ABERAMAN PC CLUB (by Aberaman Railway Station). Sec., Thomas J. James, 25 Cynon Street, Aberaman. Open each day from 9 a.m. to 9 p.m. Afternoon workmen can come in the morning. 6d. per week.

ABERCARN WELFARE BOYS' CLUB. Hon. Sec., Lgr. H. Preece, 6 Park Street, Cwmcarn, Mon.

THE DRAGON ATHLETIC CLUB. Aberystwyth. Sec., LDO D.Ll.C. Morgan, 'Gwarfelin', Llanbadern Fwr., Aberystwyth. Wed., 6.30-8.30 p.m. No Ent. fee, 3d. weekly sub. Strand-pulling, WL, Etc. Lectures by LDO Morgan on hygiene, massage, training, PC, etc. No ladies' or juvenile sections.

BLAENAVON PC CLUB (Aff.), White Horse Assembly Rooms.   Gen.

Sec., LDO Reg. Morgan, 17 Mary Street. Gent's sec., G. Gait; Ladies' Sec., Miss M. Daniels. Men, Mon., 6.45, Wed., 7.45, and Fri., 5.45 p.m. Ladies, Tues., 6.45, and Thurs., 4.30 p.m. Ent. fee 1/- and 6d. wkly. All-round PC No juvenile section.

THE 'ACE' PC CLUB (Aff.), Metal Street (opposite Metal St. School), Roath, Cardiff. Sec., LDO B. Giles, 1 Kerrycroy Street, Adamstown. Mon.-Fri., 6.30 - 10 p.m. Ent. fee 6d. and 6d. subs. per week. Muscle control, hand balancing, expander pulling, dumb-bell work, ju-jitsu, WL etc.

HEALTH & STRENGTH PC CLUB (Aff.), 9 Walker Road, Splott, Cardiff. Sec. S/LDO Nicholls, 9 Walker Road. Club nights Mon., Wed., Thurs. and Fri., 7 - 9.30 p.m. Ent. fee 1/-, covering first week's sub., and 6d., per week. Ladies' section. Also Sun. mng. at 11. Club-swinging, boxing, wrestling, JC, ju-jitsu, running, ball-punching, skipping, free ex. and table tennis. No juvenile section.

COLWYN BAY ROTARY ATHLETIC & GYMNASTIC CLUB (Aff.), Rydal School, Lansdowne Road, Colwyn Bay. Thurs., 6.30 - 9.30 p.m. Subs., 4/- per annum. Athletics and gymnastics. No ladies' or juvenile sections.

CWMDU WELFARE PC CLUB, Cwmdu Institute, Maesteg, Glam. Sec., LDO W.G. Smith, 29 Duke Street, Garth. Mon., Wed. & Fri., 6 - 9 p.m. Sub., 6d.; unemployed, 3d. Gym., WL, ju-jitsu, wrestling and all-round PC.,

CWMPARE PC CLUB (Aff.). Sec., Ivor J. Meredith, 17 Railway Terrace, Cwmpare, Treorchy, Rhondda, Glam. Mon. & Fri., 7 - 8.30 p.m. Ent. fee 6d., and 3d. weekly. 20 minutes' exs. led by A/LDO John Fox. WL, boxing, balancing, expander pulling and skipping.

HOLYHEAD BOYS' INSTITUTE, Newry Street and Beach (2 Institutes). Every evening during the week, 7.30 p.m., and 1.30 p.m. aftns, 3d. per month. WL, wrestling, Ju-jitsu, boxing, rings and dumb-bells. Also billiards. No ladies, and juveniles taken privately at first.

MONT PC CLUB. Prin., LDO David T. Owen, c/o., 'Penisarabar', Aberangel, Cemmaes Road, Mont.

ST. JAMES' A & PC CLUB (Aff.), Mon., Wed., & Fri. Ent. fee 1/-, and 6d. sub. per week. Sec., Lgr. H. Sergeant, 46 Wibham Street, Newport, Mon.

PONTYMISTER H. & S. CLUB (Aff.), Manor Road, Pontymister. Sec., Lgr. Bert Gingell, 16 Wyndham Terrace. Mon., Wed. & Fri., 6.30 - 10 p.m., and Sat. aftn. 1.30 - 4. 1/6, and 6d. per week. Wrestling, ju-jitsu, running, club-swinging, hiking, camping, cycling, WL and muscle control. No ladies' section.

PONTYPOOL PC CLUB, Clarence Hotel, Pontypool. Sec., Lgr. Richard Davies, Ash Cottage, Nr. Viaduct, Talywain. Tues. & Fri., 7 - 9.30 p.m. Ent. fee 1/1, and 6d. weekly. WL, club-swinging and vaulting horse exs. No ladies' or juvenile sections. All employed young men are allowed to join the club at the low admission fee of 7d. and 3d per week.

SEVEN SISTERS WL CLUB, at the back of The Palace, Seven Sisters (Aff. BAWLA). WL, boxing, gym, and all-round PC. Open all day and every day throughout the week. Ent. fee 2/6, and 6d. weekly contribution. Further particulars from S/LDO W.J. Morgan, MSFME, 22 Mary Street, Seven Sisters, Nr. Neath, Glam.

SWANSEA SCHOOL OF PC (Aff.). Sec., Lgr. John C. Doyle, 83 George Street, Swansea. Hon. Treas. Lgr. J.L. Macdonald, 32 Oxford Street, Swansea.

LANELAY WL CLUB. Prin. S/LDO Wm. Pritchard, 36 Nant Eirin Road, Twnyburn, Tonyrefail, Glam.

TRE-THOMAS H. & S. PC CLUB. Sec., LDO Wilfred B. Pope, 73 James Street, Tre-Thomas, Nr. Newport. Each night, 6.30 1/-, and 3d. per week. WL., wrestling, free exs., all-round PC, camping, cycling, etc. No ladies' or juvenile sections.

TRE-THOMAS CYCLING CLUB. Tours arranged every week. Sec., LDO, Wilfred B. Pope, 73 James Street, Tre-Thomas. Contributions 3d. per week (unemployed 1d. per week). Runs every Sunday starting at 11 a.m., from Lower Glyn Gwyn Street, Tre-Thomas.

THE YSTALYFERA PC CLUB (Aff.).   Sec. Ladies' section, Lgr. Mrs. M.H. Booth, 4 Office Row, Ystalyfera, Nr. Swansea, Glam.

YNYSYBWL PC CLUB, English Methodist Church Vestry.   Sec., Lgr. T.L. James. Ladies' section.

H. & S. establishments in Wales were about as numerous as those in Scotland and more so than Ireland; in England they were much more plentiful.

The H. & S. League had world-wide influence and we find clubs in Arabia, Burma, Ceylon, Hong Kong, Malta and Singapore. Not all were Colonial clubs but some were set up by the indigenous population.

2.   All-round performer: boxer, wrestler, hand-balancer, weight-lifter, Middleweight Champion of the World, Britain's Strongest Man, Heavyweight Champion of the British Empire, lecturer, and acrobat.

3.   The grading system entitled the LDO or Lgr. to a badge distinction, which did not include the Bronze (10 recruits) until later, or Silver (18), Silver Gilt (48) and Gold (100), denoted by the prefixes B/-, S/-, SG/- and G/- placed before LDO or Lgr.

4.   The challenge of a list of tests by Percy Hunt was the reviving of a tradition, which probably had its roots in the Pentathlon, popularised as far back as 1894 when French physical culturist Professor Edmund Desbonnet won the 'Attila Trophy' for all-round strength athletics, at the International Athletics Congress in New York. The tests in the contest included, apart from weight-lifting, jumping, gymnastics, bicycle riding, etc.

5.   Athletes who used their hair in a bodily lifting feat were known as 'Hair Gladiators', after circus performer Sascha.

6.   The title 'The Man They Could Not Hang', is a macabre reference to John Lee, of Babbacombe, Devon, found guilty of murder in 1884. Three attempts were made to hang him but on each occasion the trap doors failed to open, even after a carpenter had removed a portion of the woodwork. No further execution attempts were made and the sentence was subsequently commuted to life imprisonment.

7. A sensitive image for valley, mining audiences, the abdominal features of the politician were only included after consultation with show organisers.

8. Percy's solo act at the close of a display was on the whole particular to boxers; fellow Welshman, boxer Fred Dyer, for instance, would sing 'Thora', or a similar type of song, after 20 rounds of boxing, to the delight of the National Sporting Club members.

9. Competent in ju-jitsu, there is no evidence to suggest that Percy was leader of the British Ju-Jitsu Society.

10. A one-time favourite war-horse of male voice choirs, 'Italian Salad' is a pastiche of an Italian operatic final chorus of the type popular in the 19th Cent. - a kind of mock Verdi/Rossini. The composer F.G. Genee (b. 1823(4) - 1895), apparently German, (!) from (the then) Danzig, cleverly used Italian musical terms as a nonsense-type text, illustrating their meaning (*fortissimo*, *rallentando*, etc.). The piece was one of Percy's delights.

Chapter 4

1. A considered pioneering combination by Percy - although Monte Saldo had also synched his muscle movements to the rhythms of music - the musical element in his muscle control was not regularly employed and at the whim of theatre musicians it faded away from his muscle dancing routine.

2. Percy was positioned against a curtained backdrop either in the appropriate leopard skin loin-cloth, or in a black bow tie or evening wear. From these series of photographs, taken at various stages of his athleticism, came his famous age-span composite image of 'The Great Mavello' between the ages of 29 to 44. There were later ages of comparison with 29 - 48, 50 and 65.

3. The Aberavon all-rounder also attended the first Health & Strength Display, held in King's Hall, and, with a group of pupils, the first Mr. Britain contest venues in the National Sporting Club, on January 5th 1929. Other London locations included the Memorial Hall, Farringdon Street, and London Palladium.

4. Theatre prices for the H. & S. display of 1936 were: Orchestra Stalls 10/6, Royal Fanteuils 7/6, Fanteuils 6/-, Grand Circle 6/-, Pit Stalls 3/8, Circle 3/8, Balcony 2/6.

5. The introductory singing at the Holborn Empire on 17 March 1924, which Percy and Joe had attended, was commemorated by a mass recording with an additional rendition by bass-baritone Foster Richardson.

6. Born in 1881, Thomas Inch of Scarborough was mainly a heavyweight WL and made significant progress as an apparatus innovator. Noted, like many of the leading physical culturists, for his courses on BB and WL. He was also one of the first to instruct that WL be used in sport, which he called 'Miniature WL'. Britain's Strongest Man before Edward Aston.

7. Born in 1888, W.A. Pullum, proprietor of the renowned Camberwell Club, London, was, like Inch, essentially a WL. He was a British Champion in three weight categories: 9 stone, 10 stone, and 11 stone. Purchased H. & S. publications, taking over from editorial talent D.G. Johnson, who was said to have been of Welsh extraction, and appointed assistant editor George Kirkley as editor and League Organiser.

8. Beneath a photograph of the Welsh all-rounder in a Maxalding advert, in *H. & S.* of 1957, it states that Percy continues to perform the same act that he did when he appeared with Monte Saldo's son Court Saldo on a London stage in the 1920's.

9. Ivy Russell: Bent Press of 120 lb.; Two Hands Dead Lift - 377 lb.; T.H. Straight (military) Press - 110 lb.; T.H. Snatch - 110 lb.; T.H.C. and Push - 150 lb.; T.H.C. and Jerk - 176 lb.; O.H. Swing - 92 lb.; O.H. Snatch - 95lb.

Chapter 5

1. Apart from Christopher, who had a premature demise, only the youngest, Cyril, remained unmarried; Thomas, the eldest, and Albert went to live in Southampton, Eliza, Percy, Violet, Blanche and Bachelor Cyril remaining in Port Talbot.

2. Ted Jones (runner-up Mr. Wales 1948) weighed about 12 stone. He joined a group of stage performers. They toured the country calling themselves 'The Seven Volants' - whirlwind acrobats. Ted Jones was the main bearer in a pyramid act.

3. As in Percy's day judgement for both sexes: (a) Physical Proportion and deportment; (b) Presentation (posing ability); Development (muscularity); and (c) Condition of hair, skin and teeth.

4. Much change had taken and was taking place in WL systems with the decline in BAWLA's traditional all-round lifts (42, 44), most of which were 'military' in technique - the Olympic set of Two Hands Clean and Press, Snatch and Clean and Jerk - the introduction in the 1950's of Strength lifts (regarded then as the basis of BB practices) of Two Hands Curl, Press on Bench and Deep Knee Bend, and the appearance in the mid-1960's of the Power lifts. The latter lifts were an abomination to Percy in that they encouraged obesity in lifters.

5. There was no single system, but a number of systems and various principles which they held. Of particular influence was the effective, alternate use of heavy and light poundage sets operated with a day's rest between applying low counts and heavy weight, and high counts with lighter weight. Perfection of lifting in strict style was supposedly the standard, but there was doubt about this, although Percy would not have veered from strictness of lifting - it was in his blood.

6. An American contact of long standing, Ray van Cleef ran a gym 'Gateway to Health', in San Jose, California, and organised physical culture displays. He also operated a publishing business with his brother Mike. In later years Percy ripped up letters received from Ray van Cleef, the rest of the correspondence from the USA being thrown out by his wife at his death.

7. A number of women in shows also belonged to the Women's League of Health and Beauty, founded in 1930 by Mrs. Bagot Stacks and carried on by her daughter Prunella Stacks, whom Percy had met in one of their events held at the Baltic Lounge, Swansea in the late 1930's.

8. Results: 'Mr. Wales' - 1 Henry Downs, RAF St. Athan. 2 Dennis Stallard, Tonyrefail. 3 Graham Hale, Neath. 'Miss Wales' - 1 Joan Richards, Briton Ferry. 2 Elsie Baines, Portskewtt. 3 Betty Jones, Swansea. 'Junior Mr. Wales' - 1 Dave Meredith, Aberdare. 2 William St. Roas, Cardiff. 3 Hugh Roberts, Pwllheli. 'Junior Miss Wales' - 1 Jean Bridgwater, Abertillery. 2 Valerie Jones, Crumlin. 3 Mary George, Aberdare. 'Senior Mr. Wales' (over 40) - 1 William James, Port Talbot. 2 Herbert Davies, Abergavenny.

9. The significant contribution made by RAF St. Athan Physical Training School to athleticism was by National Athletics Coach Geoff Dyson, Britain's first National Coach Al Murray, and Oscar State, secretary of BAWLA and WL administrator, who installed a pilot 'circuit training' scheme devised from weight-training principles. Geoff Dyson's remarks that the athlete of tomorrow will not only require elemental cardiovascular development, but all-round muscular strength, proved to Percy the value of his own contribution to physical culture.

10. Mel Barnett: Bronze Medallist in the 1950 World Championship in Paris; chosen for the Helsinki Olympic Games of 1952 and won another bronze at the Vancouver Commonwealth Games of 1954.

11. Sid Frost (9 stone World record holder) was the prime mover with Cliff Hall (11 stone World amateur and World record holder) in establishing pre-war 1940/45 Welsh WL.

12. Jack Acocks revived post-war Welsh WL in 1946 and became first secretary and dynamic leader for some years of the Welsh Amateur Weight-Lifters' Association.

13. John Jones: Welsh record holder (Military lifts).
Walter Jones: contender for British title (Olympic set).

14. Many years younger than Percy, one of Tom George's feats was to pull a double-decker bus with a leather bit between his teeth.

15. One audience member did not grip Percy's hair properly and tore a patch of the growth from the top of his scalp leaving a balding area. Over the

years he treated the damaged roots with hand and electric massage and applications of Elliman's Universal Athletic Rub, which restored healthy growth to some extent.

Chapter 6

1. Probably the widest audience he ever reached in Port Talbot was during the all-night 'go as you please' concerts which were held in the Majestic (later Odeon) Cinema on General Election nights. After the film performance was over this popular variety show - interspersed with election results as they came in from the constituencies - began. Percy - always seeking a captive audience - was a regular at these marathons which, of course, were made obsolete by TV and its Swingometer!

2. Masters of ceremony: Mr. D. Bryn Thomas and Mr. B.K. Michaelson. Officers and working committee: Chief Inspector D.E. Jones, Chairman; Mr. B.K. Michaelson, Vice-Chairman; Inspector L. Morgan, Hon. Secretary; Mr. P.H.R. Thomas, Hon. Treasurer; Messrs. J.F. Dolan; P.H. Higgins; R. McKay; Dr. Anthony O'Connor; Douglas Scott; C. Slater; D.W. Smith; E. Spiers and D.B. Thomas.

3. Major Chidzoy was basso profundo-voiced and the father of the soprano (Mrs. Mary Gittings) Percy rescued when the lady had locked herself out of her car on Penycae.

4. In the Bovril photograph Percy is seen performing a one-hand planche on top of what is supposed to be a giant Bovril jar, which in reality was a cardboard cut-out, the balancing being done on a chair behind. All of this is barely discernible with a larger cardboard cut-out of the H. & S. League badge and motto covering about four-fifths of the area. To hopefully make clear the product as the intended main purpose of the composition, Percy holds a SMALL jar of the real thing, not a LARGE jar, in his outstretched, counter-balancing left hand, with even the trade name blurred.

5. Of the many fine portraits of the athlete there are a number which present the unusual, but it is the admirable, allegorical composition of 'Percy and the Angels', accomplished in a style reminiscent of Victorian indulgence

for picture-making in the High Art photography of the period, which stands out from the rest. The composition came about, according to Joe Manship, who was present, out of a sudden request by Percy that a photograph be taken in a kind of celebration of the H. & S. Leaguer with reference to the movement's motto. Newark Lewis dutifully obliged by selecting from an array of studio props of pillars, aspidistras and pseudo-Grecian urns, two, half-sized, plaster angels elevated upon separate square pillars, which were carefully placed, with assistance from Joe, into positions a few feet apart. Between the angel props the photographer - who suffered like his brother Harry from a stammer - gesticulated to Percy to pose on a plinth provided between the angels, which he did without hesitation. In the process of preparing to take more than one photograph a sudden violent thunderstorm erupted, the effects of thunderous clappings and sizzling flashes of lightning vibrating the studio and casting monstrous, leaping shadows in a simultaneous spectacle. Joe Manship likened the storm to the special effects in a Frankenstein movie, with Newark, hiding underneath the black hood of his camera, in the role of Frankenstein, and Percy crouching away from the lightning flashes in a kind of monster awakening position. That is how it seemed to Joe Manship.

6.   A tribute given to Yorkshire's Ronald Walker - Britain's Greatest, versatile pre-1939 lifter - in a 1948 issue of *H. & S.* which Percy kept in his music case. An acquaintance of the Welsh all-rounder, the English lifter died in his early 40's of cancer just after the war and Joe Manship believed that the poem written in 'Harpe Metre' by Lgr. D.Ll.C. Morgan, DO, ND, FFCS, (Hons.), winner of 59 Bardic Chairs, was particular to his colleague. It might be that the poem would also have been a fitting 'In Memoriam' to Percy, even though the tribute recalling the lifter's longing for the old country and shortness of his life bore no similarities to Percy's life, but much of the rest, give or take a line, rings true:

> Grieve ye not as friends forsaken,
> Though another road I've taken:
> I am come with faith to Zion
> Past the gate and last Horizon.

I have known the pains of striving;
Known the thrill of joyful living:
May it be in verse recorded—-
My Creator I remembered.

Well I loved the break o'morning,
And the russet hues of evening,
Greatly did I love the beauty
Of my old, peace-loving country.

With the strong I was apprenticed,
What I preached I also practised.
In a life devoid of falsehood
I revelled in mighty manhood.

Thus, so brief, is writ my chapter,
Time nor tide can nowise alter.
Be ye strong of faith who follow
In my steps, today, tomorrow.

        POET D. LL. C. MORGAN
Poet's Corner,
ABERYSTWYTH.

Glossary

Progressive Resistance Training: With emphasis upon WL and BB there are many variations and priorities (i.e. bulk, definition, strength, mobility, etc.), but in simple terms training with weights which are made slightly heavier as the repetitions and sets are reduced to a single rep. and single set in what is often called the pyramid principle.

Military Style: A strictly disciplined system of WL where, for example, no movement mannerisms like the use of an added impetus of a little heave to break or cheat through the limiting factor of the 'sticking point' in a lift are permitted.

DEFINITIONS OF A NUMBER OF LIFTS FROM BAWLA's 44

Lifts 3 and 4. - Right (and left) Hand Snatch

The bar shall be placed horizontal in front of the lifter's legs. The Snatch must be executed in one distinct movement, the weight being taken from the ground vertically above the head to the full extent of the arm. The bar shall pass with a continuous, non-stop movement along the body, of which no part other than the feet shall touch or graze the ground during the execution of the movement.

The weight which has been lifted must be held for two seconds in the final position of immobility, with the arm and legs extended, the feet on the same line with a maximum separation of $15\frac{3}{4}$ inches.

The lifter is permitted to support the opposite hand or arm on the knee or thigh of either leg.

Incorrect movements: A pause, supporting a hand or knee on the ground, finishing with a press-out, touching the bar with the other hand during the execution of the movement.

7 and 8. - Right (and Left) Hand Clean and Jerk

First Part: Cleaning the bar.

It shall be done in one distinct movement without any pause. The bar shall be placed horizontally in front of the lifter's legs. He shall grip it in the centre with one hand with the palm forward and pull it up in a single, clean movement from the ground to the shoulder. During this first movement, the bar must in no case touch either the shoulder or chest of the side opposite to the lifting arm,

the axis of the sternum serving as the limit line. The lifter is permitted to support the hand or fore-arm on the knee or thigh opposite the lifting arm.
Second Part: The Jerk

It shall be done in one distinct movement. The arm holding the weight shall be taken vertically above the head and held for two seconds in the final position of immobility, with the arm and legs extended, the feet on the same line with a maximum separation of $15\frac{3}{4}$ inches.

Incorrect movements: Movement finished with a press-out, a pause, support from a hand or knee on the ground, touching the bar with the other hand during the movement, supporting the bar on the shoulder. It is also forbidden, when the Jerk proper has failed after a visible effort, to make a second attempt after a fresh stop at the shoulder.

9 and 10. - Right (and Left) Bent Press

The barbell shall be taken to the shoulder in one clean movement and thence elevated to arm's length over head, as described in Nos. 13 and 14. In the pull-in to the shoulder the trunk may be bent sideways, the elbow may rest upon the thigh prior to standing erect, but should the bar be brought into contact with the body below the line of the nipples it shall be counted cause for disqualification. At the conclusion of the lift the trunk shall be erect, the lifting arm and legs straight and the heels, if separated, held not wider apart than $15\frac{3}{4}$ ins. on a plane parallel with the lifter's front.

13 and 14. - Right (and Left) Hand Bent Press (Two Hands to Shoulder)

The barbell shall be taken to the shoulder with two hands without restriction as to method and, having been transferred into one hand, shall, grasped in the centre, be elevated to arm's length overhead by means of lateral pressure. During the press from the shoulder it shall be counted cause for disqualification should any part of the bell be brought into contact with the hip.

At the conclusion of the lift...

17. - Abdominal Raise

Lying on the ground, with the back of the neck resting on the centre of the bar, the lifter, grasping the bar with both hands, shall raise himself into a sitting position. Throughout the lift the legs shall remain straight, and the bar in contact with the body, and upon conclusion the trunk shall be at right-angles to the legs. In the performance of this lift the use of a dumb-bell is not permitted, but the feet may be secured under some weighty object.

19. - Rectangular Fix

The barbell grasped with both hands (knuckles to the front) shall hang at arm's length across the lifter's front, from which position it shall be raised forward steadily until the forearms are at right angles to the upper arms. Throughout the lift the trunk must not be inclined backwards, forwards, or sideways, the shoulders must be kept quite level, the legs straight, the upper arms remain stationary and in contact with the body. No sagging of the wrists is permitted. The slightest deviation from this position shall be counted cause for disqualification.

Although a count is not insisted upon at the commencement of this lift, a pause must be observed and the lift must not be continued from the momentum gained by lifting the bar into the commencing position.

26. - Pull Over and Push on Back

Lying on the ground with the centre of the bar immediately behind the head, the bell shall be brought over the lifter's face until the upper arms rest on the ground. Once the bell clears the line of the sternum where the collar-bones meet, the discs shall not again be brought into contact with the floor. Immediately the bell is in the same position for the 'Press', then the heels may be brought close to the buttocks, and the forearms inclined forward until the bar rests across the abdomen. From this position the bell may be impelled to arm's length overhead by a quick 'bridge' formation, but at no period of the lift shall the shoulders leave the ground. At the conclusion of the lift, the arms and legs shall be straight, the buttocks on the ground.

Percy extended the 'Bridge' position in the lift to make it a feat on its own. This was achieved by moving from the shoulder area to the back of his head. Holding this position he would then slowly roll his head backwards and forwards by pushing slowly with his legs.

A powerful exercise for the neck and back for wrestler's becoming known as 'Wrestler's Bridge' and, because of its bow-shape, the 'Chinese Bridge'.

29. - Two Hands Clean and Push with Dumb-Bells

The dumb-bells shall be taken clean to the shoulders, after which the commencing position shall be assumed. This position may be taken with the feet astride, or with one foot advanced, and in either the trunk may be inclined forward. If the feet are placed astride, both legs must, at this period of the lift, be kept quite straight. If one foot is advanced, the leg corresponding to that foot must be kept quite straight. After taking up the commencing position, a pause of two seconds shall elapse; the conclusion of which shall be indicated by the referee by a sharp clap with both hands. The bells shall then be pushed to arms' length overhead. As soon as the push begins, the legs and trunk may be bent to any extent, but lowering the body vertically is not permitted.

At the conclusion of the lift...

31. - Two Hands Continental Jerk with Dumb-Bells

The dumb-bells, which must be lifted simultaneously, may be taken to the shoulders in a series of movements, and may be rested upon or against, any part of the legs or trunk in so doing. they shall thence be jerked to arms' length overhead. At the conclusion of the lift the trunk shall be erect, the arms and legs straight, and the heels, if separated, held not wider apart than $15\frac{3}{4}$ inches on a plane parallel with the lifter's front. There is no restriction in the number of jerks from the shoulders.

Note: The term **'Continental'** means that in a lift dumb-bells or barbells can be taken to the shoulders in any number of movements, resting against any part of the body.

32. - Two Hands Anyhow with Dumb-Bells

The dumb-bells shall be lifted to arms' length overhead anyhow. For example, one bell may be taken to the shoulder with two hands, thence to be jerked, or bent pressed overhead, after which the other shall be raised to full stretch of arm overhead. This is the method usually employed. At the conclusion of the lift the trunk shall be erect, the arms and legs straight, and the heels, if separated, held not wider apart than $15\frac{3}{4}$ inches on a plane parallel with the lifter's front.

34. - Two Hands Clean and Press with Barbell

First Part: The bar shall be placed horizontally in front of the lifter's legs. He shall grip it with both hands and bring it to the shoulders in a single distinct movement while either 'splitting' or bending the legs. The bar shall rest on the chest or on the arms fully bent. The feet shall be brought back on the same line with a maximum separation of $15\frac{3}{4}$ inches.

Second Part: A pause of two seconds shall be observed in this position while remaining motionless. Then the bar shall be lifted slowly and vertically without any jerk or sudden start until the arms are completely extended. When the movement is finished, a pause of two seconds shall be observed with the arms and legs extended. During the whole execution of the second part, that is to say, the Press proper, the body and head of the lifter must remain constantly in a vertical position.

Important remark: As a rule, the bar must touch the chest before the execution of the second part, which must not begin before the referee gives the signal by clapping his hands. Lifters who are unable to rest their bar on their chest, must inform the jury before the start of the contest. For this class of competitors, the starting point of the bar, as far as the Press proper is concerned, shall be the point where the collar bones meet the sternum.

Incorrect movements: Any deviation of the body or head from the vertical position; any twisting; any movement of the feet (heels lifting, etc.); any bending - however little - of the legs, and the uneven extension of the arms during the Press.

35. - Two Hands Clean and Push with Barbell

The barbell shall be taken clean to the shoulders, after which the commencing position shall be assumed. This position may be taken with the feet astride, or with one foot advanced, and in either the trunk may be inclined forward. If the feet are placed astride, both legs must, at this period of the lift, be kept quite straight. If one foot is advanced, the leg corresponding to that foot must be kept quite straight. After taking up the commencing position a pause of two seconds shall elapse, the conclusion of which shall be indicated by the referee by a sharp clap with both hands; the bell shall then be pushed to arms' length overhead. As soon as the push begins, the legs and trunk may be bent to any extent, but lowering the body vertically is not permitted.

At the conclusion of the lift...

36. - Two Hands Snatch

The bar shall be placed horizontally in front of the lifter's legs. He shall grip it with both hands and pull it in one movement from the ground vertically above the head to the full extent of the arms, while either 'splitting' or bending the legs. The bar shall pass with a continuous, non-stop movement along the body, of which no part other than the feet shall touch or graze the ground during the execution of the movement. The weight which has been lifted must be held for two seconds in the final position of immobility, with the arms and legs extended, the feet on the same line with a maximum separation of $15\frac{3}{4}$ inches. The distance between the hands is optional, but they may not, in any case, move along the bar during the execution of the movement.

Important remarks: In this lift, of which the fundamental principle is to allow only one single movement, no delay shall be permitted in the extension of the arms after the turning over of the wrists, which must not occur before the bar has clearly passed the top of the lifter's head. As soon as the lifter's arms are extended, he must recover his legs to the erect position as quickly as possible.

39. - Two Hands Clean and Jerk with Barbell

The bar shall be placed horizontally in front of the lifter's legs. He shall grip it with both hands and pull it up in a single, clean movement from the ground to the shoulders, while either 'splitting' or bending the legs. The bar must not touch the chest before the final position, it shall then rest on the chest or on the arms fully bent. The feet shall be returned to their original position, that is to say on the same line. Then bend the legs and extended them quickly, as well as the arms, so as to bring the bar to the full stretch of the vertically extended arms. The weight shall be held for two seconds in the final position of immobility, the feet on the same line, with a maximum separation of $15\frac{3}{4}$ inches. It is forbidden to repeat the jerk.

Incorrect movements: Leaning with a knee on the ground or any 'Clean' in which the bar touches a part of the body before its final arrival at the shoulders.

42. - Two Hands Dead Lift

The barbell shall be lifted from the ground in front of the legs until the lifter stands erect. Upon conclusion the legs must be straight and the shoulders taken back. Should the bar be brought to rest against the legs during the lift it shall not be counted cause for disqualification, and the manner in which the bar shall be grasped is a matter for the lifter's discretion.

The lifts described are those which Percy practised in his prime; the following, which include the addition of two further BAWLA lifts of 'Press on Bench' and 'Deep Knee Bend' moving the number from 42 to 44, are exercises used by pupils in addition to some of those described.

43. - Press on Bench

The lifter shall lie supine upon a horizontal bench with both feet in contact with the floor. The barbell shall be placed into the lifter's hand at arms' length above the chest. The width of the grip taken is limited by the requirements that the forearms shall be vertical. From this position the lifter shall lower the barbell until it is touching the chest, where it shall be held for a pause of two seconds. The conclusion of the pause shall be indicated by the referee, after which the lifter shall press the barbell to arms' length where it shall be held until the referee has signified his approval.

The press which shall be made in the lifter's own time shall be in a continuous upward movement.

During the press proper there shall be no uneven extension of the arms and the head, shoulders and buttocks to remain in contact with the bench. The feet shall remain in contact with the floor throughout the lift. At no time during the lift shall the lifter's upper arms come into contact with the bench or floor.

44. - Deep Knee Bend

The barbell shall be placed in position behind the neck of the lifter by the assistants, or taken into that position from supports. The bar shall be grasped by the lifter with both hands. From this position the lifter shall bend his knees and lower his body until the top levels of his thighs are at least parallel with the floor which point shall be indicated by the referee.

The lifter shall then resume the upright position with knees braced and trunk upright. Immediately this position is reached the referee shall give a signal.

The weight shall be held in complete control during the whole of the exercise.

A small amount of padding may be added to the central portion of the bar (not exceeding twelve inches) but the lifter shall not be permitted to wear towels and sweaters padded around the neck. Note - A straight or cambered bar may be used but in each case it shall conform with the regulations governing apparatus.

The spacing of the feet is optional and the use of supports under the heels is permissible. The maximum thickness of such supports shall be one inch.

Squat: Many variations of the above i.e. bar held in front on the chest. Legs lowered only to the position where thighs parallel to the floor, etc.

'Hack' Lift: (not official lift): Named after the great Russian wrestler Hackenschmidt, the lift is a 'Dead Lift' made behind the legs, the grip being forward or back with either hand. Reverse grip or ordinary grip.

Two Hands Slow Curl: The barbell grasped with both hands (palms to the front) shall hang at arms' length across the lifter's front, from which position it shall be lifted to the shoulders by bending the forearms completely on the upper arms.

The trunk must not bend forward, sideways or backwards throughout the lift. Legs straight, shoulders level - heels together.

'Zottman' Curl: Named after George Zottman, a German all-round strength athlete who developed powerful biceps by curling a pair of dumb-bells alternately and in a circular movement across the body, turning the dumb-bells fully to the side.

The Zottman Curl is a fine exercise working the biceps and supinators in addition to working them as flexers.

Weight-Training: Called 'Miniature Weight-Lifting' (loosely defined between WL and BB with barbells and dumb-bells in use) by weight-lifting and body-building expert Thomas Inch, he was one of the first to instruct its use for all kinds of sports. The term 'Weight-Training' was introduced later by rival W.A. Pullum. NOTE - While old-timers like Percy Hunt had long followed unreservedly such teaching in the use of the system for sports, it was not until the early 1950's that so-called experts of the day re-evaluated 'Weight-Training' as suitable for track and field events (circuit training) and not until later for other forms of sport.

Indian Clubs: Used at least two centuries ago by the British Army. Their use was originally a standard piece of apparatus for physical exercise.
Two clubs were swung in many intricate movements and were made in various designs and weights, with exhibitions popular at the beginning of the century revealing the physical benefits of such training.
Percy was a master at 'Indian Club' swinging, using a lighter class of clubs suitable for suppleness and rhythmic speed in his act.

Kettle Bells: The solid and hollow globes with handles attached originated in the last century from kettles filled with ballast before the prominence of dumb-bells. 'Kettle Bells' were used by Percy in one of his juggling acts.

'In-Klein' (Incline) Bench: An adjustable bench used mainly for abdominal work, the apparatus taking its name from the great German-born strongman and BB specialist Siegmund Klein (known to Percy through correspondence), who influenced its use by installing it in his New York studio. The home-made apparatus used in the gym was in the manner of an 'In-Klein' bench.

Weighted Shoes: First used in a pre-Christian times by the Greeks and Romans, iron boots were first patented in the USA in 1938, although they were used as a standard exercise in the St. Mary's Street gym years earlier.

The ingenuity of construction from miscellaneous items is typical of exercising implements incorporated into the gym. The iron boots were thus made from two roughly cut strips of heavy iron plate screwed to similar-sized pieces of soft wood and attached to each length of wood was a metal heel guard with two leather straps for securing the feet.

The exercise itself had the pupil lie alternately supine and procumbent, and in these positions the shoes were lifted upwards and downwards separately and then together, and if further weight was needed the shoes were joined by an iron rod with additional disc poundage, making sure in both positions to point the feet at the apex of each movement - Percy insisted upon this as it fully extended muscle and sinew.

BODY-BUILDING TERMS USED IN THE GYM BY PUPILS

Multi-Sets: Variations favoured by the advanced BB allowed sets to be used for different reasons i.e. bulk, definition, strength, etc.

Muscle Priority: When encrgy is greatest at the beginning of a work-out, the weaker parts of the body are given prime attention, which in turn leads to the following.

Split Work-Outs: Preference is then given to different areas of the body at different work-outs.

e.g. Legs in the morning on one particular day. The upper body another day.
       More advanced BB's in the gym would have 'Split Work-outs' the same day.

Forced Reps: Performing a greater count than the weight would normally allow, either by 'Cheating' (adjustment of levers) or by assistance from a training partner.

Flushing: Retaining the 'pump' (of blood) in the origins or insertions of the muscles e.g. biceps and deltoid exercise.

A great deal of work can be achieved with all muscle groups closely linked especially where origins/insertions overlap, however careful selection and repetition is necessary in order not to strain ligaments/tendons, etc. Recovery period must be adjusted and watched closely.

Sticking Point: A phrase used in respect of a repetition where maximum effort is needed to keep momentum going at the point of the exercise when muscles are at their full potential. Often adjustment of gravity or cheating method are used to complete the repetition.

NOTE - Percy had no real liking for any of the methods, particularly the latter three with their links to 'cheating' past the 'sticking point', and the puffed-up muscle tissue achieved by 'flushing'.

Bibliography

Institutions

The British Museum Library; City of Glasgow District Council Libraries Department; Devon County Council; Neath Port Talbot County Borough Council; The Queen's University of Belfast; Records Office, London; Royal College of Music, London; The Royal Regiment of Wales; The South Wales Borderers and Monmouth Regtl. Museum; South Wales Miners' Library; Theatre Museum, London; University of Dublin; Welsh Folk Museum; West Glamorgan Area Records Office, West Glamorgan County Council; Welsh Music Information Centre.

Periodicals and Newspapers

The Aberavon and Port Talbot News; The Cambrian Daily Leader; Glamorgan Gazette; Health & Strength magazine, Annuals and H. & S. League Guide and Pocket Companion; British Amateur Weight-Lifters' Association magazine; Port Talbot Guardian; Rhondda Leader; South Wales Evening Post; South Wales Guardian and Amman Valley Chronicle; South Wales Weekly Argus.

Books, Diaries and Pamphlets

C.T. Atkinson, The History of the South Wales Borderers; Prof. Hywel Francis, History Workshop - Workers' Libraries; J. Ivor Hanson, Profile of a Welsh Town; Colin Hughes, Mametz; John Vivian Hughes, Margam Castle; London Theatres and Music Halls 1850 - 1950; William Rees, A Story of the Ancient Borough of Aberavon; Traditional Ballads in Welsh and English; War Diaries of the South Wales Borderers; David A. Webster, Barbells and Beafcakes, The Iron Game.

Index